2nd Edition

BTEC FIRST

Public Services

Nick Cullingworth

Nelson Thornes

Published in 2006 by:
Nelson Thornes Ltd
Delta Place
27 Bath Road
CHELTENHAM
GL53 7TH
United Kingdom

09 10 / 10 9 8 7 6 5

A catalogue record for this book is available from the British Library

ISBN 978 0 7487 8390 8

Cover photograph by © David Hoffman Photo Library/Alamy
Illustrations by Pantek Arts Ltd
Page make-up by Pantek Arts Ltd, Maidstone, Kent
Printed and bound in Croatia by Zrinski

Contents

Introduction

Millions of people work in Britain's public services. They include firefighters, police officers, soldiers, sailors, air crew, prison officers, civil servants, teachers and nurses. Their work is varied, exciting, demanding, responsible – and vitally important. In Britain the importance of the public services is widely recognised and billions of pounds are spent on them. They provide secure, relatively well-paid jobs, and excellent careers for the right people. Because of these advantages many people want to work in the public services – and this is where BTEC First Public Service courses come in. These courses tell you what the public services are all about, and prepare you for public service work. They won't ensure that you get into a public service - but they will get you off to a flying start by giving you knowledge and skills you need, both for public service work and for further studies.

How do you use this book?

Covering the units of the new 2006 specification, this book has everything you need if you are studying BTEC First certificate or diploma in Public Services. Simple to use and understand, this book is designed to provide you with the skills and knowledge for you to gain your qualification. We guide you through your qualification using a range of features that are fully explained over the page.

Which units do you need to complete?

For the BTEC First Diploma in Public Services you are required to complete 3 core units and 3 specialist units.

Core Units	Specialist Units
Unit 1 **Uniformed Public Services Employment**	Unit 4 **Citizenship, the Individual and Society**
Unit 2 **Public Service Skills**	*Unit 5 **Public Service Workplace Welfare**
Unit 3 **Unformed Public Service Fitness**	Unit 6 **Adventurous Activities and Teamwork for the Public Services**
	Unit 7 **The Value of Sport and Recreation in the Public Services**
	Unit 8 **Land Navigation by Map and Compass**
	Unit 9 **Law and its Impact on the Individual**
	Unit 10 **Crime and its Effects on Society**
	*Unit 11 **Community and Cultural Awareness**
	Unit 12 **Driving and its Relationship to the Public Services**
*Units 5, 11 & 14 are not included in this book but can be found on the BTEC First Public Services Tutor Resource.	Unit 13 **Expedition Skills**
	*Unit 14 **Fundamentals of Nautical Studies**

Is there anything else you need to do?

1. Do all the work your tutors set you.
2. Never be afraid to ask for help if you need it.
3. Develop your fitness, 'people skills' and sense of responsibility.
4. Get wise to the Internet, and use the Internet wisely.
5. Visit the public services, and meet the people who work in them.

We hope you enjoy your BTEC course – Good Luck!

Turn over now for your guide to the features of this book.

Features of this book

Learning Objectives

At the beginning of each Unit there will be a bulleted list letting you know what material is going to be covered. They specifically relate to the learning objectives within the 2006 specification.

Grading Criteria

The table of Grading Criteria at the beginning of each unit identifies achievement levels of pass, merit and distinction, as stated in the specification.

To achieve a **pass**, you must be able to match each of the 'P' criteria in turn.

To achieve **merit** or **distinction**, you must increase the level of evidence that you use in your work, using the 'M' and 'D' columns as reference. For example, to achieve a distinction you must fulfil all the criteria in the pass, merit and distinction columns.

Activities

are designed to help you understand the topics through answering questions or undertaking research, and are either *Group* or *Individual* work.

UNIT 1

Uniformed Public Services Employment

This unit covers:

- the purpose, roles and responsibilities of uniformed public services
- jobs and conditions of service within the uniformed public services
- application and selection processes for uniformed public services
- initial training and opportunities for career development within uniformed public services.

Many hundreds of thousands of people are employed in the UK's uniformed public services. For example, there are over 100,000 uniformed people working in the British Army, more than 40,000 in the Royal Navy, and more than 50,000 in the RAF. In 2005 there were over 141,000 police officers and 70,000 civilian staff working for the police. There are around 48,000 prison officers and 33,000 firefighters.

This unit introduces you to the uniformed public services, the work they do, and the application procedures you have to go through if you want to work in them. You will also learn something about basic training in the public services, and the ways in which you can be promoted.

grading criteria	To achieve a **Pass** grade the evidence must show that the learner is able to:	To achieve a **Merit** grade the evidence must show that the learner is able to:	To achieve a **Distinction** grade the evidence must show that the learner is able to:
	P1 describe the roles, purpose and responsibilities of two contrasting uniformed public services	**M1** explain the role, purpose and responsibilities of two contrasting uniformed public services	**D1** evaluate the role, purpose and responsibilities of a uniformed public service
	P2 describe the type of work done in three different jobs within a named uniformed public service	**M2** explain in detail the work of a job within a uniformed public service	**D2** evaluate both the potential and the limitations for their own career development within their chosen uniformed public service
	P3 describe the current conditions of service for a given job within a uniformed public service	**M3** explain the process of applying for a given job within a uniformed public service	
	P4 describe the current conditions of service for a given job within a uniformed public service	**M4** comment on their own suitability to complete basic training and for their career development within a chosen uniformed public service	

activity
INDIVIDUAL WORK
(1.1)
Which of the following describes a role of the police?
(a) Patrolling the streets
(b) Treating everybody fairly
(c) Doing what the government tells them to do
(d) Proving that they are not wasting public money.

UNIT 1

case study

1.1

Examples of uniformed public services

Fire and rescue service	Military
Coast Guard	Army
NHS Nursing	Royal Air Force
Military Police	Royal Navy
Police	HM Customs and Excise
Prison Service	Ambulance

activity
GROUP

(a) Divide the public services listed into the three types (1), (2) and (3).
(b) Note down the main jobs you think each one does.
(c) Compare your answers.

keyword

Uniform – dress of a distinctive design or fashion worn by members of a particular group and serving as a means of identification; broadly: distinctive or characteristic clothing.

A public service is a non-profit-making organisation set up to protect or help people. A uniformed public service is one where most of the people working in it wear a **uniform**.

link

Links to unit 2, page 120

i

www.policereform.gov.uk *(Police Reform Act 2002)*

remember

Law is a complicated subject. Donıt get bogged down in detail, and ask your tutor for guidance if you feel you need it.

progress check

1. Give an example of a role, a purpose and a responsibility for a public service.
2. List as many differences as you can between civilian and military public services.
3. Give two reasons why public services have mission statements.
4. Why is it hard for the public services to please the user and the taxpayer at the same time?
5. What is 'accountability' and why does it matter?
6. Give as many examples of 'conditions of service' as you can.
7. Why are the selection processes for the uniformed public services so difficult and complicated?
8. State three possible uses of a CV.
9. Explain two types of career development within a public service.
10. What is the value of self-appraisal?

Case Studies
provide real life examples that relate to what is being discussed within the text. It provides an opportunity to demonstrate theory in practice.

An **Activity** that is linked to a Case Study helps you to apply your knowledge of the subject to real life situations.

Keywords
of specific importance are highlighted within the text in blue, and then defined in a 'keyword' box to the side.

Links
direct you to other parts of the book that relate to the subject currently being covered.

Information bars
point you towards resources for further reading and research (e.g. websites).

Remember boxes
contain helpful hints, tips or advice.

Progress Checks
provide a list of quick questions at the end of each Unit, designed to ensure that you have understood the most important aspects of each subject area.

Acknowledgements

The author and publishers would like to thank the following for permission to reproduce material:

Bendrigg Trust; Buckinghamshire County Council; CPS; Department for Culture Media and Sport; Department for Transport; Driving Standards Agency; DVLA; Greater Manchester Police; Hampshire Fire and Rescue Service; The Home Office; HSE; London Ambulance Service; Office for National Statistics; Outward Bound; The Ramblers Association; West Yorkshire Fire and Rescue Service.

Ordnance Survey Mapping reproduced by permission of Ordnance Survey on behalf of HMSO. © Crown copyright 2006. All rights reserved. Ordnance Survey Licence number 100017284.

Crown copyright MoD material is reproduced with the permission of the Controller of the HMSO and the Queen's Printer for Scotland. Licence number C2006009492.

Photograph credits: Corel 414 (NT), p.23; Barbara Oenoyar/Photodisc 16 (NT), Kevin Peterson/Photodisc 33 (NT), Tom LeGoff/Digital Vision HU, p.56; Ingram ILV2CD5 (NT), Digital Vision 17 (NT), Photodisc 67 (NT), Corel 498 (NT), Corel 36 (NT), p.72; © Jack Sullivan/Alamy, p.115; © Martyn Barnwell/Alamy, p.139; Digital Vision XA (NT), p.149; Photodisc 14 (NT), p.176; Corel 760 (NT), p.197; Corel 275 (NT), p.208; Photodisc 72 (NT), p.225; PA Empics, p.234; Ashley Cooper/Corbis, p.262; © Jack Sullivan/Alamy, p.282; Ingram PR V2 CD6, p.316; Corel 275 (NT), p.325.

Every effort has been made to contact copyright holders and we apologise if any have been overlooked.

I have had a great deal of help in preparing this book. In particular I would like to thank Claire Hart and Jess Ward, who expertly got the project up and running, and gave me motivation and advice when I needed them. In the later stages the book was ably overseen by the production editor, Vanessa Thompson and copy edited by Elaine Bingham, who gave invaluable help. Proof-reading was carried out by Jan Morris, with an eagle eye and a great deal of discernment and understanding. I also wish to thank Keith Courtney and Cris Cullingworth, who have given me the benefit of their technical knowledge and long experience. Finally I would like to give my greatest thanks to Loretta – for everything she has done.

Nick Cullingworth

Uniformed Public Services Employment

This unit covers:

- the purpose, roles and responsibilities of uniformed public services
- jobs and conditions of service within the uniformed public services
- application and selection processes for uniformed public services
- initial training and opportunities for career development within uniformed public services

Many hundreds of thousands of people are employed in the UK's uniformed public services. For example, there are over 100,000 uniformed people working in the British Army, more than 40,000 in the Royal Navy, and more than 50,000 in the RAF. In 2005 there were over 141,000 police officers and 70,000 civilian staff working for the police. There are around 48,000 prison officers and 33,000 firefighters.

This unit introduces you to the uniformed public services, the work they do, and the application procedures you have to go through if you want to work in them. You will also learn something about basic training in the public services, and the ways in which you can be promoted.

grading criteria

To achieve a **Pass** grade the evidence must show that the learner is able to:	To achieve a **Merit** grade the evidence must show that, in addition to the pass criteria, the learner is able to:	To achieve a **Distinction** grade the evidence must show that, in addition to the pass and merit criteria, the learner is able to:
P1 describe the roles, purpose and responsibilities of two contrasting uniformed public services	**M1** explain the role, purpose and responsibilities of two contrasting uniformed public services	**D1** evaluate the role, purpose and responsibilities of a uniformed public service
P2 describe the type of work done in three different jobs within a named uniformed public service	**M2** explain in detail the work of a job within a uniformed public service	**D2** evaluate both the potential and the limitations for their own career development within their chosen uniformed public service

grading criteria

To achieve a **Pass** grade the evidence must show that the learner is able to:	To achieve a **Merit** grade the evidence must show that, in addition to the pass criteria, the learner is able to:	To achieve a **Distinction** grade the evidence must show that, in addition to the pass criteria, the learner is able to:
P3 describe the current conditions of service for a given job within a uniformed public service	**M3** explain the process of applying for a given job within a uniformed public service	
P4 describe the current entry requirements and the selection stages for a given uniformed public service	**M4** comment on their own suitability to complete basic training and for their career development within a chosen uniformed public service	
P5 complete an application form and curriculum vitae accurately for a given job within a uniformed public service		
P6 describe the initial training programme for a given uniformed public service		
P7 describe what opportunities are available for career development within a given public service		

The Purpose, Roles and Responsibilities of Uniformed Public Services

A public service is a non-profit-making organisation set up to protect or help people. A uniformed public service is one where most of the people working in it wear a **uniform**.

keyword

Uniform
dress of a distinctive design or fashion worn by members of a particular group and serving as a means of identification.

keyword	**Purpose** overall aims.

keyword	**Roles** jobs and the work done.

keyword	**Responsibilities** duties; and how the public services make sure they give a good service.

Every uniformed public service has a **purpose**, **roles** and **responsibilities**.

There are three main kinds of uniformed public service:

1. the emergency services
2. the armed forces
3. other kinds of uniformed service.

The roles, purpose and responsibilities of a public service are interrelated. Figure 1.1 below shows how this works with the police.

In Figure 1.1 the main roles of the police come under the headings 'Priority 1' and 'Priority 2'. These are the jobs the police do when they are keeping us safe and fighting crime. The neighbourhood policing under 'Priority 3' is also a role of this kind.

The purpose of the police is a general statement about why we have the police in the first place. That is given in the middle of Figure 1.1.

Figure 1.1

Roles, purpose and responsibilities of the police

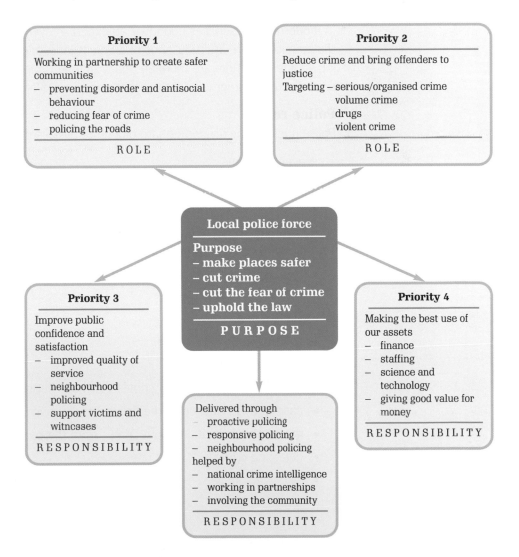

Priority 1

Working in partnership to create safer communities
- preventing disorder and antisocial behaviour
- reducing fear of crime
- policing the roads

ROLE

Priority 2

Reduce crime and bring offenders to justice
Targeting – serious/organised crime
           volume crime
           drugs
           violent crime

ROLE

Local police force

Purpose
– make places safer
– cut crime
– cut the fear of crime
– uphold the law

PURPOSE

Priority 3

Improve public confidence and satisfaction
- improved quality of service
- neighbourhood policing
- support victims and witnesses

RESPONSIBILITY

Delivered through
- proactive policing
- responsive policing
- neighbourhood policing
helped by
- national crime intelligence
- working in partnerships
- involving the community

RESPONSIBILITY

Priority 4

Making the best use of our assets
- finance
- staffing
- science and technology
- giving good value for money

RESPONSIBILITY

keyword

Resources
money, staff,
equipment and
knowledge.

The responsibilities of the police are to do their job as well as they can with the **resources** available. These come mainly under Priorities 3 and 4.

We will now look at roles, purpose and responsibilities individually, and in more detail.

activity

**INDIVIDUAL WORK
(1.1)**

Which of the following describes a role of the police?

(a) Patrolling the streets

(b) Treating everybody fairly

(c) Doing what the government tells them to do

(d) Proving that they are not wasting public money.

Roles

In modern public services nobody is an expert at every type of work done by that service. There are thousands of different jobs, and the work done in each job is different. There are therefore many different roles – and these roles are all specialised – in other words, they concentrate on different types of work.

Police roles

Police roles can be divided up into different specialised roles – for example:

1. Preventing crime

   - educating people so they avoid the risk of being victims of crime

   - advising on security

   - involving young people in 'diversionary' schemes which make them less likely to commit crime

   - researching patterns of crime so they can understand criminals and the way they behave.

2. Fighting crime

   - catching criminals

   - carrying out drugs raids

   - collecting evidence about crimes that have happened

   - passing this evidence to the Crown Prosecution Service

   - gathering information about crimes from the public and from informers

   - detecting crime

   - catching criminals.

Roles of the Royal Marines

The Royal Marines are a branch of the Royal Navy. They have two main roles:

1. *Fighting role*. They carry out swift, small-scale military operations in order to protect the interests of the United Kingdom, its armed forces, or the armed forces of allied countries. They were used in the Iraq war in 2003. Their main roles during that operation were:

   - launching an amphibious assault on the Al Faw peninsula
   - commanding a US Marines expeditionary unit.

2. *Deterrent role*. Because the Royal Marines are seen as a very effective fighting force, they also have a role as a deterrent: that is, they discourage enemies from trying to attack the UK, UK forces or UK interests. This probably reduces the threat of war.

Purposes of uniformed public services

The purposes of a public service are the overall aims of the service. In the UK these are laid down by law.

Information about the purposes of a uniformed public service comes in two forms:

1. **Mission statements**
2. Laws.

Mission statements

Every uniformed public service has a mission statement, and two examples of them are given in Case study 1.1.

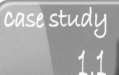

keyword

Mission statement
a phrase or sentence which (a) says what a public service aims to do and (b) tries to give a good public image of the service.

---

case study 1.1 — Mission statements

1. Metropolitan Police

Our mission
- To make places safer
- To cut crime and the fear of crime
- To uphold the law

Our vision
- To make London the safest major city in the world

Our values
- To treat everyone fairly
- To be open and honest
- To work in partnership
- To change to improve

(*Source*: www.met.police.uk)

2. Prison Service

Statement of purpose

Her Majesty's Prison Service serves the public by keeping in custody those committed by the courts. Our duty is to look after them with humanity and help them lead law-abiding and useful lives in custody and after release.

Our vision

- To provide excellent prison services that are the best in the country
- To work towards this vision by securing the following key objectives

Objectives

We protect the public by:

- Holding prisoners securely
- Reducing the risk of prisoners re-offending
- Providing safe and well-ordered establishments in which we treat prisoners humanely, decently and lawfully
- Providing an effective custody and escort service to the criminal courts, which supports their efficient operation.

In securing these objectives to adhere to the following principles:

Our principles

In carrying out our work we:

- Work in close partnership with others in the Criminal Justice System to achieve common objectives
- Obtain best value from the resources available using research to ensure effective correctional practice
- Value diversity, promote equality of opportunity and combat unlawful discrimination; and
- Ensure our staff have the right leadership, organisation, support and preparation to carry out their work effectively.

(*Source*: www.hmprisonservice.gov.uk)

activity

GROUP WORK

(a) Make a collection of mission statements from as many uniformed public services as you can. Put them on a wall display.

(b) Imagine you are teaching a citizenship class for people wishing to get UK citizenship. Choose mission statements from two different uniformed services and explain in the simplest possible language exactly what they mean.

(c) Write down the four purposes of the Prison Service in order of their importance and discuss why you have put them in that order.

Laws

The purposes of public services are laid down by law. This is so that everybody (inside and outside those services) knows what they are supposed to do, how they are supposed to do it, and where the limits of their power lie.

Examples of such laws are:

Law is a complicated subject. Don't get bogged down in detail, and ask your tutor for guidance if you feel you need it.

- The Police Reform Act 2002
- The Armed Forces Discipline Act 2004
- The Army Act 1955.

Here is a brief summary of the Police Reform Act 2002:

> An Act to make new provision about the supervision, administration, functions and conduct of police forces, police officers and other persons serving with, or carrying out functions in relation to, the police; to amend police powers and to provide for the exercise of police powers by persons who are not police officers; to amend the law relating to anti-social behaviour orders; to amend the law relating to sex offender orders; and for connected purposes (Home Office website).

You can see that the Act (law) aims to make the police more professional and cost-effective, to increase some of the powers of the police, and to allow community support officers (who are not police but wear uniforms and go on patrol) to be employed.

www.army.mod.uk
www.opsi.gov.uk (Armed Forces Discipline Act 2000)
www.policereform.gov.uk (Police Reform Act 2002)

activity
INDIVIDUAL WORK
(1.2)

(a) Print off part of a law which lays down the purpose of a public service.

(b) Show what part of the service's work is linked to the requirements of that law.

(c) Explain how successful you think the public service is in fulfilling that law.

(d) Outline any problems the service may have in carrying out that part of the law.

Responsibilities of uniformed public services

The responsibilities of a uniformed public service are to give the best possible service at the lowest possible cost.

In Figure 1.1 the responsibilities of the police include:

■ good finance: using money wisely; keeping a proper record of what is spent; making their accounts 'transparent' (so they can be inspected and people know how the money has been spent)

■ looking after their staff and making sure there are enough good staff for the job they are supposed to do

■ using science, technology, IT and other effective up-to-date ways of combating crime

■ working in partnership with the community, other crime-fighting agencies (such as HM Revenue and Customs), and using national crime intelligence (national database of crime information).

activity
GROUP WORK
(1.3)

(a) Find out how much your nearest police force spent in the last year.

(b) Have a group discussion on the subject: 'Is the money we spend on the police worth it, or should we spend it in other ways?'

keyword

Taxes
money collected by the government to pay for public services

The reason why cost matters is that the money that pays for the public services comes mainly from **taxes**. These can be general taxation such as income tax, excise duty and VAT, and local taxation such as the council tax.

Figure 1.2 outlines the responsibilities of a uniformed public service. This responsibility has two sides to it. The top half of the diagram is concerned with the responsibility to provide a good service. The bottom half of the diagram concerns the supply of money and the responsibility not to waste that money.

Citizens and taxpayers are of course the same (i.e. ordinary people), but they appear twice on the diagram because most of us have two conflicting priorities. As citizens we want the very best police service that money can buy, but as taxpayers we don't want to pay for it! Either way, the responsibility of the police is towards ordinary people. They must try to provide a good service, and they must try to do it as cheaply as possible.

Figure 1.2

Responsibilities of a
uniformed public service

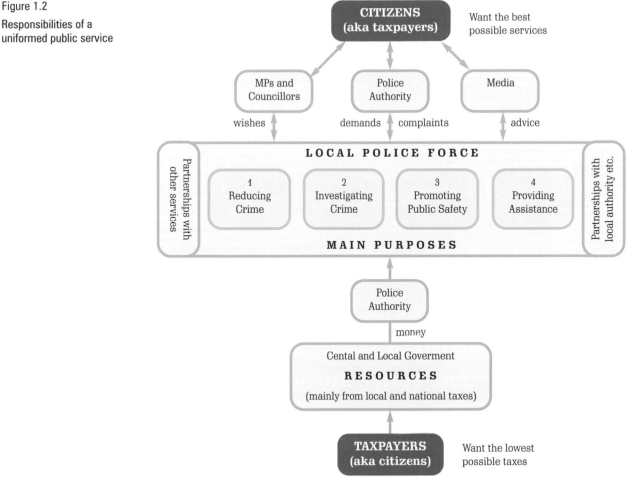

Accountability

Accountability is to do with ways of ensuring, and checking, that public services are carrying out their responsibilities.

Uniformed public services have three main kinds of accountability:

1. *Legal accountability*. This means following the law, and being seen to follow the law. In the case of the police this is very strict. For example, the police have:
   - the local police authority whose job is to oversee their work
   - inspections by Her Majesty's Inspectors (employed by the Home Office) to make sure they are doing their work correctly
   - inspections by the Audit Commission (to make sure they are spending their money wisely and legally)
   - the Independent Police Complaints Commission
   - the media, who may publicise the fact if police officers break the law.

2. *Professional accountability*. This means doing the job in an efficient, fair and conscientious manner. For example, if there was discrimination or harassment within a force there are various ways this could be dealt with:

Accountability
Working in such a way that other people can see what you have done, how you've done it, and what it costs. It usually means keeping good records and making them available for inspection.

keyword

- through an employment tribunal (a kind of court which tries cases of discrimination, harassment and unfair treatment at work)
- through the police authority
- through the police association (an organisation looking after the welfare of police officers).

Discrimination and harassment are illegal as well as being unprofessional. But other poor work practices which may or may not be illegal can be dealt with:

- through the police discipline code (a strict set of disciplinary rules)
- informally, or by a supervisory officer.

3. *Political accountability*. The police are not supposed to support any political group or party. The public or the media will normally complain if they appear to show political bias. The elected councillors in a police authority are chosen from a mix of political parties, with most coming from the party which won most votes in the local elections.

It can cause serious problems for a public service if they are not accountable, because they can be accused of human rights violations and even war crimes.

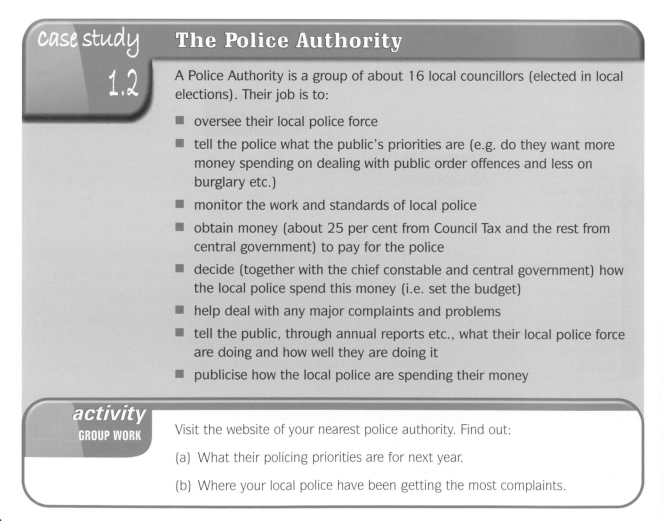

case study 1.2   The Police Authority

A Police Authority is a group of about 16 local councillors (elected in local elections). Their job is to:

- oversee their local police force
- tell the police what the public's priorities are (e.g. do they want more money spending on dealing with public order offences and less on burglary etc.)
- monitor the work and standards of local police
- obtain money (about 25 per cent from Council Tax and the rest from central government) to pay for the police
- decide (together with the chief constable and central government) how the local police spend this money (i.e. set the budget)
- help deal with any major complaints and problems
- tell the public, through annual reports etc., what their local police force are doing and how well they are doing it
- publicise how the local police are spending their money

activity
GROUP WORK

Visit the website of your nearest police authority. Find out:

(a) What their policing priorities are for next year.

(b) Where your local police have been getting the most complaints.

Other bodies which keep an eye on how well the police carry out their work are:
- Pressure groups – e.g. Liberty, Greenpeace, Stonewall
- Members of Parliament
- the Commission for Racial Equality.

Responsibility and diversity

The responsibilities of public services change as society changes. The uniformed public services used to contain more than their fair share of white males; now they are making a big effort to be as diverse as society and treat all people (whether employees or the general public) equally. The services are responsible to the whole of society, and government ministries, such as the Home Office, the Ministry of Defence, the Department for Communities and Local Goverment, formerly the Office of the Deputy Prime Minister and others, have targets and monitoring systems to try to make sure that these social responsibilities are met.

Why accountability matters

The public services are staffed by human beings and often suffer from a shortage of money, while their workload tends to go up all the time. This means that the service they give can sometimes sink to unacceptable levels. Systems of accountability tell the government and the public when things are going wrong in a public service establishment, so someone can do something about it. An example of this openness is given in Case study 1.3.

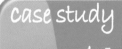

case study 1.3 — Lindholme Immigration Removal Centre

(From the report of a full unannounced inspection of Lindholme Immigration Removal Centre in 2004)

'Perhaps the most shocking aspect of the inspection was the filthy and dilapidated state of many of the communal areas. Paint was peeling, floors had ingrained dirt, and all of the telephone rooms – very important for detainees' contact with the outside world – were in a disgraceful state.'

(*Source*: www.homeoffice.gov.uk/justice)

activity
INDIVIDUAL WORK

Imagine you work at Lindholme. List:

(a) As many possible reasons for these problems as you can.

(b) Ways in which the prison service might ensure that they carry out their responsibilities better in future at Lindholme.

Jobs and Conditions of Service within the Uniformed Public Services

> **Job description**
> information about a job, sent out to applicants.

Jobs

Jobs are the posts that people hold in the public services. Each job has a name. The type of work that people do depends on the job – different jobs involve different types of work. Because the uniformed public services are so big, and their work so varied, there are many different jobs, and many different types of work. The type of work that goes with a particular job is usually described in a **job description**.

An example of a uniformed public service job description is given in Case study 1.4.

---

case study 1.4

Coastguard Watch Assistant (CWA) – job description

■ To undertake user checks on all communication systems and equipment, reporting faults/problems as appropriate.

■ To undertake, as supervised, 1st line non complex fault rectification (e.g. fuse and indicator bulb replacement) on communication systems and equipment; preparing defect reports for faults requiring higher level attention.

■ To operate the Action Data System (ADAS) recording incident and routine messages; amending front end data base information as directed.

■ To monitor and respond to CH16 and GMDSS distress, safety, and urgency calls, logging all available information, reporting all such calls to the WO/WM and taking broadcast action as required.

■ To initiate and monitor, as directed, SAR and related emergency service activities.

■ To perform basic chart work plotting functions in support of SAR and other operations, including the production of basic search plans.

■ To respond to routine and 999 telephone calls, including logging and reporting to the WO/WM.

■ To undertake routine admin tasks.

■ To participate in SAR accident prevention projects and PR events as required.

(*Source*: www.mcga.gov.uk)

---

activity
INDIVIDUAL WORK

(a) Using the internet find out the meanings of the abbreviations in this job description.

(b) Imagine you are telling a friend about this job vacancy. Using your own words, try to persuade him or her to apply for it, by describing the type of work.

A person's job includes:

- the things they do during an average day
- the reasons why they do those things
- exceptional or non-routine work they may be called upon to do
- the way they work with their colleagues and the public
- the advantages and drawbacks of the job as they see it.

case study 1.5

Emergency Medical Dispatchers – London Ambulance Service

Emergency medical dispatchers and emergency call handlers are the first link in the vital emergency response chain, receiving urgent calls and mobilising ambulances. They are also sometimes directly involved in saving lives by talking a caller through an emergency procedure over the phone, while the ambulance is on its way.

Emergency medical dispatchers/call handlers take the essential details of every call quickly and accurately, sometimes from people who are very distressed. They must stay calm and reassuring, while thinking fast and using their initiative. Some ambulance services split the control role into call handlers and dispatchers.

Quotations from a dispatcher:

'The details of the call come through to the sector controller who decides on the nearest ambulance crew. I pass them the call by computer if they are on station, or by radio if they are on the road. The crews can respond very quickly and the difficult part is to give them all the information they need about the patient before they arrive at the address.'

'It's a demanding and challenging job and you need to able to multi-task and deal with some very complex situations. I think you need good listening skills and the willingness to do whatever you can to help.'

'The best part about this job is that you are helping people, particularly older people who are often anxious not to cause a fuss, even when they are in considerable pain. It's good when we can make them comfortable.'

(*Source*: London Ambulance Service)

activity
GROUP WORK

(a) Read the case study and note down the questions you would ask an emergency medical dispatcher working with the ambulance service.

(b) Interview someone who works for a public service, and note down what they say. Try to include word-for-word quotations, to get a real feeling of what the job is like.

(c) Write up your findings, for someone who might be interested in working for that service.

By far the best way to find out about the work people do in a uniformed service is to talk to them about it. One way to organise this is to ask your tutor to invite visiting speakers from the uniformed public services to tell you about their jobs. Another way is to fix up a work placement or period of work shadowing with a public service. This is not always easy to do, but it is well worth making the effort if you are seriously interested in public service work.

keyword

Conditions of service
things like hours, pay, holidays, pension and health arrangements that go with the job.

Conditions of service

Every job in the uniformed public services has **conditions of service**. These are legally binding on both the employer and employee.

Case Study 1.6 shows a typical outline of conditions of service for a uniformed public service job: a Fire Control Operator in the Mobilising and Communications Centre (MACC) of the West Yorkshire Fire and Rescue Service.

case study 1.6 — Fire Control Operators

Main Conditions of Service Applicable to Fire Control Operators

Salaries:
Salaries are paid 4 weekly and payment is made by direct credit to your bank account or building society account.

Hours of duty:
Your hours of duty average 42 per week normally worked on a rotating shift basis within a prescribed watch-keeping system, the shifts commencing at either 0900 hours or 1800 hours. The 42 hour week is organised as 2×9 hour day duties followed by 2×15 hour night duties then 4 days off duty.

REST AND BREAK

Accommodation:
Whilst on duty both day and night the rest areas are mixed and used by men and women at the same time.

Initial training:
The periods for trainee Fire Control Operators training, are Monday to Friday 0900 hours to 1700 hours.

Place of work:
The Mobilising and Communications Centre based at FSHQ, Birkenshaw, Bradford.

Maternity leave:
Maternity leave is granted on a standard scale to all women and in accordance with the relevant sections of the National Joint Council for Local Authorities Fire Brigades, Scheme of Conditions of Service.

Paternity leave:
Paternity support leave of 5 working days (for personnel conditioned to the shift system this will be 4 duty shifts) shall be granted to the child's father or the partner or the nominated carer of an expectant mother at or around the time of birth. A nominated carer is the person nominated by the mother to assist in the care of the child and to provide support to the mother at or around the time of birth.

Pension:
From the date of commencement of your employment, you will be deemed to be a contributor to the Local Government Pension Scheme at the rate of 6% of your pay. You may, however, opt out of the scheme.

Probation:
From the date of your appointment you will be subject to a probationary period. The length at the discretion of the Service shall not be less than 12 months but is usually a standard 2 years.

Union membership:
The recognised body for most Fire Service personnel is the Fire Brigade's Union (FBU). [Membership is optional].

Uniform:
Uniform is provided and must be worn while you are on duty.

(*Source*: www.westyorksfire.gov.uk)

activity
GROUP WORK

(a) Each person chooses four headings from the conditions of service above.

(b) Write clear definitions of all the main words.

(c) Set a short quiz on key terms for conditions of service for another group in the class and make them do the quiz.

(d) Answer questions from other groups.

Collect careers leaflets issued by the service you are interested in.
Visit the official website of a uniformed public service.
Contact a Recruitment Section of a uniformed public service.

Application and Selection Processes for Uniformed Public Services

People who want to work in the uniformed public services have to go through a lengthy application and selection process – whatever the job is that they are applying for.

Most uniformed public service jobs are popular. For this reason some services do not recruit all the time, but only when they need new applicants. It is therefore a good idea to ring a service before applying and ask them if they are recruiting at that time.

Entry requirements

Uniformed public services usually have a clear idea of the kind of applicant they want, so they usually state **entry requirements** for applicants. These state the kinds of person they are looking for.

> **keyword**
>
> **Entry requirements**
> a list of information about the kind of applicant a public service is looking for. Sometimes entry requirements are called a 'person specification', or 'job criteria'.

---

case study 1.7

Emergency Medical Technician – London Ambulance Service

To become an EMT you must:

- Be aged between 21 and 45.
- Have a stable employment or education record.
- Be able to communicate effectively with people from different backgrounds.
- Be physically fit with good eyesight.
- Have held a full, manual British driving licence (with no more than 3 points) for at least two years.
- Be resident in or near the Greater London area or prepared to relocate.

(*Source*: www.londonambulance.nhs.uk)

---

activity
INDIVIDUAL WORK

(a) What is meant by 'stable employment or education record'?

(b) What is meant by 'people from different backgrounds'?

(c) Why do they set age limits – and do you think they are justified in doing so?

Each uniformed public service has different entry requirements. You can find them on their websites. As the requirements change sometimes, make sure that the information you get is up to date!

Selection stages

For the uniformed public services selection is divided into a number of different parts, called stages. During these stages each aspect of your abilities, character or qualities needed for the job is investigated or put to the test.

An example of a selection process is given in Figure 1.3. The diagram shows the order in which each stage is carried out, and the comment at the right-hand side is a description of each selection stage.

Figure 1.3

Basic selection process – firefighter

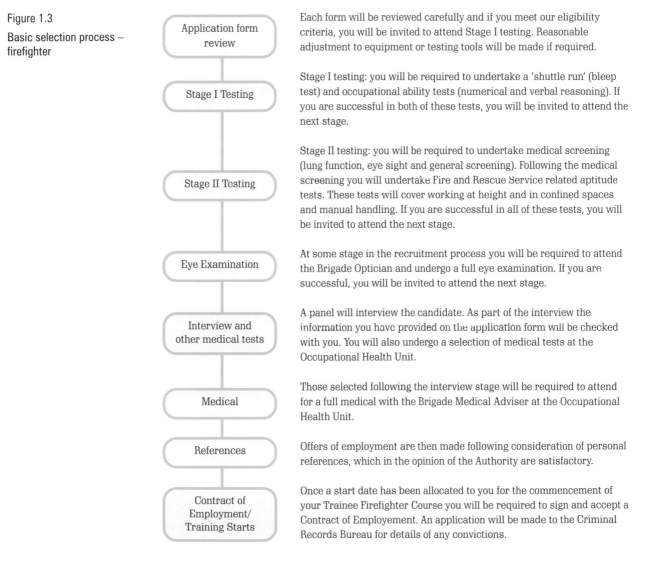

Application form review	Each form will be reviewed carefully and if you meet our eligibility criteria, you will be invited to attend Stage I testing. Reasonable adjustment to equipment or testing tools will be made if required.
Stage I Testing	Stage I testing: you will be required to undertake a 'shuttle run' (bleep test) and occupational ability tests (numerical and verbal reasoning). If you are successful in both of these tests, you will be invited to attend the next stage.
Stage II Testing	Stage II testing: you will be required to undertake medical screening (lung function, eye sight and general screening). Following the medical screening you will undertake Fire and Rescue Service related aptitude tests. These tests will cover working at height and in confined spaces and manual handling. If you are successful in all of these tests, you will be invited to attend the next stage.
Eye Examination	At some stage in the recruitment process you will be required to attend the Brigade Optician and undergo a full eye examination. If you are successful, you will be invited to attend the next stage.
Interview and other medical tests	A panel will interview the candidate. As part of the interview the information you have provided on the application form will be checked with you. You will also undergo a selection of medical tests at the Occupational Health Unit.
Medical	Those selected following the interview stage will be required to attend for a full medical with the Brigade Medical Adviser at the Occupational Health Unit.
References	Offers of employment are then made following consideration of personal references, which in the opinion of the Authority are satisfactory.
Contract of Employment/ Training Starts	Once a start date has been allocated to you for the commencement of your Trainee Firefighter Course you will be required to sign and accept a Contract of Employement. An application will be made to the Criminal Records Bureau for details of any convictions.

Applying to uniformed public services

The application procedure for many uniformed public service jobs is long and complex. They aim to get to know as much as possible about you before they decide whether to accept you or not.

case study 1.8   Applying for a job as a police officer

Stage 1

If you are interested in joining the police you should first of all find out more about police work and whether you would like it. The best way to do this is to visit the police, explain your plans to them, and ask their advice.

In addition you should consider some long term preparation – for example, practising the kinds of tests you will have to do in stage 2 below, and getting yourself fit.

To apply for a job as a police officer you must be at least $18^1/_2$ years old. Check that there is nothing (e.g. disability, bad health, serious criminal record) which will lead to immediate rejection.

Next you should find out which of the 43 police forces in the country are recruiting. The best way to do this is to telephone their recruiting sections. You should then give them your details and ask them to send you an application pack. If they want you to write to them for a pack, do as they say.

As soon as you know which police force you are applying to, find out as much as you can about the force and the area it covers.

Police application forms are long and complex, and divided into many parts. They must be filled in correctly, to a high standard, following all instructions. The completed forms must reach the police before their deadline.

Then you wait. Applications to the police can take many months to be checked.

Your application form shows that:

- you can understand and follow instructions
- you understand how to present yourself in a way that would impress the police recruiters
- you understand what police work is about
- you may well have the qualities the police are looking for.

If your application form is poor, inaccurate or untruthful, or if it shows that you are not suitable or eligible to join, you will be rejected at this stage. If you are not rejected, you will go on to the next stage.

Stage 2

You will be invited to attend a police assessment centre. You will be sent material to prepare you for the activities you will do there. You should study this material carefully before you go to the centre.

At the centre you will be assessed on numerical reasoning, verbal logical reasoning, competence in writing, and on five 'core competences' which are linked to personal skills and qualities. These are: Respect for Diversity, Teamworking, Personal Responsibility, Resilience and Effective Communication. The five core competences are assessed by people at the assessment centre using role plays and simulations.

The purpose of this stage is:

- to show that you are numerate enough for the job
- to show that you are literate
- to show that you have good reasoning skills
- to show that you are not sexist or racist and respect people whose backgrounds are different from yours
- to show that you can work with others
- to show that you are able to take on responsibilities and can be trusted
- to show that you can adapt well to strange situations
- to show that you communicate well.

Stage 3
If you are successful in the assessments you will be invited for a medical examination. (This will add to the information about your health already given on your application form.)

The purpose of this is to show that you are healthy enough to carry out the work without taking too much time off, or damaging your own health.

Stage 4
If you have passed your medical examination you will be invited for a fitness test. You will be tested on 'dynamic strength' and 'endurance fitness', and you will be expected to reach a level which is needed to do your work as a police officer.

The purpose of this is to show that you are fit enough to work long hours and deal with emergencies where physical action is needed.

(*Source*: This outline is adapted from material found at www.policecouldyou.co.uk)

activity
GROUP WORK

(a) Discuss and note down all the reasons you can think of why the police application process is so complex.

(b) The police employ many people besides police officers. Research the types of work the police offer for people who are not police officers.

(c) Application procedures keep changing. Write off to your favourite public service and get them to send you their latest application pack.

Application forms

Application forms for uniformed public services must be filled in correctly – and truthfully.

Only high-quality application forms – neat, written in good English, clearly stating facts (and opinions, where asked for) – stand a chance of success.

Police application forms are long and complicated and have several sections. Applications for some other jobs, such as infantry soldier, or RAF gunner, are much simpler.

You can obtain application forms by writing off to the public service of your choice, or – in some cases – by downloading them from the internet.

Advice on filling in application forms

1. Photocopy the whole form, and fill in the photocopy first, making sure that you have got everything right.

2. Get someone such as a tutor to check through the photocopied form and make sure that it will give a good impression.

3. Take note of any alterations which may be suggested.

4. Fill in the proper form, using black ink, and following any other instructions on how it should be filled in.

5. Take your time: it must be done as neatly and accurately as possible.

6. Make sure you give examples or other evidence for your 'skills and abilities' section.

7. If you have to make a correction, rule a single line through the error and write the correct wording in the nearest space. Never use 'tippex'.

8. When you have finished, check – then get someone else to check – that you have not missed anything out.

9. Post the form in a clearly addressed envelope, well before the final deadline.

Curriculum vitae

A curriculum vitae (CV) is a document, produced by you, giving the main facts about you which would interest an employer.

When applying for a job in a uniformed public service, you are not normally required to send a curriculum vitae.

However, you need to prepare a CV:

- to pass your BTEC First
- to apply for some jobs or work placement experience
- to record information about yourself so that you can copy it straight onto an application form, instead of having to think about it.

It should end up looking a bit like the one shown in Figure 1.4.

remember

There are smart computer programs for doing CVs. And once it is done, all you will ever need to do is update it.

Figure 1.4
Example CV

CURRICULUM VITAE

FAMILY NAME:	Whitehouse	**TELEPHONE:**	01326 839625
OTHER NAMES:	Mary Louise	**DATE OF BIRTH:**	16 November 1990
ADDRESS:	32 Fleet Street Weston on Sea Suffolk WS23 4WH	**NATIONALITY:**	British

EDUCATION

Date	School/College	GCSE	Grades
09/2000–06/2006	Weston High School	English Language	D
		English Literature	E
		Mathematics	D
		French	D
		Geography	E
		Combined Sciences	D
		Craft, Design & Technology	E
		PE	B
		Religious Studies	F
09/2006–present	Cramwell College	BTEC First Diploma in Public Services	Results not yet available

EMPLOYMENT

Dates (most recent first)	Employer	Type of work	Reason for leaving
March 2006 (for two weeks)	Weston Fire and Rescue Service	Work placement: observation and piloting exercises	End of placement (after two weeks)
November 2005 –	Patel's Newsagents High Street Upper Weston	Filling shelves Helping customers Working on till Stocktaking Supervising paper deliveries	Not applicable
November 2004	Patel's Newsagents	Paper girl – delivering Sunday papers	Became shop assistant in November 2002.

OTHER ACTIVITIES/ INTERESTS

2000–2005	Member of Guides. Went on walking and canoeing activities.
2005	Successfully completed Duke of Edinburgh Silver Award and started on Gold Award.
2001 onwards	Voluntary work at Nevada Riding Stables, Weston (grooming, cleaning stables, helping new riders).
June 2005	Came fourth in Junior section of regional show-jumping competition at Colchester, Essex.

I have represented my school and college as a middle distance runner in athletics competitions.

REFEREES

The following people, who are not related to me, would be willing to act as referees:

1. Mrs Amina Patel
    Patel's Newsagents
    High Street
    Upper Weston
    WS23 5WH

2. Mr Rio Ferdinand
    Course Tutor
    BTEC First Diploma in Public Services
    Cramwell College
    Task Road
    Cramwell
    CL3 8KO

activity
INDIVIDUAL WORK (1.4)

(a) Get an application form for a uniformed public service job and fill it in correctly.

(b) Produce an accurate, up-to-date curriculum vitae for yourself.

Initial Training and Opportunities for Career Development within Uniformed Public Services

Initial training is usually basic and designed to give you a fundamental understanding of the job.

Typically, initial training starts as soon as you join the service, continues for a number of weeks, and is followed by a probationary period, which may last for a year or two. During this probationary period the recruit will be watched and helped by a 'mentor' – a more senior employee who knows all about the job. Initial training is more complex, and lasts longer, for the police than it does for most other uniformed public services. In the armed forces initial training for officers is much longer and more classroom-based than the initial training for other ranks.

Initial training usually concentrates on developing skills and knowledge which are needed for carrying out the job effectively.

case study 1.9 — Training for Immigration Officers

Initial training consists of 5 weeks for passport control officers and 8 weeks for immigration enforcement officers. This covers classroom and practical work and includes site visits. The training period supports the development of a wide range of skills and knowledge, including:

- immigration legislation
- customer care
- professional practice
- interviewing
- report writing.

New immigration officers are also provided with support through mentoring offered by more senior staff.

At the end of the initial training period new entrants begin their first posting with intensive support from colleagues. The major ports and centres of employment have a team dedicated to continuous training; practice differs in smaller teams.

The UK Immigration Service (UKIS) also offers assistance for further job-related training depending on the specific role or functional specialism of the staff concerned. This may include the development of language skills.

All new entrants must serve a period of probation, which would normally be a year in length.

(*Source*: www.prospects.ac.uk/links)

(a) Find out as much as you can about the five bullet points.

(b) Which of the following methods do you think would be suitable for teaching each of them, and why?

Role-plays and simulations

Self-appraisal

Classroom instruction

Work shadowing

Case studies

Figure 1.5

Soldiers on basic training

keyword

Basic training/initial training
training for new recruits giving general skills which are needed for almost every job in that service.

keyword

Manager
a person who organises, motivates and directs other employees.

Basic training

Basic training (sometimes called **'initial training'**) is the training that recruits do when they join a uniformed public service.

Career development

Career development in a public service takes two forms:

1. 'Upward' movement (promotion) leading to higher rank, higher pay and greater responsibility

2. 'Sideways' movement (transfer) leading to specialisation in a particular field of work.

At the present time (2006) the organisation of some public services is changing. For example, in the fire and rescue service, 'generic occupational standards' have replaced the old 'rank structure'.

Upward career development is from firefighter to crew **manager** to watch manager, and so on. Sideways career development might be from technical fire safety to fire investigation. This kind of development involves gaining new skills and knowledge, and can bring more job satisfaction.

Career development in the armed forces follows a similar principle. Salaries increase by increments (small amounts) every year. Promotion, which is on merit, is from one rank to the next. Promotions for soldiers are up the following rank structure:

■ New recruits

■ Private

■ Lance Corporal

■ Corporal

■ Sergeant

case study 1.10

Basic training for soldiers

A: Fieldcraft

How to look after yourself and your equipment; how to live in the field, and how to observe, detect and report an enemy.

B: Weapon Training

How to use and fire the SA80 rifle at distances of up to 300 metres.

C: Nuclear, Biological and Chemical

First aid and defensive measures against NBC (Nuclear, Biological and Chemical) warfare.

D: Military education

Military history, welfare and financial advice.

E: Recreation, Adventurous and Initiative Training

Outdoor pursuits, including team sports and 'Outward Bound' activities aimed at character development.

F: Physical Fitness and Endurance Training

As well as the organised sport in the training programme, there is time to enjoy the many facilities of the ATR. All have gymnasiums and squash courts, and there is plenty of opportunity to play team games.

G: Drill

Foot and Arms Drill building up to the Passing Out Parade which relatives and friends will be invited to attend.

H: Administration

Your own personal administration is an important factor in ensuring that you are well organised and can concentrate on your military training without being distracted.

activity
GROUP WORK

(a) Get into pairs and grade yourself and your partner out of 10 for each of the skills A–H on a piece of paper.

(b) Swap your papers and justify your grades to your partner. Try to reach agreement for each one.

- Staff Sergeant
- Warrant Officer Class II
- Warrant Officer Class I .

But career development for soldiers in the sense of increasing their skills is also very important. The training of infantry soldiers that takes place after their initial training is part of their career development. The qualifications can lead them to 'sideways' development where they specialise in different kinds of soldiering.

case study
1.11

Training

You'll be thoroughly trained and gain real skills as a soldier. We won't just teach you when to salute and how to use a gun. Our training will bring out your self-confidence, teach you to think on your feet and give you some valuable qualifications:

- Earn recognised qualifications such as NVQs (or SVQs) and BTECs.

- Get practical qualifications, like your driving licence or even your motorcycle or HGV licence.

- Keep on training all the way through your time in the army – learn about new equipment and how to handle different situations.

- Gain skills that will stand you in good stead for life – as well as being vital for your everyday work.

(*Source*: Army website: www.army.mod.uk)

activity
INDIVIDUAL WORK

Contact the recruitment office/section of a uniformed public servce and ask them:

(a) How people get promoted.

(b) What employees have to do if they want to change the type of work they do (e.g. from traffic policing to scenes of crime examination).

How do I know if I can do it?

Training

To comment on your own suitability to do training you must consider (a) what you have to do, (b) whether you can do it and (c) whether you would enjoy doing it.

Your comments should include some evidence to support them. For example: 'I would enjoy military education because I always enjoyed history at school and like reading about battles which took place in the past.'

activity
INDIVIDUAL WORK
(1.5)

(a) Look at Case study 1.11 on page 26, then answer the following questions:

A. Fieldcraft

What experience do I have of camping, walking and navigation?

When have I shown good powers of observation?

B. Weapon Training

Have I ever fired a gun? Would I enjoy improving my marksmanship?

C. Nuclear, Biological and Chemical

Am I interested in basic science?

(b) Make up, and answer, similar questions for items D to H.

Career development

Your ability to develop your career will depend on:

1. your desire for promotion
2. your motivation and ability to gain new skills
3. your ability to get on with other people.

Promotion

Whether a person gets promoted in a public service depends on whether:

- they want to be promoted (and apply)
- they can learn new skills
- they can take on new responsibilities
- there is a system (rank structure) which enables people to get promoted from one level to the next
- there are vacancies in the next level up
- the applicant has a good work record
- the applicant can do well in tests and interviews
- the applicant has the right mix of leadership and teamwork qualities
- the applicant is a good communicator.

Evaluating career potential

People who gain promotion and develop their careers successfully often do so because they know their own abilities well, and plan for the future.

Self-appraisal, or evaluation, is used in public service training to make people more aware of their strengths and limitations, and to show them how they should develop. After each training activity recruits evaluate their own performance and learn from it.

case study 1.12

Promotion in the Metropolitan Police – constable to sergeant

Career structure:

- Police Constable
- Police Sergeant
- Police Inspector
- Chief Inspector
- Superintendent
- Chief Superintendent

After successful completion of a 2-year probationary period, you have to register your interest if you wish to apply for promotion.

You then take the following examination, which is in two parts:

Objective Structured Performance Related Examinations (OSPRE)

Part 1 of the promotion process (OSPRE) for Constables to Sergeants usually takes place in March each year. This consists of a 2.5 hour exam (multiple choice). If successful Part 2 of the promotion process (OSPRE) takes place approximately 6 months later, which consists of a number of interactive exercises.

For the Metropolitan Police Service, after successful completion of OSPRE Parts 1 and 2, you have to obtain a recommendation for promotion from your commander. (This recommendation is based mainly on your work record.) You will then have to either apply for individually advertised posts or be put in the 'posting panel' in which there are a number of officers matched up to a number of vacancies throughout the Metropolitan Police Service.

The promotion exams are in two parts. Part 1 tests knowledge of the law; Part 2 tests 'management and supervisory potential' (e.g. dealing with people and planning).

The qualities looked for in sergeants are:

- Strategic perspective (able to understand the long-term aims of policing)
- Planning and organising (efficient and effective; makes sure that people do what they are supposed to do)
- Community and customer focus (aware of the needs of the public)
- Openness to change (able to listen, learn and adapt)
- Effective communication (good at explaining, advising, persuading etc., and at paperwork)

- Problem solving (able to think clearly and sort out difficulties)

- Respect for diversity (non-sexist, and showing respect to people of all cultures)

- Commitment (hard working).

activity
GROUP WORK

(a) Note down the advantages and disadvantages (from your own point of view) of getting promoted in a public service such as the police.

(b) Exchange your notes with the group, and compare your ideas.

Career limitations could take the form of lack of interest, confidence or ability to do a particular job. The main thing you need to know about limitations is that they can almost always be overcome, if you have the desire to do it!

activity
INDIVIDUAL WORK (1.6)

Test yourself on the following questions.

(a) What will be the likely changes in the work of (my chosen public service) in five years' time?

(b) What evidence could I give an interviewer that I am good at planning and organising?

(c) What would my strengths and weaknesses be if I was working with the public?

(d) Can I give an example of when I listened to someone's advice and changed my behaviour because of it?

(e) Have I ever been able to persuade someone to do something for their own good?

(f) What evidence could I give that I relate effectively with people from other ethnic groups?

(g) What should I be doing now to make myself more likely to be employed by the public service of my choice?

progress check

1. Give an example of a role, a purpose and a responsibility for a public service.
2. List as many differences as you can between civilian and military public services.
3. Give two reasons why public services have mission statements.
4. Why is it hard for the public services to please the user and the taxpayer at the same time?
5. What is 'accountability' and why does it matter?
6. Give as many examples of 'conditions of service' as you can.
7. Why are the selection processes for the uniformed public services so difficult and complicated?
8. State three possible uses of a CV.
9. Explain two types of career development within a public service.
10. What is the value of self-appraisal?

UNIT 2

Public Service Skills

This unit covers:

- the purpose and importance of teamwork in the public services
- using a range of interpersonal communication skills
- understanding various methods of instruction

The public services are made up of teams. If you don't like being in a team, think again about your choice of career.

In this unit you will learn quite a lot about teamwork. And you will also learn about the things that go with it such as communication.

Good communication means speaking, reading and writing effectively. But it goes further than that – it is the key to influencing people, leading people, and making friends with them. It has a lot to do with promotion and success in public service.

Finally, you will learn how to instruct people. If you work in the public services you will often have to tell people things – and this has to be done in a clear and relevant manner that holds their attention.

grading criteria

To achieve a **Pass** grade the evidence must show that the learner is able to:	To achieve a **Merit** grade the evidence must show that, in addition to the pass criteria, the learner is able to:	To achieve a **Distinction** grade the evidence must show that, in addition to the pass and merit criteria, the learner is able to:
P1 describe the purpose and importance of teamwork using examples from at least two contrasting public services	**M1** explain the importance of teamwork in at least two contrasting public services	**D1** analyse the importance of teamwork in a specified public service
P2 participate in different team-building activities	**M2** analyse the application of interpersonal communication skills in a chosen public service	**D2** evaluate the effective use of interpersonal and communication skills in a given public service
P3 describe the effectiveness of various methods of interpersonal communication skills	**M3** demonstrate effective instruction skills	

grading criteria

To achieve a **Pass** grade the evidence must show that the learner is able to:	To achieve a **Merit** grade the evidence must show that, in addition to the pass criteria, the learner is able to:	To achieve a **Distinction** grade the evidence must show that, in addition to the pass criteria, the learner is able to:
P4 demonstrate use of interpersonal skills to communicate with personnel in given situations		
P5 describe the qualities of a good instructor and how they are used		

The Purpose and Importance of Teamwork in the Public Services

Public services work in **teams**. They may not be called teams – they could be crews, squads, units, regiments, task forces, partnerships, departments, sections, shifts, watches, outfits, offices or think tanks – but they still work as teams.

The purpose of teamwork

The purpose of **teamwork** is to do the job for which the team was set up. Teamwork aims to achieve the best possible results, as quickly as possible, as easily as possible and as cheaply as possible.

The importance of teamwork

The obvious importance of teamwork in the public services is that everybody does it, and everybody belongs to at least one team. (An individual can, of course, belong to several teams at the same time.)

The underlying importance of teamwork is that – if it is done well – it brings major advantages:

- for the public service itself
- for the people working in it
- for the people the service works for.

Figure 2.1 shows the importance of teamwork in a uniformed public service in four main areas:

Figure 2.1

Advantages of teamwork

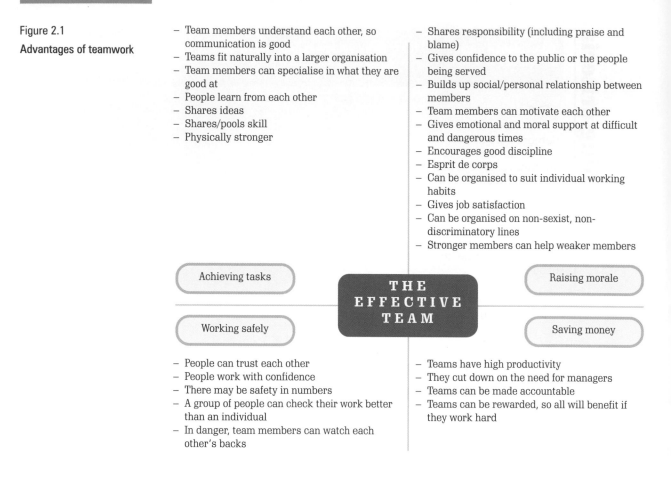

- Team members understand each other, so communication is good
- Teams fit naturally into a larger organisation
- Team members can specialise in what they are good at
- People learn from each other
- Shares ideas
- Shares/pools skill
- Physically stronger

- Shares responsibility (including praise and blame)
- Gives confidence to the public or the people being served
- Builds up social/personal relationship between members
- Team members can motivate each other
- Gives emotional and moral support at difficult and dangerous times
- Encourages good discipline
- Esprit de corps
- Can be organised to suit individual working habits
- Gives job satisfaction
- Can be organised on non-sexist, non-discriminatory lines
- Stronger members can help weaker members

Achieving tasks

Working safely

THE EFFECTIVE TEAM

Raising morale

Saving money

- People can trust each other
- People work with confidence
- There may be safety in numbers
- A group of people can check their work better than an individual
- In danger, team members can watch each other's backs

- Teams have high productivity
- They cut down on the need for managers
- Teams can be made accountable
- Teams can be rewarded, so all will benefit if they work hard

- *Achieving tasks*. Good teamwork gets things done. It saves time and work is done to a higher standard.

- *Raising morale*. Good teamwork makes people feel good about themselves and their work. It raises 'morale' – i.e. courage and confidence.

- *Working safely*. People can check each other, and look out for each other.

- *Saving money*. People work harder in teams. They give more service for less money.

Teamwork in the armed forces

case study

2.1

Army teams

'Fighting and other military operations on land are fundamentally a group activity. Even when deployed alone or dispersed, soldiers are part of a team. The effectiveness of the team depends on every individual, seen or unseen, playing their part to the full, and contributing to the cohesion of the whole.'

(*Source*: the Military Covenant: www.army.mod.uk/ servingsoldier/)

activity
GROUP WORK

(a) Why is a group of people more effective at fighting than an individual? Discuss and note down as many reasons as you can.

(b) Why are soldiers part of a team even if they are deployed alone?

Different kinds of army team

The army is divided into many different kinds of unit, all of which are either teams, or made up of teams.

From Figure 2.2 it is clear that any soldier is a member of a platoon, a company, a regiment, a brigade and a division. When the soldier is with the platoon or troop he (for infantry soldiers are always male) is with a team of people he knows well. The bigger units, such as regiments and brigades, are entirely made up of teams. If you took the teams out of the army there would be nobody left!

Purpose of army teamwork

The purpose of army teamwork is:

■ to make the army easier to command

■ to make the army more versatile and adaptable (i.e. it can fight big battles or small operations)

Figure 2.2
Main army units

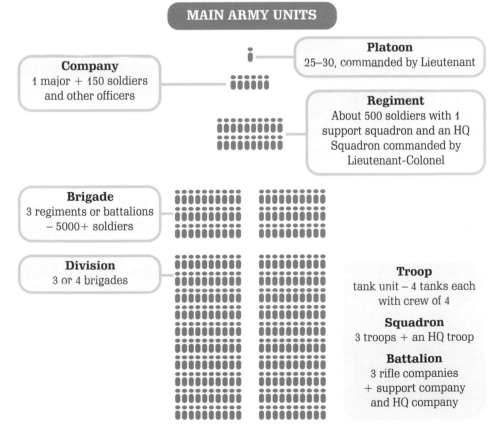

MAIN ARMY UNITS

Company
1 major + 150 soldiers
and other officers

Platoon
25–30, commanded by Lieutenant

Regiment
About 500 soldiers with 1
support squadron and an HQ
Squadron commanded by
Lieutenant-Colonel

Brigade
3 regiments or battalions
– 5000+ soldiers

Division
3 or 4 brigades

Troop
tank unit – 4 tanks each
with crew of 4

Squadron
3 troops + an HQ troop

Battalion
3 rifle companies
+ support company
and HQ company

keyword

Specialise
to concentrate on one particular kind of work.

- to enable units to **specialise**
- to enable fast accurate communications (either orders from above, or information and feedback from below)
- to improve morale – everybody is among team-mates and knows where they belong.

Importance of army teamwork

Army teamwork is important because:

- the army trains and fights more effectively
- units of the army can be sent to different parts of the world, without weakening the army as a whole
- everybody knows what they need to know, when they need to know it
- units can fight or work independently if they have to
- it enables individuals to find a role which satisfies them and uses their skills
- it makes it clear who is responsible for what
- it is good for discipline
- individuals enjoy working with people they know – i.e. team-mates.

Specialist teams

In the army there are many teams and organisations which have special skills. They keep the regimental system (outlined in Figure 2.2) working well.

case study 2.2 — Army teams with special skills

Logistics/engineers/artillery/medical

Units drawn from these corps are often used to support regiments, battalions, divisions and brigades where necessary (depending on the requirements of a specific situation).

Corps

A corps is a collection of different regiments or groupings that share a common area of interest or expertise.

Specialist units

Taking on a variety of very specific tasks, specialist units are formed when certain army needs cannot be met through existing army units.

(*Source*: www.army.mod.uk)

activity
INDIVIDUAL WORK

(a) Visit www.army.mod.uk and find the names of 10 different army teams.

(b) Why is it important that every team has a name?

Examples of team achievement

One feature of teams is that they can achieve great things in difficult circumstances. The Royal Navy's rescue of Russian sailors from a trapped submarine in August 2005 is a good illustration of this.

---

case study

2.3

Royal Navy rescue mission

PETROPAVLOVSK-KAMCHATSKY, Russia, (AFP) - A British undersea robot cut free a Russian mini-submarine in a dramatic operation that saved seven sailors trapped for three days 190 meters (625 feet) under the Pacific Ocean.

The rescue, some 75 hours after the Priz AS-28 mini-sub became snagged on the seabed during military exercises, was completed with just hours left in oxygen supplies for the seven crew.

Russian ships had tried unsuccessfully on several occasions to haul up both the mini-sub and the anchored cables of an underwater coastal defence antenna in which it had become snagged.

But the British Royal Navy team, which arrived Sunday at the site roughly 70 kilometers (45 miles) south of the port of Petropavlovsk-Kamchatsky, used a high-tech Scorpio unmanned submersible to attack the cables and an abandoned fishing net.

Within two hours, the Scorpio had cut the stricken craft free and Russian navy spokesman Igor Dygalo was able to announce: 'The submarine resurfaced and the seven submariners are alive.'

(*Source*: http://news.yahoo.com)

---

activity

GROUP WORK

(a) Choosing one uniformed public service each, collect information about five teams from that service.

(b) Put up a wall display showing what the teams do and why they do it.

The importance of teamwork in the army

The army is an organisation which places high value on teamwork. Some analysis of this is given below:

1. *Teamwork is a tradition*. Even in Roman times armies formed teams and groups (legions etc.) in order to fight more effectively. These groups were the origins of the present system of brigades, regiments and other units. The modern British army is also a highly traditional organisation. Regiments and battalions have a long history, and there is an outcry when they are disbanded or merged to save money (see Case study 2.4).

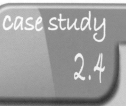

case study 2.4   Black Watch homecoming

By Terry Land

SCENES of jubilation greeted the homecoming to the UK today of 200 soldiers from the Black Watch after completing a six-month mission in Iraq.

But the celebrations and emotional reunions with relatives and friends were tarnished by bitterness over the proposed disbandment of the battalion and the deaths in Iraq of five of their colleagues.

(*Source*: The Sun: www.thesun.co.uk/)

activity
INDIVIDUAL WORK

(a) Why did some people feel bitter about the plan to disband the Black Watch in 2004?

(b) Do you think they were right to feel bitter about it?

---

keyword

Morale
confidence; team spirit and the will to succeed.

keyword

Self-esteem
feeling good about yourself.

---

2. *Teamwork is good for morale*. Soldiers in warfare work under stress, and there is always the possibility that will have to kill, or be killed. Good **morale** protects soldiers against fear and depression, and keeps them cheerful in danger and hardship. The team has a collective responsibility if something goes wrong, so that no one individual has to take all the blame. Equally, each team member shares in its success. Teamwork builds loyalty and trust, increasing confidence and effectiveness.

3. *Teamwork brings job satisfaction*. Job satisfaction means the enjoyment of work. Sharing a task is a good way of getting to know other people; it gives you something to talk about, and can lead on to friendship. Getting the respect of other team members raises **self-esteem** and if the teamwork goes well, you get a feeling of achievement.

4. *Teamwork is effective*. For physical tasks teams are effective because they have more physical strength than one person. For problem solving they are better because 'two heads are better than one' and groups of people can brainstorm problems. In emergencies teams can act quickly if they have good training and decisive leadership.

Problems with teamwork

Teamwork will always be used in the army. But there are times when teamwork runs into problems. The team fails to meet its targets, its work is of poor quality, or the team members are unhappy.

This can happen for a number of reasons:

- External
  - the team is expected to do too much work, too quickly
  - the team is being asked to do something which it is not able to do, or which is morally wrong
  - the team is under-resourced – i.e. it is not getting enough equipment, people or money
  - the team is getting too much criticism and is not valued
  - the team is getting confusing instructions
  - the team has achieved what it set out to do, and there is no more to be done
  - the wrong people have been chosen to join the team.
- Internal
  - team members do not have the skills or ability to do what is expected of them
  - the team is badly led
  - some people are doing all the work and others are slacking
  - team members do not like or respect each other
  - team members are adopting destructive roles
  - there is bullying or some other sign of low morale.

In extreme cases, teamwork can go badly wrong. This is suggested in the case study below (though the truth of what happened at Deepcut Barracks is yet to be established).

case study
2.5

Deepcut Barracks

The Scotsman, Wednesday, 30 October 2002

THE Ministry of Defence was accused yesterday of conducting a prolonged campaign to withhold the truth, by the families of young soldiers whose violent deaths are a mystery.

The bereaved relatives of four soldiers who died at the Deepcut barracks, Surrey, protested at the House of Commons, claiming the deaths had been labelled suicide by senior officers to protect the reputation of the armed forces.

They claimed documents were destroyed and conflicting statements were made as army officials tried to cover up what had happened.

They also stepped up a campaign for an independent public inquiry into the deaths, focusing on the four suspicious fatal shootings at Deepcut.

The father of Private Geoff Gray said all his son's clothes were destroyed after his death in September. Also, log books recording the serial number of the SA-80 rifle he was using were destroyed within hours of him being found with two gunshot wounds to the head.

(*Source*: news.scotsman.com/)

activity
GROUP WORK

(a) What failings of teamwork are suggested by the case study?

(b) Write a list of rules for good teamwork, to be used for cadets or young soldiers.

The importance of teamwork in the police

Like the armed forces, the police are made up of teams, and there is no police officer who does not belong to one or more teams.

Police teams are often specialised in their roles. Most do 'core' police work, but there are also many teams which are concerned with the smooth running of the police force itself.

Police teams include:

- *Management teams*: these organise people and strategy (major, long-term planning of police work)

- *Administration teams*: these run police stations, handle paperwork, deal with money, accountancy etc.

- *Specialist teams* comprising experts in all the different aspects of policing

- *Partnerships* (teams including people outside the police), which work with the community, other public services, and the public.

Police teams do not work in isolation. They are advised, or even told what to do, by management teams, and they themselves may direct or advise teams working under them or in cooperation with them. On organisation charts, like the examples from Avon and Somerset Police in Figure 2.3, they are linked through tree diagrams. On the tree diagrams, which can be seen in full on

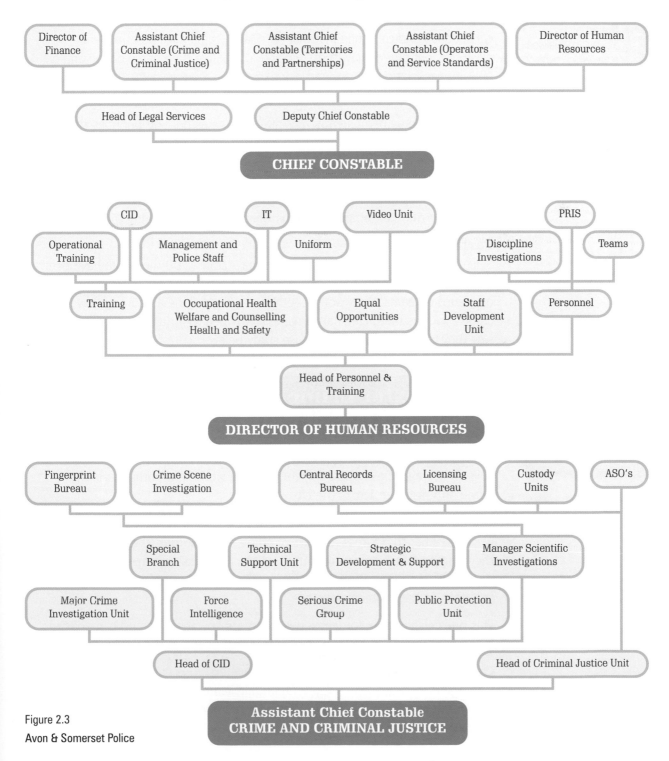

Figure 2.3
Avon & Somerset Police

> **keyword**
>
> **Personnel**
> staff or employees.

> **keyword**
>
> **Squad**
> a small, specialised team which can act quickly.

www.avonandsomerset.police.uk, the roots of the trees have the highest rank, and the leaves the lowest. Normally, a team has a leader, who may be the line manager of the team members. But not all police teams are wholly made up of police officers: many include support **personnel** of various types too.

Some teams exist to carry out actions – e.g. drug and vice **squads**, or armed response units. Others, e.g. Force Intelligence are more involved in planning, consultation and collecting information. Many teams have a permanent existence, but others may form, disband, or change their name depending on policing needs at any given time. For example, a team investigating a murder may be disbanded once that murder is solved.

The work done by permanent teams may change as policing priorities (the police work which people think is most important) change. For example, after the London bombings of July 2005, 10,000 police were involved in the investigations. It was said that many other major investigations came almost to a standstill at this time. The extra police had to leave their normal teams and go and work with other temporary teams which were set up during that emergency.

Partnerships

Since the passing of the Crime and Disorder Act in 1998 the police have been heavily involved in crime and disorder reduction partnerships. These are teams or groups of teams which work together to cut down the amount of 'low level crime', such as theft, criminal damage, rowdy behaviour and drug abuse. The way they work is outlined in the case study below.

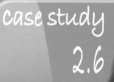

case study 2.6

Manchester Crime and Disorder Reduction Partnership (CDRP)

The Crime and Disorder Reduction Partnership (CDRP) is the union of several key agencies in Manchester who are working together to tackle crime and disorder across the city.

The Crime and Disorder Act 1998 requires the local council and police to work together to address matters of crime and disorder. The Act outlines the position that by working with all of the agencies that are affected by, or deal with crime and disorder, we can produce better and more effective solutions to the problems we face.

This partnership, therefore, includes the city's key agencies and is managed by an Executive Partnership Group (EPG) that oversees the work undertaken.

On a day-to-day basis the work of the partnership is carried out by the Crime and Disorder Team, Youth Offending Team (YOT), the Drugs and Alcohol Action Team (DAAT) and the Manchester Multi Agency Gang Strategy (MMAGS).

These teams address the separate aspects of the partnership work, and are responsible for ensuring that the objectives and aims outlined in the Crime and Disorder Strategy are met.

The CDRP is supported by a number of agencies across the city. They include:

- Manchester City Council
- Greater Manchester Police
- South Manchester Primary Care Trust
- Central Manchester Primary Care Trust
- North Manchester Primary Care Trust
- National Probation Service, Greater Manchester
- HM Prison Manchester
- Crown Prosecution Service
- Greater Manchester Police Authority
- The Community Network
- Manchester County Fire Service
- Criminal Justice Board
- And... you, the community!

(*Source*: Greater Manchester Police www.makingmanchestersafer.com)

activity
GROUP WORK

(a) Why is it important for crime and disorder reduction partnerships to have members from different public services and organisations?

(b) Contact a member of a local crime and reduction partnership and find out more about their work.

Team-building activities

Team-building activities are used by the public services to help train new recruits – and others – in teamwork skills.

A team-building activity starts with a group of people who are not a team, and gives them a shared task. The purpose of the task is to force them to cooperate so that they start working together and helping each other as members of a team should. Very often the task is not useful in itself: its aim is simply to change a group into a team. An example is given below:

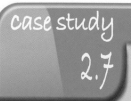

case study 2.7

Team-building exercise: The Web

Purpose:

To teach students to depend on others to solve a problem. It involves using physical trust, group problem-solving skills, long-range planning.

Materials:

String (heavy – will not break easily).

A hoop for the centre (not essential).

Rules:

Each team member must go through every section of the web – which means:

■ They cannot go around the trees.

■ They cannot go under the web (between the web and the ground).

■ They cannot go over the web.

■ They cannot go between the web and the tree.

Additional rules:

A team must use all sections once before they can be reused.

Sections that are not large enough for any of the bodies on a team to go through are exempted spaces (shaded on diagram).

When passing through the web you cannot touch the string (the spider will be alerted).

Possible strategies:

The most difficult people to get through the web are the first and the last person, so they should be selected with respect to their size and the size of the sections closest to the ground. Heavier people might be 'passed' in the middle so that there are people on both sides to send and receive.

(*Source*: www.krellinst.org)

Figure 2.4

The web – a team-building exercise

Shaded holes (which are too small to pass through) can be left out of activity.

Cord or rope 'web'

hoop

7 ft

ground

activity

GROUP WORK

(a) Discuss why an activity like 'The Web' can help to build teams.

(b) Take part in a team-building activity and say what you think you gained from it.

Using a Range of Interpersonal Communication Skills

keyword	**Interpersonal communication skills** reading, writing, listening, speaking and non-verbal communication.

Interpersonal communication skills are used all the time in the public services and in most other kinds of work.

The way these work are illustrated in Figure 2.5.

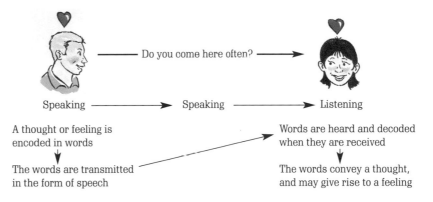

Speaking — Speaking — Listening

A thought or feeling is encoded in words

The words are transmitted in the form of speech

Words are heard and decoded when they are received

The words convey a thought, and may give rise to a feeling

If the communication is effective, the thoughts and feelings of the speaker will be recreated in the mind of the listener

Writing

Message

My name is Anne

Reading

Thoughts and feelings are encoded in words

The words are transmitted in the form of writing

Words are read and decoded when they are received

The words convey a thought, and may give rise to feelings

Figure 2.5

Communication process

If the communication is ineffective, the thoughts and feelings of the writer are not recreated in the mind of the reader.

Reading

Public services expect applicants to be able to read well enough to do the job. Young soldiers who join the infantry aged 16 won't have to read as much, or as quickly, as, say, police recruits or trainee paramedics, but they are still expected to have some reading skills:

case study 2.8 — The BARB test

Except for those who wish to train in certain technical employments, an applicant's eligibility for service and/or to qualify for a particular form of training will be determined by the results achieved on the Army Entrance Test (known as BARB). The test assesses an applicant's ability for training by using computer touch-screen question and answer techniques.

(*Source*: Army website)

activity
INDIVIDUAL WORK

(a) Take the BARB test, or a test like it. Make a note of any problems you had.

(b) Which communication skill, or skills, does BARB test?

Types of reading

There are three kinds of reading: skimming, scanning and detailed reading. All are needed in the public services – especially by people like the police or probation officers, who sometimes have to deal with large amounts of written material.

Skimming is looking through something quickly to find out what is in it. We do this if we are thinking of buying a newspaper or magazine and want to see what it is like. In a uniformed public service people skim documents, letters, reports etc., just to see if they are worth looking at in more detail.

How to skim:

1. Read the title and the main headings of the document to find out what it is about.

2. Read the first sentence of each paragraph.

3. Stop skimming once you have a general idea what the document is about.

Scanning is used when you are looking for particular information in a piece of writing – especially a long piece such as a book, report or document. We scan if we are looking up a telephone number in a phone book, or a train time on a timetable. Once we have found the relevant bit, we collect the facts we want and the job is done.

How to scan:

1. Decide on the key word or words you are looking for – e.g. 'fire and rescue service'.

2. If it is a book or report, look in the contents to find the relevant chapter, or the index to find relevant pages for your key word(s).

3. Check the headings to see if they contain your key word(s).

4. Once you have found the right page, look down it and only stop when you see the key word(s).

5. Note or memorise the facts you want – then go off and do something else.

Detailed reading – if you work in a uniformed public service you will sometimes need to read documents, or parts of documents, carefully and in detail. For example, if you were in the police and you were reading transcripts of an interview of a suspect, you might want to read them through very carefully indeed to make sure you fully understood what was being said, and to pick up on hidden meanings, contradictions, lies or inconsistencies in what the suspect had said. Equally, if you were in the army and you wanted to memorise some written instructions from a senior officer, you would have to read them very carefully to make sure you fixed them in your mind and understood exactly what you were supposed to do.

How to read in detail:

1. Try to read the document in a place where you have some peace and quiet, and can concentrate.

2. First, skim the document to get a general feel of what it is about.

3. Then, go through it line by line and word by word, pausing after each sentence or two to make sure you've understood it.

4. If you have not understood something, re-read it.

5. Go back over the document if you think you have missed something.

6. After you have read the whole lot, test yourself by running through the document in your mind.

7. If you really need to be sure you understand it, write yourself some notes on the main points, and any questions you have about it.

8. If the document is extremely important, read it through several times in the day and give it some thought.

Barriers to effective reading

Effective reading is reading which gives you, with minimum effort, the information that you want. But sometimes reading is difficult, especially when you are reading for work rather than pleasure. The reasons why reading can be difficult are called barriers to effective reading.

These barriers are of three main types:

1. Barriers in ourselves
   - tiredness
   - not in the mood
   - would rather be doing something else
   - keep thinking about something else
   - cannot concentrate
   - lack of interest
   - lack of reading skills.

2. Barriers in the text
   - the text is at the wrong level (too easy or too difficult)
   - the text is boring (i.e. the content is irrelevant, or contains too much or too little detail)
   - the text is annoying (it expresses ideas, or uses words, that we don't like)
   - the text is badly constructed (sentences and paragraphs are too long or too short)
   - poor punctuation (e.g. too many or too few commas, semi-colons etc.)
   - poor layout (the font is too big or small; the colour of the paper is wrong etc.)
   - the text is in a second or foreign language.

3. Barriers in the environment
   - bad lighting
   - uncomfortable chair
   - noise distractions
   - the room is too hot, cold, stuffy etc.

Writing

An ability to write is needed in public service work. But it is quality that matters, not quantity. The writing that you do, if you are working in a uniformed public service, must be 'fit for purpose'. In other words it should be:

- in a suitable format
- written in a suitable style and tone
- relevant
- concise
- clear
- accurate
- as brief as possible.

Many uniformed public service jobs, at an operative level (e.g. infantry, gunners, ambulance technicians etc.) do not involve much writing. Others, for example in police management or in HM Revenue and Customs, may require much more.

If you work in a uniformed public service you will find that there are rules on the format that most written communication takes. For example, if you write an official letter in the army, it must have a certain format. The same is true of reports. Even memos have rules about the format and the kind of information they contain.

Emails

These are widely used for brief written communications to people in different offices, branches, centres etc. and are sent electronically, through the computer, to any part of the world. They should be worded briefly and clearly:

```
Jane and Julie,

The Liaison Committee meeting tomorrow, 15 May, begins
at 11.30am. Copies of the Agenda and the previous
meeting's minutes are attached.

See you both at the meeting,

Johara

Ext 7259
```

Memos

Memos (called 'loose minutes' in the army) are used when giving information or directives to people within the same public service organisation. Often they are very informal:

MEMO

From: PC Josh Milligan
To: PC Michael Adebaye

Date: 26/6/06

Mike

There is a meeting of the Community Liaison Committee on Thursday 2 March at 6.30pm. You said you might want to come along and make a few points!

See you
Josh

A memo is like an email, but is usually sent through the internal post. If it is confidential it should go in an envelope.

Letters

Letters written in the uniformed public services are almost always formal or semi-formal. The rule is that, if you know the name of the person you are writing to, you should write a semi-formal letter, otherwise you should write one which is completely **formal**.

(a) Semi-formal letter

> Marburton Police Station
> Letsby Avenue
> Marburton
> West Yorkshire
> MN1 3BD
>
> 3 March 2006
>
> Mr D.G. Rothwell
> Department of Public Services
> Mayhem College
> Erringden
> West Yorkshire
> EN3 12FD
>
> Dear Mr Rothwell
>
> **Proposed police station visit**
>
> Thank you for your letter of 27 February 2006 suggesting a visit to this police station for your BTEC First Diploma Students.
>
> This will be no problem provided that the students are in groups of no more than ten and are accompanied by a member of staff. Suitable dates will be Tuesday 7 March or Tuesday 14 March, at 10.30am in either case. You will be met by PC Gwen Shaw, our Youth Liaison Officer and she will show your students round. There will be a question and answer session at the end of the visit.
>
> I would be grateful if you could confirm that these arrangements are suitable for you.
>
> Yours sincerely
>
> *Sgt James Wainwright*

Note the following points:

- the 'Dear Mr Rothwell' at the beginning and the 'Yours sincerely' at the end
- the polite, friendly yet businesslike tone
- the brief heading saying what the letter is about
- the three paragraphs: one introducing the subject, one giving details, and one finishing off.

The letter is typed on a computer, and a copy kept on disk.

(b) Formal letter

Loamshire Fire and Rescue Service
Meltdown Fire Station
Ladder Street
Meltdown
MN1 3RF

9 September 2006

The Sales Department
Backdraught Publications Ltd
Hydrant House
Water Street
Sherburn in Elmet
SN12 1OU

Dear Sir or Madam

Could you please send me a copy of your recently published book: *Health Risks in Burnt-out Buildings: A Guide for Fire Investigation Teams*.

I enclose a cheque for £14.50 including package and posting.

Yours faithfully

Abdul Rahman

Station Training Officer

Completely formal letters are used when you know nothing about the person you are writing to. For example:

Reports

Reports are pieces of writing, split into sections, which outline a situation, give information about it and suggest what ought to be done. In the armed forces reports are sometimes called 'briefs' or 'submissions'.

Usually, reports are about problems. It might be something minor, like problems with the car park, or it might be something major such as 'Repeat Victimisation in the West Midlands'. Most reports are short, but some reports involving a lot of research, such as some government reports, can be hundreds of pages long.

The structure of a report should include:

- Title page (name and date of report, who wrote it, and who it is intended for)
- Contents (list of sections and page numbers)
- Introduction (a brief outline of what the report is about, and how the information was obtained)
- Findings (research on the problem and what was discovered about it)
- Conclusion (the writer's opinions)

■ Recommendations (things that ought to be done – e.g., if the report is about car parking, change the layout of the car park, put up a barrier, introduce smart cards etc.).

The paragraphing of reports should be in the following style:

1. Sub-heading
   a Sub-sub-heading
   b (1) Sub-sub-sub-heading
      (2)
           (a) Sub-sub-sub-sub-heading

Speaking (verbal communication)

Speaking is an essential interpersonal communications skill. Its use varies from extreme formality (for example on ceremonial occasions such as passing-out parades) to the almost complete informality used by teams whose members know each other well.

When speaking to superior officers greater formality may be required (for example 'Sir' or 'Madam'), and the language should be more 'correct'. Otherwise, most speech is relaxed and informal.

In the public services you have to learn to speak so you can be understood by your colleagues, the public, and anyone else you come in contact with. It is extremely important in public service work to be able to speak clearly so that you can be instantly understood by your colleagues – especially in the armed forces and the emergency services, where a misunderstanding can be a matter of life and death.

Regional and other accents should not be a problem, unless they prevent people from understanding you.

Verbal communication in the uniformed public services can be either one-way or two-way.

One-way verbal communication

This takes the form of lectures, presentations, instruction, briefings and speeches. In most cases an individual is speaking to a group, and the group listens in silence unless questions or comment are asked for by the speaker.

A *lecture* is a spoken explanation or 'lesson' on a subject – usually knowledge or skills needed for the job. Often it is part of a series of lectures.

A *presentation* is like a lecture but is more likely to be a one-off. It is often accompanied by visual aids – e.g. PowerPoint, overhead projectors and so on.

Instruction tends to be lectures in a practical setting – for example, when you are being taught how to use equipment or act in specific situations (e.g. riot control).

Briefings are instructions on what to do on a particular day, or in a particular situation. For example, the police may use briefings when planning a drugs raid.

Speeches are used on ceremonial or special occasions, and their main purpose is to raise morale or 'esprit de corps'.

Reprimands and verbal warnings could also be considered a form of one-way verbal communication, and are given by line managers or superior officers to their subordinates to enforce discipline.

link

There is more about this in 'Techniques of Instruction' later on in this unit.

Two-way verbal communication

Discussion, debates, arguments, meetings, conversation and chatting are all forms of two-way verbal communication. By far the largest part of our speaking takes place in these two-way formats, whether at work or in our social and private lives.

Some types of two-way verbal communication are more formal than others.

A *discussion* is a conversation on a serious topic, often with a serious aim, such as sorting out a possible disagreement

A *debate* is a formal kind of discussion which is not needed in most uniformed public service work.

Arguments are (in this context) discussions which have gone wrong, and should be avoided between colleagues in the uniformed public services as they lead to ill-feeling – or worse.

Meetings play a very important role in decision making in the uniformed public services. They are formal discussions, controlled by a chairperson, and the decisions are written down in the form of minutes (a report of the meeting).

Conversation and *chatting* are forms of two-way verbal communication which are done for pleasure, or to be sociable. They are not part of official duties, but they are important ways of relating to people on a personal level, both inside and outside work.

Verbal communication is, in the workplace, done for a purpose. It takes such forms as questions, replies, requests, commands, instructions, complaints, advice, telling off, showing appreciation and so on. Each of these 'speech functions' is a skill that we have been learning from our earliest years, but some of them are particularly important in public service work. Training and development in these skills takes place in many public services.

For example, questions are essential as a means of gathering information, especially in organisations such as the police, HM Revenue and Customs, the ambulance service and the prison service.

The two main types of question are closed questions and open questions.

Closed questions

These expect the answers 'yes' or 'no'. They begin with verbs, i.e. words like 'Did', 'Were', 'Do', 'Are' or 'Have'.

These questions gather single items of information. They take up little time. They have some special uses in public service work – for example, carrying out surveys and questionnaires where the answers are going to be turned into statistics.

Example: 'Did you vote in the last election?'

Open questions

These questions begin with 'Where', 'What', 'Why', 'Who', 'Whose', 'When' and 'How'. They encourage people to speak at length. They are used for interviews, police questioning etc.

Example: 'Why were you carrying a knife?'

Sometimes requests or even commands can be used in place of questions – e.g. 'Could you tell me what you were doing last night at nine o'clock?' or, 'Explain what you did after you put the bomb in the rucksack'. In these cases, tone of voice would be very important.

Tone

Tone of voice is connected with:

- the feeling expressed in the voice (e.g. excitement, impatience, anger etc.)
- the loudness of the voice
- the changes of pitch in the voice – 'high' or 'deep'.

Tone can tell us the purpose of a spoken sentence (e.g. the pitch of a question rises at the end).

Example: 'Are you going out tonight?'

If one word in a sentence is louder than the others, we say it is emphasised or stressed. This can affect the meaning of the sentence.

Compare:

'*Don't* let me see you do that again!'   (I'm getting angry)

'Don't let *me* see you do that again!'   (I'm covering my back)

'Don't let me see you do *that* again!'   (I'm focusing on the action, but I'm not angry)

Audience

Audience awareness is important in verbal communication. We don't necessarily speak to our friends like we speak to our parents. People who work in the uniformed public services change the way they speak according to who they are speaking to. Police officers may speak to members of the public differently from

Audience
any listener or listeners (occasionally it can mean readers).

keyword

the way they speak to their colleagues. Other factors may also influence the way a person speaks to another person, in a uniformed public service – for example:

■ the age of the listener

■ the sex of the listener

■ the number of listeners

■ the situation in which the person is speaking (time, place, urgency, other people present etc.)

■ the subject the person is speaking about

■ the state of mind of the speaker

■ the state of mind of the listener

■ the listener's knowledge of English

■ the relationship between the speaker and the listener.

Standard and non-standard English

Standard English is normal correct English, used for speaking or writing. This is the best kind of language to use in most public service work. Other types must only be used in certain situations.

Slang

This means certain words which we use when talking to people we know well, but which are inappropriate when talking to clients, customers and other people we meet formally.

Slang includes 'swear words'. It should not be used in writing, except to close friends, or if you are writing someone's exact words for some reason, or in things like plays and novels.

Jargon

Jargon is used a lot in the work place or within different organisations or professions. Often a person from outside may find it difficult to undertstand what is being said.

keyword

Jargon
language specific to a particular job.

case study 2.9 | Jargon

Protocols have been agreed between the YOT, its *statutory partners* and other organisations, outlining the *level of service*, *human resources issues* and *funding arrangements*.

activity
INDIVIDUAL WORK

(a) Put the sentence above into the simplest English you can.

(b) What are the advantages and disadvantages of using jargon?

(c) Why do some people not like slang?

Verbal presentations of basic information

If you are standing in front of a group of people telling them about something to do with work, check the following points:

- Can everybody see and hear you?

- Is your language suited to the audience?

- Have you thought about and planned what you are going to say beforehand?

- Do you have any visual aids so that they can see, as well as hear, what you are talking about?

- Are you going to answer questions as you go along, or answer them all at the end?

Meetings

Meetings are a form of organised group discussion and are important in public service teamwork. Meetings often follow fairly strict rules, usually in order to save time. The aim of meetings is to find out what people think about something – it may be a plan, a problem, or simply the progress of their work that week. As with most group discussions, it is important in meetings to know when to speak, when to listen, and to be prepared to give and receive ideas. Language is more formal than a chat among friends, but less formal than a job interview.

Barriers to verbal communication

A number of factors can make speech communication difficult. These can relate to the speaker, the listener or the environment.

Problems with the speaker can include:

- unclear pronunciation – the words are spoken in such a way that the listener cannot recognise or understand them

- not loud enough – the speaker is shy or has a soft voice

- language not suited to listener – the speaker is using words the listener does not understand

- content not suited to listener – either the speaker is saying things the listener dislikes so much that he/she will not or cannot listen (e.g. the speaker may be racist or sexist), or the speaker is so boring that the listener's mind wanders

- ambiguity – the words or ideas are confusing and could have more than one meaning.

Problems with the listener can include:

- deafness

- language differences

- unable to understand the words or ideas being spoken

- distracted by strong emotion, bored, thinking about something else, unable to concentrate etc.

Problems with the environment can be:

- noise or other people speaking
- high stress levels (e.g. in a life-threatening emergency)
- distance or poor acoustics
- the speech is being transmitted by telephone, radio etc., and reception is poor.

In operational situations where both the speakers and listeners are well trained (e.g. in the armed forces), environmental problems are likely to be the main barriers to verbal communication.

In operational situations such as those that apply in Iraq, language barriers between the uniformed public service and civilians are the main difficulty in verbal communication. Soldiers have to rely on very simple expressions, such as 'No problem', which many people understand, learn a few words of Arabic, or make use of interpreters who, if they come from the local community, may be a security risk and cannot always be trusted or able to pass on a message accurately.

Listening skills

In public service work you often have to listen to other people; it may be briefings, instructions, questions, complaints or requests. Listening attentively and politely is a skill.

It is also a skill to absorb the information and remember what you have been told. In many situations note-making skills are useful. You are advised to develop your note-making skills and to use them when interviewing people, or listening to lectures, connected with your course.

Non-verbal communication

When we meet somebody for the first time we know (or think we know) a lot about them from the way they look or behave. These signs and signals that we notice are all part of non-verbal communication (NVC).

NVC includes:

- gestures
- facial expressions
- posture (the way we stand or sit)
- self-presentation – dress, hairstyle etc.
- some experts also consider it includes tone of voice, and a range of grunts, throat-clearing etc.

An understanding of NVC is important for members of a uniformed public service. It helps them to give a good impression to others, and also to understand the ways other people feel towards them. For example, a police officer can sometimes tell by reading the signs of non-verbal communication whether a member of the public is looking for a fight or whether they are lying.

Figure 2.6
What are they thinking?

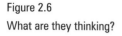

activity
GROUP WORK
(2.1)

(a) Research the use of reading, writing, listening, speaking and NVC in a public service. Keep a record of what you have found out.

(b) Draw conclusions about the use of these skills, and the circumstances in which they are most effective.

(c) Explain where there may be problems in communication in the service you have studied.

(d) Give a joint presentation on your findings to others in your group.

Evaluating communication in a public service

If you really want the low-down on public service interpersonal communication you should visit a public service and watch people at work, or talk to someone who has experience of working there. You should ask questions such as:

■ When is it better to use speech at work, and when is it better to use writing? Why?

■ What are the advantages and disadvantages of using email in a uniformed public service?

■ What are the main issues in communicating with people from ethnic minorities?

■ Is there any sexism in the workplace?

- What are the difficulties of hearing and being heard when fighting a fire? How are they overcome?
- What are the main things the police have to remember when questioning suspects?
- What are the difficulties of communicating with people who are drunk or under the influence of drugs?
- What communication problems can arise in team meetings?
- What communication skills do employers look for in applicants to the uniformed public services?

activity
GROUP WORK (2.2)

Visit a public service and

(a) Ask them the questions above (and any others you can think of).

(b) Note down what you learn.

(c) Share your findings with others.

How to improve your interpersonal skills

Interpersonal communication skills are something you should try to get better at year on year. They are the key to success in work, study and in your personal life.

Figure 2.7

Posture – some main points

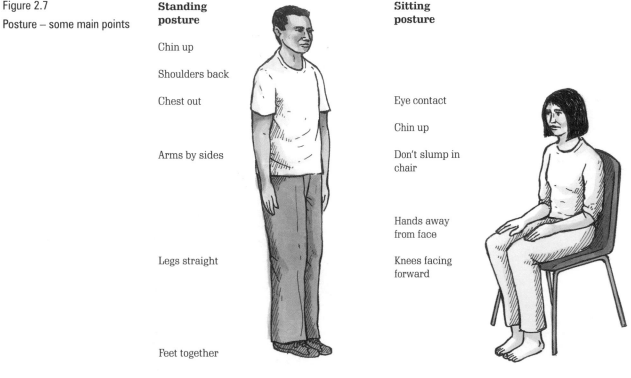

Standing posture

Chin up

Shoulders back

Chest out

Arms by sides

Legs straight

Feet together

Sitting posture

Eye contact

Chin up

Don't slump in chair

Hands away from face

Knees facing forward

Table 2.1 Improving your personal skills

Reading	Writing
Get practice at skimming and scanning	Try to make your handwriting fast and legible
Read as much as you can for pleasure – it doesn't matter what – quantity is more important than quality	Train yourself to be fast and accurate on the keyboard
Don't move your lips when reading silently	Use the spellcheck and grammar check on the computer
Learn how to make notes from written material	If your spelling needs improving, learn to spell the common words, or words to do with public service, first!
Get yourself a place at home where you can read in peace	

Verbal communication (speech)	Listening
Speak clearly and confidently	Learn how to take notes. Read it up in a book on study skills, or ask your tutor (or someone) to give you some tips. Practise taking notes in lessons and get good at it. Being able to take (and make) notes is the most important study skill you will ever learn.
Always go to practice interviews etc. – in order to get feedback	
Look for part-time jobs where you have to deal with the public.	

Body language in interviews

- Avoid twitching your face unnecessarily.
- Make eye contact about half the time when you are listening to someone, and about a quarter of the time when you are talking to someone.
- Keep your hands away from your face.
- Don't chew gum in formal situations.
- Dress smartly and not too unconventionally.
- Think about how close you should stand to people.
- Learn how to do a firm handshake.

---

activity
GROUP WORK (2.3)

Take part in each of the following whenever you get the chance:

(a) mock job interviews

(b) role play

(c) presentations/instruction

(d) discussions/meetings

(e) questioning a member of the public services

(f) organising a group task.

Understanding Various Methods of Instruction

Instruction is a kind of teaching which is widely used in the public services. Sometimes the instruction is one to one and sometimes the **instructor** may teach a large group of learners.

Qualities of a good instructor

A good instructor has:

1. **Charisma**

2. Knowledge of the subject

3. Teaching skills and techniques.

The best instructors have all three of these. Each quality is about equally important in making up a 'good instructor'.

Charisma is partly inborn (e.g. good looks, pleasing voice) and partly a collection of social skills (e.g. sense of humour) we develop as we grow up. Subject knowledge and teaching skills are learned, and developed through experience.

Personal qualities in an instructor include:

- *Confidence* – the ability to talk clearly and freely in front of a group of people. Body language matters here. Standing straight, facing the group, making eye-contact, varying the tone of voice, moving about the teaching area – all these give the feeling that you mean business. So too does a smart appearance, although this is less important than being safely and suitably dressed (e.g. in a workshop, or on a mountain).

- *Attitude* – an instructor should treat all learners in the group fairly and equally, while remembering that they are individuals with individual needs (for example, some may need more help or explanation than others). Instructors should expect – and show – good discipline. This means giving respect to the learners and getting it in return. Their attitude should be fair, firm and friendly. They should be hard-working and conscientious in their teaching and they must respect any confidential knowledge they have about any of the students or learners.

- *Enthusiasm and interest* – instructors should be enthusiastic about their subjects and keep up to date with new developments in their subject area. They should expect their students to learn and they should be keen to learn themselves. They should also enjoy teaching, and show that they enjoy it. They should try to motivate their students by assessing their work regularly and praising it when it deserves praise.

Instructor
a teacher of practical or job-related skills and knowledge.

keyword

Charisma
personality, attractiveness, or leadership qualities.

keyword

Techniques of instruction

Lessons should be planned, and should fit into a well-organised course. The instructor should write lesson plans. A simple example is given below.

Table 2.2 Lesson plan for slopes

Instructor: Tilda Field
Subject of class: Slopes
Time and date of session: 9.10–10.10 am, Monday 13 March 2006
Week number: 22
Students: BT Group III: 10 trainees ages 16–17 who are preparing for an Initial Training expedition (15 miles in hilly terrain)
Aim: Students will learn to recognise different kinds of slope on a 1:25000 OS map, and draw conclusions which will help them to plan the timing of their expedition.

Time	Topic	Instructor activities	Learner activities	Comment
9.30–9.45	Slopes	Introduce topic through Q and A What's a slope? How does it affect you when walking? Which is worse – going up or down? Why? How does it affect planning? How do we measure the steepness of slopes? What are the safety implications? How are slopes shown on the map? Teacher puts correct student answers on board	Answer questions. Expected answers: – The side of a hill – a slope slows you down – tiring when going up; could be dangerous going down, if steep – it affects the planned time of the walk – 1 in 3 (or whatever) – safety – more of a problem in wet snowy weather, or if there are rocks Using contours Students note main points	Don't let David answer all these questions. He knows this stuff, and it'll stop the others from learning
9.45–10.00	Slopes on maps	Teacher gives out maps – 1 between 2 Teacher gives out question sheet giving 10 grid references, all pinpointing different kinds of slope. Explains exercise Teacher walks round seeing how students are getting on	In pairs, students note down the types of slope corresponding to each grid reference under the headings 'description of slope' and 'direction faced' and grade in danger 1–5 (safe to dangerous)	Stress that maps must be looked after – no pencilling on maps Don't let Chloe and Danny pair off – she'll do all the work
10.00–10.05		Teacher invites answers after student pairs have exchanged work Teacher sorts out any problems – e.g. that the direction of slope is shown by the direction in which contour heights are facing	Students exchange work Notes made on any points of difficulty	Give Nasreen an equipment list
10.05–10.10		Teacher recapitulates and asks students to get information on the extra time needed to walk up or down steep slopes. End of session		

Note that in this example students have already learnt various things about map-reading (e.g. grid references). The activities fit into a wider programme and prepare them for a full-day mountain expedition which they have to do.

Assessment of instructors

In this unit you will have to instruct someone about something, and you will assessed by your tutor or someone else. Below is a list of the kinds of things on which instructors are assessed:

activity
INDIVIDUAL WORK
(2.4)

(a) Draw up a checklist of the skills and qualities that make a good instructor.

(b) Carry out a written assessment of one of your own instructors or tutors based on this checklist.

- the suitability of the topic
- the quality of your planning
- the quality and suitability of your visual aids
- the interest and appropriateness of the practical activity
- the confidence with which you start your piece of instruction
- the clarity of your delivery
- your timing
- the accuracy of your information
- the steps you take to make sure your learners have understood each part of your session
- the understanding you show of your learners
- your management of the group
- your summing up and conclusion.

Instructing a class

When instructing a class, you should:

- Give your tutor or assessor copies of any handouts etc. that you give your class.
- Keep your cool whatever happens.
- Use visual aids.
- Try not to ramble on too much.
- Follow the sequence: Explain, Demonstrate, Imitate, Practise.
- Progress from what the student knows to what the student doesn't know.
- Don't be afraid to ask for questions from your listeners.
- Don't panic!

activity
INDIVIDUAL WORK
(2.5)

Give a short period of instruction (5–10 minutes) to one or more people on a topic which interests you. (This may be a practical skill, such as operating a camping stove or installing a smoke alarm, or it may involve theoretical knowledge – e.g. a brief talk on the uses of electronic tagging for offenders.)

progress check

1. State three ways in which teamwork can benefit a public service as a whole.

2. State three ways in which teamwork can benefit the people who work in a public service.

3. State three ways in which teamwork in a public service can benefit the public.

4. Outline the roles of a good team leader.

5. What is a partnership?

6. Give three reasons why teamwork can be unsuccessful.

7. Name the three types of reading and give an example of when each type should be used.

8. Give three differences between formal and informal speech.

9. What is jargon and when should it not be used?

10. 'Instructors should know about their subject and should be able to motivate the learner.' Which of the two is more important – and why?

Uniformed Public Service Fitness

This unit covers:

- the major body systems associated with health and fitness
- basic nutrition and its effect on health
- public service fitness tests and the requirements of the public services
- developing and completing a personal fitness training programme

You have to be fitter than average to work in almost all uniformed public services. In this unit you will learn how to get fit and stay fit.

First you will learn about the human body in relation to health and fitness, and the importance of eating the right foods.

Then you will find out about the fitness tests the uniformed public services use and the kinds of fitness they are looking for. You will learn about entrance fitness tests and the regular annual fitness tests which are compulsory in many uniformed public services.

Finally, you will try to increase your personal fitness, using planned programmes to improve your fitness and health – and your chances of getting into a uniformed public service.

grading criteria

To achieve a **Pass** grade the evidence must show that the learner is able to:	To achieve a **Merit** grade the evidence must show that, in addition to the pass criteria, the learner is able to:	To achieve a **Distinction** grade the evidence must show that, in addition to the pass and merit criteria, the learner is able to:
P1 produce an annotated diagram describing the major body systems associated with health and fitness	**M1** explain the short- and long-term effects of exercise on the major body systems	**D1** recommend improvements to own performance in a public service fitness test
P2 describe the purpose and function of each food group	**M2** explain the importance of good nutrition to health	**D2** evaluate own performance on completion of the training programme.

grading criteria

To achieve a **Pass** grade the evidence must show that the learner is able to:	To achieve a **Merit** grade the evidence must show that, in addition to the pass criteria, the learner is able to:	To achieve a **Distinction** grade the evidence must show that, in addition to the pass criteria, the learner is able to:
P3 explain the components of fitness relating them to a public service fitness test	**M3** analyse own performance in a public service fitness test	
P4 undertake a fitness test used by the public services	**M4** explain the methods used when planning a fitness training programme	
P5 describe the factors of health and safety which could affect own training programme		
P6 plan and undertake a training programme to improve own performance in a public service fitness test.		

Major Body Systems Associated with Health and Fitness

Body systems

Body systems are linked **organs** which work together to keep us alive. If they work well, they also keep us healthy and fit.

keyword

Organs
particular parts of the body which do a special job. The heart, brain, lungs and glands are all organs, each with a different function.

Skeletal system

The body has 206 bones in it. These contain minerals and calcium, but are alive and can grow and mend themselves. Some contain marrow, a kind of jelly which makes blood cells.

Bones are linked by joints. Some joints, such as those which connect different parts of the skull, will not move at all. Others, such as finger joints, are hinged so that they will only move in one direction, while shoulder joints (for example) are ball-and-socket joints which will move in any direction. Moving joints are lubricated by cartilage (a sort of gristle) and synovial fluid.

Table 3.1 Summary of systems, organs and main functions

Name of system	Main organs	Main functions
Cardiovascular system	Heart, blood, vessels	Supplies oxygen, nutrients and water to the body
Respiratory system	Nose, windpipe, lungs	Breathing and absorbing oxygen
Digestive system	Mouth, oesophagus, stomach, small intestine, large intestine, rectum	Processes food into nutrients the body can use, then gets rid of waste
Nervous system	Brain, spinal column, nerves	Gathers information; decides and controls actions
Skeleton	Bones, marrow, cartilage, ligaments	Supports and protects the body and its organs
Muscles	Muscles, tendons	Provide movement and strength
Endocrine system	Glands – pituitary, thyroid, thymus, adrenals, ovaries/testes	Enables the body to grow, develop, reproduce, protect and defend itself
Urinary system	Kidneys, ureters, bladder, urethra	Purification and waste disposal
Skin	Epidermis, dermis	Protection
Immune system	Circulatory system and lymph system; white blood cells	Cells and chemicals which protect the body against infection

Figure 3.1

Joint showing cartilage and synovial fluid

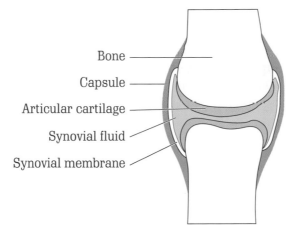

Bone

Capsule

Articular cartilage

Synovial fluid

Synovial membrane

Muscular system

There are three kinds of muscle: smooth muscle, which makes up veins, arteries and the intestines; heart muscle, only found in the heart; and ordinary muscle which makes up about 40 per cent of our body weight. Muscles are made of long thin cells which contract (shorten) when we want to move. There are two types of cells: 'fast twitch' which give us strength and are used in sprinting and weight-lifting, and 'slow twitch', which give us stamina and are used in walking or long-distance running.

Muscles are fastened to bones by natural cables called tendons. When the muscle contracts and pulls the tendon, the bone moves.

Figure 3.2
Muscles

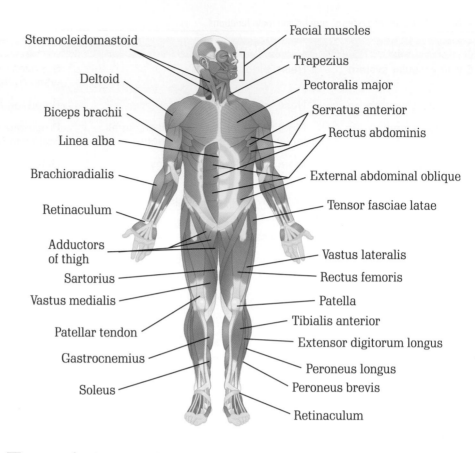

Sternocleidomastoid
Facial muscles
Trapezius
Deltoid
Pectoralis major
Biceps brachii
Serratus anterior
Linea alba
Rectus abdominis
Brachioradialis
External abdominal oblique
Retinaculum
Tensor fasciae latae
Adductors of thigh
Vastus lateralis
Sartorius
Rectus femoris
Vastus medialis
Patella
Patellar tendon
Tibialis anterior
Gastrocnemius
Extensor digitorum longus
Soleus
Peroneus longus
Peroneus brevis
Retinaculum

The respiratory system

This supplies oxygen to the blood. Fresh air goes down the windpipe or trachea, splits to go down the bronchi and enters the lungs. Here the oxygen is absorbed into millions of capillaries.

Figure 3.3

The respiratory system

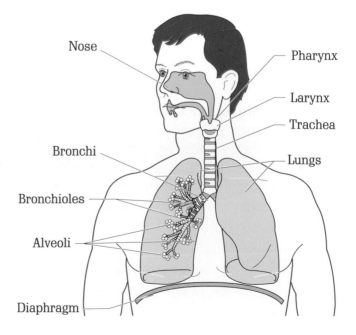

Nose
Pharynx
Larynx
Trachea
Bronchi
Lungs
Bronchioles
Alveoli
Diaphragm

The cardiovascular system

This consists of the heart, blood, arteries, veins and capillaries.

The heart is a pump made of muscle which moves 20,000 litres of blood around the body every day. It beats about 70 times a minute, speeding up when we are active – or stressed – and slowing down when we relax.

Blood is made of a liquid called plasma, which carries red blood cells, white blood cells and platelets. The red blood cells carry food and oxygen; the white blood cells attack viruses and bacteria, and the platelets make the blood clot.

There are three kinds of blood vessel – arteries, veins and capillaries. Arteries carry blood out of the heart, and veins carry blood back to the heart. Capillaries are tiny blood vessels which supply the muscles and organs with nutrients and oxygen.

Figure 3.4
The cardiovascular system

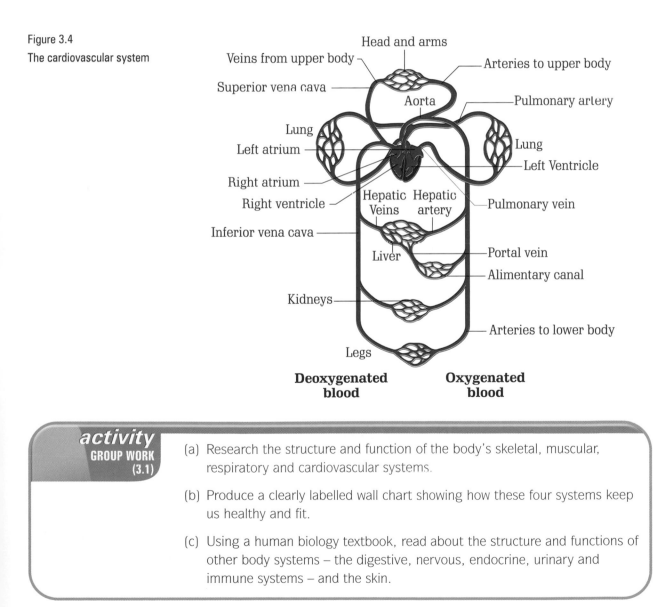

activity
GROUP WORK
(3.1)

(a) Research the structure and function of the body's skeletal, muscular, respiratory and cardiovascular systems.

(b) Produce a clearly labelled wall chart showing how these four systems keep us healthy and fit.

(c) Using a human biology textbook, read about the structure and functions of other body systems – the digestive, nervous, endocrine, urinary and immune systems – and the skin.

The effects of exercise

To understand the effects of exercise we also need to understand what the body is doing when it is at rest – that is when we are lying down, relaxing or asleep.

The body at rest

At rest some systems, such as muscles and joints, do very little. Parts of the brain and nervous system are less active. The heart beats (on average) at 70 times a minute. Blood travels evenly to different parts of the body. Breathing is slow and regular, bringing a steady intake of oxygen. Digestion is more rapid when we are resting, and so is the urinary system. Some parts of the endocrine system, such as the pituitary and thyroid glands, are relatively active when we are at rest and produce more hormones – for example, for growth and general protection of the body.

Figure 3.5

Body systems when a person is at rest

The person is resting.
The arrows show whether the activity of the body systems goes up or down while the body is at rest.

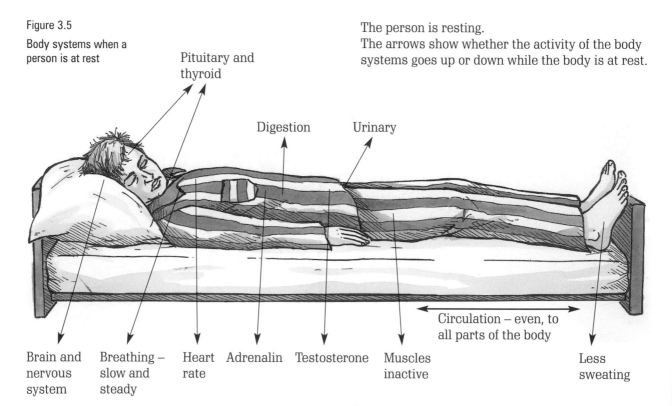

Pituitary and thyroid

Digestion   Urinary

Circulation – even, to all parts of the body

Brain and nervous system   Breathing – slow and steady   Heart rate   Adrenalin   Testosterone   Muscles inactive   Less sweating

Short-term effects of exercise on the main body systems

The short-term effects of exercise last while we are doing the exercise and for a short time afterwards. Some effects, such as increased heart rate, slow down within minutes; others, such as the stiffness caused by a build-up of lactic acid in the muscles, may take a couple of days to go away.

Shortly after exercise finishes there is an increase in appetite and a decrease in blood pressure. There is also a desire to rest, so that other body systems – e.g. the endocrine and urinary systems – can resume normal service.

Table 3.2 Short-term effects of exercise on the main body systems

Name of system	Changes caused by exercise	Reasons
Cardiovasuclar system	This becomes much more active. The heart beats much faster – up to 160 beats a minute. Blood vessels supplying muscles get wider. Blood is diverted away from digestion and the urinary system and goes to the muscles, lungs and skin instead.	The muscles need extra oxygen and nutrients to convert into energy so that they can work harder. Other less urgent needs of the body are set aside. The skin gets more blood so that the body can keep cool, since muscle movement generates a lot of heat.
Respiratory system	Breathing gets faster and deeper.	More air gets into the lungs to give more oxygen to the blood. Blood from the lungs goes to the heart, then out to the muscles.
Digestive system	Becomes inactive. But some nutrients are supplied to the blood by the body's fat stores.	The blood normally used for absorbing nutrients from the digestive system goes to the muscles instead. The breaking down of fat gives extra energy to the muscles.
Nervous system	The cerebellum controls balance; the cerebrum controls movement – both are active, but divert atttention away from other body functions.	The brain and nerves are occupied by controlling the body's movements, and processing feedback resulting from those movements (e.g. pain).
Skeleton	This moves during exercise. Fluid lubricates the joints, and the bones are strengthened by repeated impact.	These changes protect the bones against breakages, the joints against damage, and enable the muscles to have a bigger effect.
Muscles	Are highly active during exercise.	In prolonged exercise the 'slow-twitch' cells are most active; in sudden bursts of intense exercise the 'fast-twitch' cells are most active.
Endocrine system	The adrenal glands produce extra adrenalin. More testosterone is produced. Insulin goes down.	These hormones raise blood sugar levels and increase energy and aggression. Chemicals produced in the brain make you feel good.
Urinary system	Less active during exercise.	The blood it needs is diverted elsewhere.
Skin	Gets more blood and heats up.	Allows sweat glands to function – to cool the body down and eliminate wastes from blood.
Immune system	No short-term effects.	

Long-term positive effects of exercise on the major body systems

Cardiovascular system:

- There is an increase in size, number and capacity of blood vessels which increases the blood flow to muscles.
- More capillaries (small blood vessels) form round the heart, strengthening it.
- There is a decreased heart rate, but more blood is pumped round with each stroke (heartbeat).
- Regular exercise protects against cardiovascular heart disease (e.g. high blood pressure) and heart attacks.

Respiratory system:

- The capacity of the lungs increases. An increase in the size of blood vessels to the alveoli means that more oxygen can be taken in more quickly.

Digestive system:

- There is evidence that regular exercise over a period of years reduces the risk of getting bowel cancer.

Nervous system:

- There are benefits in coordination. People who exercise regularly when young are less likely to fall in old age. Regular exercise reduces the risk of depressive mental illness.

Skeleton:

- Regular exercise brings a small increase in bone mass. It is good for the joints, and protects against osteoarthritis.

- Exercise in under-20s may protect against osteoporosis in later life.

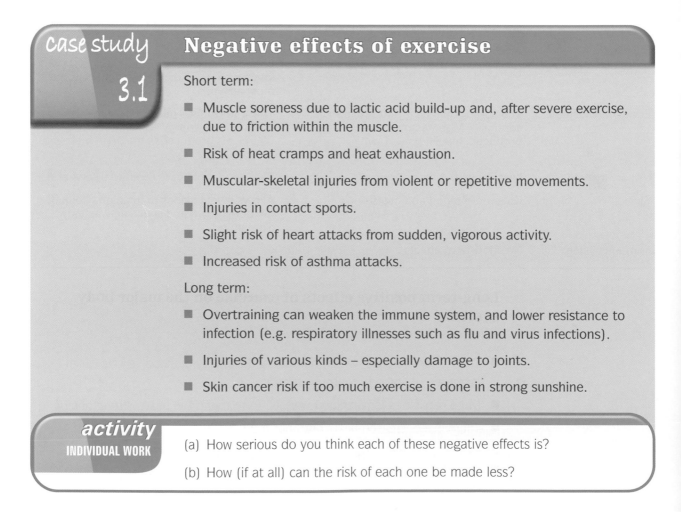

case study 3.1 — Negative effects of exercise

Short term:

- Muscle soreness due to lactic acid build-up and, after severe exercise, due to friction within the muscle.

- Risk of heat cramps and heat exhaustion.

- Muscular-skeletal injuries from violent or repetitive movements.

- Injuries in contact sports.

- Slight risk of heart attacks from sudden, vigorous activity.

- Increased risk of asthma attacks.

Long term:

- Overtraining can weaken the immune system, and lower resistance to infection (e.g. respiratory illnesses such as flu and virus infections).

- Injuries of various kinds – especially damage to joints.

- Skin cancer risk if too much exercise is done in strong sunshine.

activity
INDIVIDUAL WORK

(a) How serious do you think each of these negative effects is?

(b) How (if at all) can the risk of each one be made less?

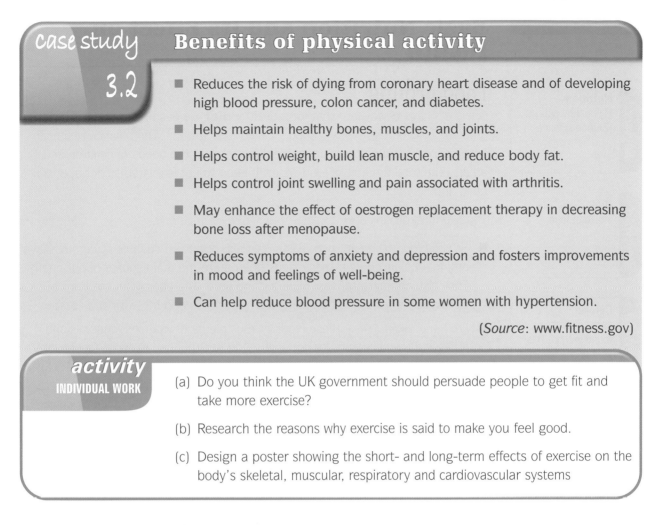

case study 3.2

Benefits of physical activity

- Reduces the risk of dying from coronary heart disease and of developing high blood pressure, colon cancer, and diabetes.

- Helps maintain healthy bones, muscles, and joints.

- Helps control weight, build lean muscle, and reduce body fat.

- Helps control joint swelling and pain associated with arthritis.

- May enhance the effect of oestrogen replacement therapy in decreasing bone loss after menopause.

- Reduces symptoms of anxiety and depression and fosters improvements in mood and feelings of well-being.

- Can help reduce blood pressure in some women with hypertension.

(*Source*: www.fitness.gov)

activity

INDIVIDUAL WORK

(a) Do you think the UK government should persuade people to get fit and take more exercise?

(b) Research the reasons why exercise is said to make you feel good.

(c) Design a poster showing the short- and long-term effects of exercise on the body's skeletal, muscular, respiratory and cardiovascular systems

Muscles:

- Ligaments and tendons are strengthened by regular exercise. Hard training increases both the numbers and sizes of muscle cells. Endurance training increases the numbers and sizes of 'slow-twitch' muscle cells, and may convert some 'fast-twitch' cells into 'slow-twitch' cells.

Endocrine system:

- Regular exercise gives some protection against breast cancer and diabetes.

Urinary system:

- None.

Skin:

- None.

Immune system:

- Moderate exercise strengthens the immune system, by encouraging the production of white blood cells, and moving them round the body.

Basic Nutrition and its Effect on Health

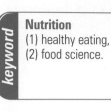

keyword

Nutrition
(1) healthy eating,
(2) food science.

keyword

Diet
intake of food.

keyword

Calorie
a unit of energy
found in food. This
energy can be used
by the body, or
stored in the form
of fat.

Food groups

Scientists have discovered that for a healthy **diet** we each need to eat the right amounts of five main types of food – called food groups. The balance is similar for all people, though there are some differences in the needs of children and adults. The total amount of food we each need to eat is related to our age, sex, build and how active we are.

The five food groups are:

■ *Starchy foods* – bread, rice, pasta, cereals, potatoes, couscous, yam, cassava etc. In a balanced diet, these kinds of food are the main source of our energy. They also contain vitamins, minerals and fibre. The energy (in the form of **calories**) is released at a steady rate, which is good for work and sport.

■ *Fruit and vegetables* – these foods give us plenty of vitamins, minerals and fibre, and are necessary for good all-round health. They make us feel healthy and alert and help to protect us against a wide range of illnesses, from colds to cancer. The fibre in them is helpful for digestion and enables us to absorb nutrients better. They usually contain very little fat but some, such as beans, peas and nuts are rich in protein. The amount of energy (calories) is fairly low.

■ *Milk and dairy foods* – these provide proteins, vitamins, minerals and fat (unless the milk has been skimmed, or the cheeses are low-fat). They are important in the growth of children and in maintaining good health as adults. They are a good source of energy, but cream and full fat cheese contain a high number of calories.

Figure 3.6
All five are needed!

- *Meat, fish, nuts, beans and lentils* – meat, poultry, fish, eggs, nuts, peas, beans, chickpeas and lentils are important sources of protein, vitamins and minerals, especially iron and zinc. They are very important both for growing children, and for rebuilding tissue and keeping us healthy as adults.

- *Fats and sugars* – these foods give large amounts of energy and are very high in calories. They are eaten for pleasure because they are tasty and filling. We need small amounts of fats and sugars to help transport vitamins, digest protein or provide minerals, but we do not need to add them to our food.

Other needs are:

- *Salt* – salt is used for many things in the body, especially in enabling the nerves to carry messages. Many people enjoy the taste of salty food, but like fats and sugars it is found naturally in other foods and does not need to be added.

- *Water* – at least two litres of water (or watery drinks) should be drunk each day – more when it is hot, or if you are doing sport or hard physical work. Water is needed for all the processes (called metabolism) which take place in the body. If we drink nothing we die after three or four days.

---

activity
GROUP WORK (3.2)

(a) Mount an exhibition, suitable for schoolchildren of a particular age, about the five food groups and why we need them.

(b) Note down what you have eaten in the last three days. Have you eaten the right amounts of the five food groups?

---

keyword

Nutrient
any chemical in food which is used by our bodies.

Nutrition and health

The active ingredients of food are called **nutrients**. The five main types of nutrient are carbohydrates, proteins, fats, vitamins, and minerals.

Table 3.3 The five main nutrients

Carbohydrates	Proteins	Fats	Vitamins	Minerals
These are starches and sugars. We need them for energy	Our muscle and other organs are mainly made of protein	Fats are needed for many metabolic (chemical) processes and for storing energy	Vitamins protect us against many illnesses and ensure alterness and good health	Small amounts of many minerals are needed in the body's chemistry

keyword

Fibre
stringy material found in food. It is not a nutrient, but it helps digestion.

A healthy diet must have the right proportions of these nutrients in our diet (together with **fibre**, water and salt). The easy way to do this is to eat the right percentage (by weight) of each food group.

Figure 3.7

Percentage of each food group in a healthy diet

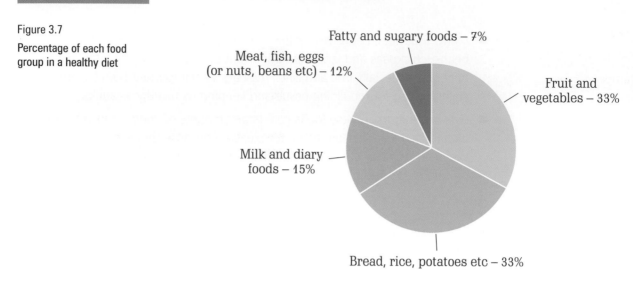

For children and young people who are still growing the ideal proportion of milk and dairy foods is slightly higher.

Amounts of food

The amount of food suitable for an individual is linked to their age, sex, lifestyle, build and amount of muscle.

On average men need more food than women and young people need more food than older people.

There are many tables and charts on the internet showing what people should weigh in relation to their height.

Table 3.4 Daily calorie intake

Age group	Men	Women
15–18	3000	2200
Over 51	2300	1900

Weight control

The uniformed public services prefer to recruit people who are the right weight for their height (i.e. within acceptable limits). If a person eats the right number of calories, and does enough physical activity to burn them up, they should be able to stay at the right weight. If they eat more calories than they use up, they will gain weight. If they eat fewer calories than they burn up, they will lose weight. The healthy option is to reach the right weight and keep at the right weight by ensuring that the number of calories going in is – on average – the same as the number used up.

Good nutrition

Each class of nutrients is needed to keep us healthy (see Table 3.5).

Table 3.5 Good nutrition

Nutrient type	Role	
Carbohydrates	Provide energy	
	Construct the body's organs and nerve cells	
Proteins	Needed to build the body and its organs	
	Form large parts of cells and connective tissue – e.g ligaments and tendons	
	Make enzymes which allow the body's chemical reactions to take place	
	Make hormones, chemicals which are released by glands into the bloodstream and determine behaviour and development	
	Carry nutrients from the blood into the cells of the body	
	Help the balance of fluids and electrolytes (dissolved chemicals)	
	Provide antibodies and heal wounds	
	Contain calories and can provide energy	
Fats	Make up part of cell membranes and help to control what goes in and out of the cell	
	Some types protect against cancer and heart disease	
	Supply large amounts of energy and can be stored in the body	
Vitamins	A:	Protects against infection; good for the eyes; deficiency can cause anaemia
	D:	Deficiency can cause rickets, or stunted growth
	E:	Deficiency causes problems with the nervous system and anaemia
	K:	Helps the blood to clot properly
	B1:	Deficiency causes a disease called beri-beri – body fluids accumulate; mental confusion; paralysis
	B2:	Deficiency causes skin problems; vision problems (oversensitive to light)
	B3:	Deficiency causes a disease called pellagra; leads to weakness, mental confusion, diarrhoea and skin problems
	B6:	Deficiency causes anaemia and convulsions
	Folic acid:	Protects immune system, and spina bifida (deformed spine in foetus leading to paralysis)
	B12:	Deficiency can lead to paralysis
	C:	Deficiency leads to a disease called scurvy – weak bones, anaemia, depression. Good for immune system
	Vitamins B and C are water-soluble and have to be taken in frequently, as the body can't store them.	
	Vitamins A, D, E and K are fat soluble and can be stored in the body	
Minerals	Calcium: needed for bones, teeth blood and nervous system	
	Chromium: protects the heart; protects against diabetes	
	Copper: good for blood and nervous system	
	Iodine: needed by the thyroid gland; essential for good growth, development and mental health; deficiency causes cretinism	
	Iron: needed to prevent anaemia	
	Magnesium: fights depression	
	Manganese: needed for healthy growth	
	Phosphorus: needed for bones	
	Potassium: used in transmitting nerve messages	
	Selenium: protects against some cancers	
	Sodium: used in regulating fluids; essential for nervous system – used, like potassium, to transmit messages	
	Zinc: good for growth and for the immune system	
	These are present in a balanced diet and do not normally need to be added	

Health problems caused by poor nutrition

Poor nutrition is sometimes called malnutrition. In its most extreme form it is linked with starvation, and has devastating effects in many poor countries, especially in Africa.

In Europe and America there are also a number of serious health problems connected with poor nutrition and unhealthy eating.

Obesity

Obesity is defined as being 145 per cent (or more) of the correct weight for your height – in other words, about half as much again as you should be. Overweight is defined as being 120 per cent of your correct weight for your height – i.e. about a fifth too much. The problem of obesity has increased greatly over the past 30 years. It is associated with poor nutrition – eating too much fatty and sugary food. The effects of obesity are to reduce the sufferer's quality of life, by limiting their activity and causing them to suffer socially (sometimes through discrimination). Obesity also shortens life expectancy by increasing the risk of heart disease, high blood pressure, diabetes and some other illnesses. Obesity is normally curable with the help of a qualified dietician and, perhaps, a change of lifestyle.

Diabetes

Diabetes is a condition which happens when the pancreas gland does not produce enough of a hormone called insulin. Insulin gets sugar out of the blood and into the cells of the body, where it is processed so that it can be used as energy later on. Type 1 diabetes, which is usually diagnosed amongst children and young adults, means that sufferers have to inject themselves with insulin. Type 2 diabetes starts, more commonly, later in life and can normally be controlled by eating a low-sugar and balanced diet, or by a combination of tablets and healthy eating. There is a small risk of diabetes starting in pregnant women. Type 2 diabetes is getting more common in the UK. Risk factors include diets high in fats and sugar, and heavy drinking.

Hypoglycaemia

This is a feeling of weakness, shakiness, loss of concentration or poor vision which takes place due to low levels of glucose in the blood. It can often occur during periods of high activity, or when people with diabetes have taken too much insulin and/or eaten too little food. If it becomes a problem the sufferer should see a doctor, as in some people it may be an indication of the early signs of diabetes. It can be prevented, or reduced, by eating complex carbohydrates, such as bread, potatoes or rice. If a person is suffering from a 'hypo' they should be given carbohydrates or, in more serious cases, a fast acting sugary drink. Alcohol, especially spirits, can also cause hypoglycaemia.

Cholesterol

Cholesterol is a kind of fat. It is needed by the body, but only in small amounts. Unfortunately foods like red meat, hamburgers, butter, eggs and cream contain a lot of 'saturated fats' – fats which contain cholesterol. In some people (but not all) eating too much of these fat-rich foods can cause a build-up of cholesterol in the blood vessels. This build-up, in the form of 'plaques' or coatings, narrows the arteries and makes the heart have to work harder to pump blood round the body. This in turn leads to high blood pressure and a greater risk of heart disease, heart attacks and strokes. The best way to reduce this risk is to eat less fatty food, and get more exercise. Certain foods, such as oily fish (herrings, mackerel and sardines), and carbohydrate food such as oats, cut the amount of cholesterol in the bloodstream – so eating these can reduce the risk of plaques forming. Cholesterol and clogging of the arteries is not normally a problem for people under 30, but the damage can start at an early age. If it gets too bad arteries and the heart may have to be operated on – e.g. with a 'heart by-pass'. For this reason people who feel they may be at risk from cholesterol-related illness should see the doctor before the symptoms appear.

Blood pressure

Blood is pumped round our bodies under pressure. The pressure is highest when the heart squeezes the blood out, and lowest when it is filling up again. A blood pressure reading is therefore expressed like a fraction, with the higher pressure (the 'systolic' pressure) over the lower pressure (the 'diastolic' pressure).

A normal blood pressure is 120/80 or less. Anything higher than 140/90 is high blood pressure, or hypertension. Low blood pressure is not normally a problem unless people are injured, in shock, or undergoing an operation. Blood pressure rises gradually with age. High blood pressure is linked to eating too much fat and sugar (see 'Cholesterol' above) and not taking enough exercise. It can cause heart attacks, strokes and kidney damage. High blood pressure is a life-threatening condition, but usually, the sufferer cannot feel it. This is one major reason why older people should have regular health checks.

Heart disease

Heart disease is linked to cholesterol and high blood pressure. The risk of heart disease can be reduced by cutting down on fatty foods, fried foods, cheese and eggs, and by eating more fruit, vegetables and complex carbohydrates. Regular exercise also cuts down the risk of heart disease. Heart disease can take various forms, leading to shortness of breath, pains called angina, and heart attacks. It is the main form of death among older people, especially men.

Many illnesses are blamed on poor nutrition: there is, for example, a link between many forms of cancer and the food we eat. A balanced diet of fresh food, with plenty of fruit, vegetables and complex carbohydrates, moderate amounts of meat, and low amounts of fat and sugar, provide the healthiest nutrition.

activity
GROUP WORK
(3.3)

Research and draw up a cheap healthy diet, suitable for a young person who has just left home.

www.nal.usda.gov (US government nutrition website)
www.fsmed.org

Public Service Fitness Tests and the Requirements of the Public Services

keyword	**Components of fitness** types of fitness. Five are 'heath-related' and five are 'skill-related'.

Most uniformed public services have fitness tests for applicants, and many have them for their employees. To prepare for these tests it is helpful to understand the different **components of fitness**, as well as the different kinds of test.

Health components

These are linked to general health. They are:

- *Cardiovascular fitness* – a healthy heart, healthy blood vessels and healthy lungs. If you have good endurance, don't get tired easily, and are rarely short of breath, you have a good standard of cardiovascular fitness.

- *Body composition* – the relationship between the amount of fat in your body, and everything else in your body, given as a percentage. Fifteen per cent body fat is about right for the uniformed public services.

- *Flexibility* – being able to bend easily at the joints. It depends on the condition of tendons, ligaments, muscles and bones.

- *Muscular strength* – the ability of muscles to act strongly in a short period of time (e.g. when lifting heavy weights).

- *Muscular endurance* – the ability of muscles to continue working for long periods of time without resting.

Skill-related components

These are learned abilities.

- *Agility* – the ability to change direction rapidly when running.
- *Balance* – the ability to avoid falling over.
- *Coordination* – the ability to do several movements at the same time.
- *Speed* – being able to move or react quickly.
- *Power* – the ability to make sudden, forceful movements.

Different kinds of test

Different uniformed public services set different fitness tests for their applicants. These depend on the physical requirements for the job. The fitness tests for marine commandos, for example, are much tougher than fitness tests for the prison service.

Tests have a habit of changing, so to get up-to-date information, visit the services' official websites, or, better still, contact them.

case study 3.3

Prison service fitness test (for applicants)

1. Height and Weight
We'll measure your height and your weight to find out your Body Mass Index, which will tell us if you're overweight or not. If you are overweight, we'll let you know how much weight you need to lose to join us and advise you on the best way to reach your target. This is as much in your interest as ours because being within the right weight limits will make you healthier as well as helping you pass the next tests.

2. Grip Strength
For this test, we'll measure the strength of your forearm muscles by asking you to squeeze a measuring device as tightly as you can in one hand at a time.

3. Endurance Shuttle Run
To find out how well your energy lasts, we'll ask you to run faster and faster over a 15-metre course until you reach your target level.

4. Dyno
Here, we want to know how strong your upper arms and upper body are. So we'll ask you to do some pulling and pushing.

5. Speed Agility
Prison Officers have to be able to run from one part of the prison to another. So, to test your ability to do that, we'll ask you to run round an obstacle course and change direction quickly.

6. *Shield*

This test involves holding a 6-kilogram shield and practising control and restraining techniques.

Figure 3.8 shows how the prison service fitness test relates to the various components of fitness.

Part of fitness test	Fitness component(s) tested
Height and weight	Body composition
Grip strength	Muscular strength
Endurance shuttle run	Cardiovascular fitness
Dyno	Power
Speed agility	Coordination/speed/balance
Shield	Muscular strength/coordination

Figure 3.8

The prison service fitness test – and fitness components

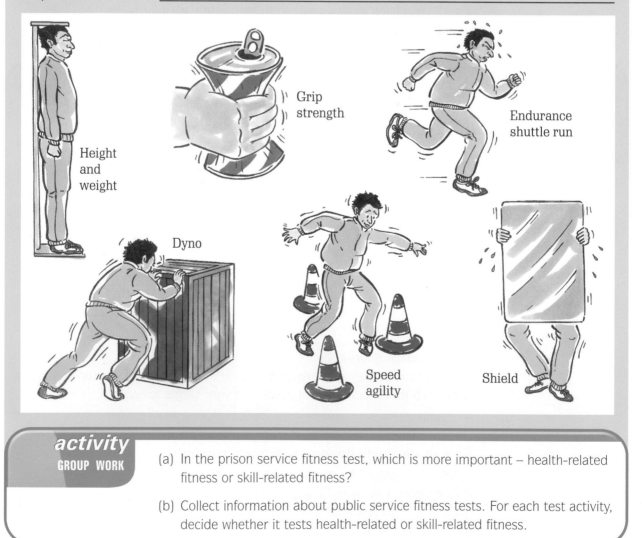

activity

GROUP WORK

(a) In the prison service fitness test, which is more important – health-related fitness or skill-related fitness?

(b) Collect information about public service fitness tests. For each test activity, decide whether it tests health-related or skill-related fitness.

Taking a test

In many cases your college will organise fitness tests which are as similar as possible to real public service fitness tests. Take the tests, and record the results.

Another option is to visit a public service, talk to the people who run the tests and have a go yourself. When you take the test, record your results, and see how they compare with the results they expect from applicants. If you do a fitness test away from college, make sure it is properly witnessed if you want it to count towards your BTEC course.

If you are not used to fitness tests, or are worried about your health, see a doctor first.

activity
INDIVIDUAL WORK
(3.4)

Do a uniformed public service fitness test under supervision.

Analysing your fitness test results

When you do your public service fitness test you must record and keep your result for each of the activities you do.

You then need to find out what the normal standards are for a suitable public service, and compare your result with those standards.

Case study 3.4 gives a minimum standard expected for applicants to the police and the fire and rescue service for one of their fitness tests: the shuttle run.

case study 3.4

Endurance

In this element you will be asked to run to and fro along a 15 metre track in time with a series of bleeps.

…

You will run until you can no longer keep up with the set pace. You will need to reach a minimum of four shuttles at level 5 to pass.

(*Source*: www.policecouldyou.co.uk)

Shuttle Run Test. The shuttle run requires you to run to and fro along a marked track 20m long, keeping up with a series of bleeps on an audiotape.

The timing of the bleeps start off slow and get progressively faster, so that it becomes progressively harder to keep up with the bleeps.

To pass this test you must reach Level 9.6, which equates to 45 VO$_2$ max.

The test takes approximately 10 minutes and will be fully explained on the day of the test.

(*Source*: www.westyorksfire.gov.uk)

Table 3.6 Example of an analysis of a shuttle run test

Score on shuttle run	Service applied for	Possible analysis
8.4	Police	It appears that my performance in this test is well above the minimum required by the police. I am encouraged by this, but that doesn't mean that there isn't room for improvement. I know that if I do well in this test, it will give a good impression and show that I am a serious candidate.
8.4	Fire and rescue service	This is not good enough – yet I felt I was trying my best. I have been jogging twice a week for the past two months and I thought I would do better in this than I have done.

activity
INDIVIDUAL WORK

Examine and comment on each aspect of your result in a public service fitness test.

Ways of improving fitness test results

There are many ways of improving your performance in a fitness test. What you choose to do depends on your needs and motivation.

Possibilities are:

- Practise the test activities – especially if they involve agility, balance, coordination or some other aspect of skill-related fitness. Skill-related fitness can be improved with practice.

■ Carry out fitness training to improve aerobic fitness, or strength training to improve strength.

■ Eat a healthier diet (this might mean examining your present diet and suggesting improvements).

■ Stop smoking and/or drinking.

---

activity
INDIVIDUAL WORK
(3.5)

Show how you could improve your standard in a public service fitness test, and plan ways of making those improvements.

Developing and Completing a Personal Fitness Training Programme

Health and safety first!

Health and safety should always be in the forefront of your mind when planning and carrying out a fitness training programme.

Figure 3.9 shows the main aspects of health and safety you should think about when planning your training.

Figure 3.9

Health, safety and training

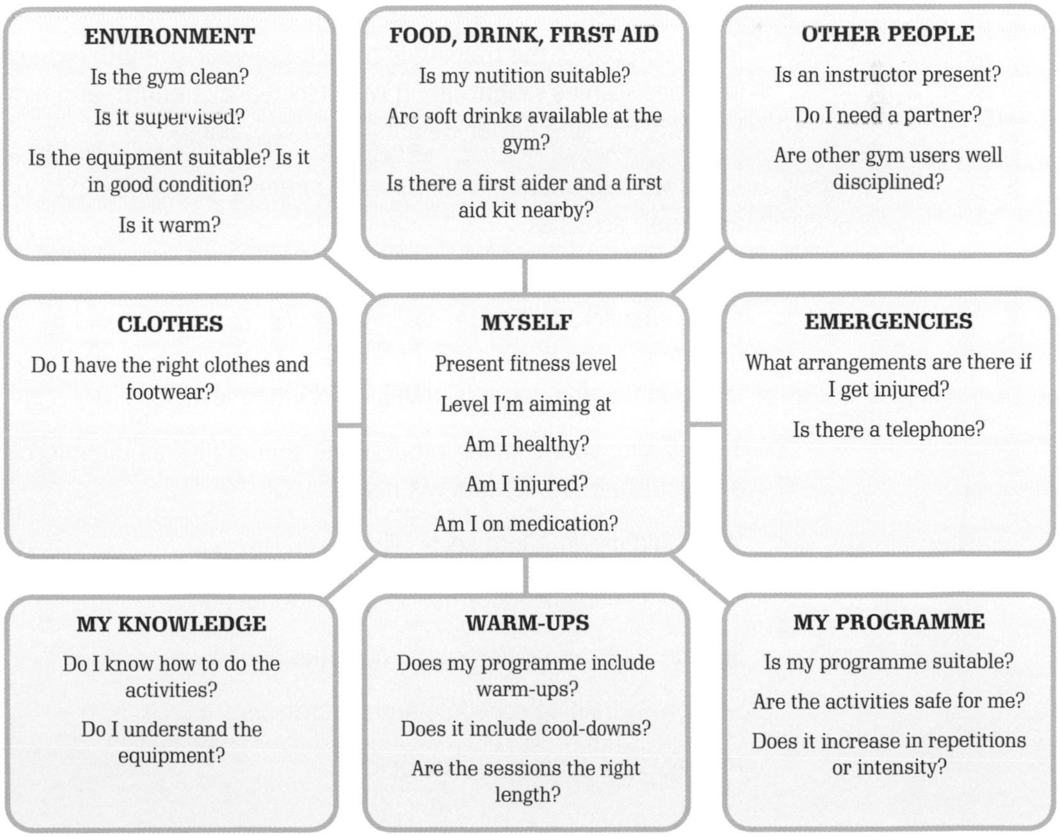

ENVIRONMENT

Is the gym clean?

Is it supervised?

Is the equipment suitable? Is it in good condition?

Is it warm?

FOOD, DRINK, FIRST AID

Is my nutrition suitable?

Are soft drinks available at the gym?

Is there a first aider and a first aid kit nearby?

OTHER PEOPLE

Is an instructor present?

Do I need a partner?

Are other gym users well disciplined?

CLOTHES

Do I have the right clothes and footwear?

MYSELF

Present fitness level

Level I'm aiming at

Am I healthy?

Am I injured?

Am I on medication?

EMERGENCIES

What arrangements are there if I get injured?

Is there a telephone?

MY KNOWLEDGE

Do I know how to do the activities?

Do I understand the equipment?

WARM-UPS

Does my programme include warm-ups?

Does it include cool-downs?

Are the sessions the right length?

MY PROGRAMME

Is my programme suitable?

Are the activities safe for me?

Does it increase in repetitions or intensity?

As you go through your fitness programme, make a note of any health or safety issues which come up.

---

activity
**INDIVIDUAL WORK
(3.6)**

Visit a sports centre and ask someone who works there what the main risks are in fitness training.

Training programmes

There are many kinds of training programme, and some are more suitable for public service fitness tests than others. The one that is best for you depends on your own present level of fitness, and the kind of test you hope to do. Many public services give advice on the best type of training programme for their tests. They tend to go for increases in both aerobic fitness and strength, and increase in intensity as time goes on. The most popular training of this type is circuit training.

Circuit training

Most training programmes for uniformed public service fitness tests are circuit training. This means you do a number of different activities in each training session. If the purpose of the training is to improve your aerobic fitness (endurance and stamina), you should gradually increase the number of times (repetitions) you do each activity.

If the purpose of the training is to increase your strength, you should pick activities such as weight-lifting which increase strength, and aim to increase intensity (i.e. lift heavier weights as you go along).

If you want to improve your all-round fitness, you should pick both aerobic and anaerobic activities.

At all times you must remember that training without knowledge and planning can be dangerous. Ensure safety as much as possible, and get the advice of qualified professionals before you start. Make sure you write something about safety in the plan for your training programme.

The plan for your training programme should give all the information that you, and your tutors/assessors will need.

You could divide it into sections:

Section 1: Personal information and introduction

Section 2: A description of the activities

Section 3: Training schedule and record sheet

A suggested outline is given below.

SECTION 1

Name:

Age: In years and months

Situation now: Give height, weight, sporting activities and any other relevant details about your health and fitness

Future plan: Which public service you want to join, and when

Fitness need: Develop all-round fitness

Introduction

Explain the purpose of the plan (one or two sentences). This is probably that you want to get yourself fit enough to take the fitness test of your choice.

Say how long the plan will take (this example lasts 12 weeks).

Say how long each training session will be.

State where and when your training sessions will take place.

Outline what steps you have taken to ensure that your training is safe.

Describe the exercises you will include in your fitness programme (examples are given in Case study 3.5).

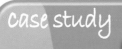

case study 3.5 — Exercises for fitness programme

Press Ups
Start in prone position with straight line from ankle to shoulder. Avoid sagging or raising backside. Look down throughout the exercise. Chest should be lowered until elbows are at 90°. Avoid locking shoulders on return to starting position. Breathe out on exertion.

Half Press Ups
Start in prone position with straight line from knees to shoulder and cross feet at ankles. Avoid raising backside. Continue as per full press up.

Lunge
Start with feet shoulder width apart. Hold dumbbells to side throughout. Keep trunk upright during the session with the spine in a neutral position. Step forward and bend front leg to 90°. Straighten back leg, but avoid locking knee. After set repetitions, change to other leg. Breathe freely during the exercise.

Triceps Press
Using a box or other suitable support, adopt a reverse press-up position. By allowing the elbows to flex, lower the body so that the buttocks are close but not touching the floor, then return to the start position keeping the hips high.

Sit Ups

Start in supine position. Bend legs and keep heels close to backside. Keep lower back on floor throughout the exercise. Maintain a gap between chin and chest, with hands on thighs or temples. Don't grip behind the head. Raise head and shoulders 30°. Breathe out on curling up.

Squat

Stand with feet shoulder width apart, keeping spine neutral. Bend legs so that thighs are parallel with the floor. Keep hands by the head throughout the exercise. Avoid locking knees on return to starting position. Breathe out on the way down.

Dorsal Raise

Lie face down on the floor concentrating on keeping your spine in neutral alignment, with your head in line. Your arms are to the side palms upwards, keeping your feet in contact with the floor, lift your shoulders and chest clear of the floor, keep looking down to keep your head in line. This is a slow squeezing action, do not jerk. Return to the start position under control. To increase the difficulty of the exercise, move your arms up so that fingers touch your temples with elbows out to the side.

Stair Running

This is simply using a staircase to create a high intensity aerobic exercise. If you can't get to the gym and use the Stairmaster spend time at home running up and down the stairs. Push hard on the way up, take it steady on the way down.

Chester Step Test

The step used in the 'Chester Step Test' (a test used to predict aerobic fitness) is a twelve-inch step, which equates to a standard exercise bench. It would therefore make sense to train on at least that size although a higher step would not be a problem.

(*Source*: www.hantsfire.gov.uk; triceps press – www.westyorksfire.gov.uk)

---

activity
INDIVIDUAL WORK

(a) Which of these activities develop aerobic fitness, and which develop strength?

(b) Research the Harvard and Chester step tests. Note down the procedures of both. What is the difference between them?

SECTION 2

keyword

Repetitions ('reps') the number of times you do a particular exercise during a training session.

This section should set out the circuits you intend to do, and the progression (planned increase of **repetitions**).

Table 3.7 Circuits and progression

Circuit	Progression 1	Progression 2	Progression 3	Progression 4	Progression 5	Progression 6
Press-ups	10 reps	15	20	25	30	35
Standing squats	10 reps	15	20	25	30	35
Lunges	10 reps	15	20	25	30	35
Triceps press	10 reps	15	20	25	30	35
Jog on spot	30 secs	40 secs	50 secs	1 min	1 min	1 min
Dorsal raise	10 reps	15	20	25	30	35
Stair run	5 reps	6	7	8	9	10

The circuit is the activity; the progression is the number of repetitions or – in the case of jogging on the spot – the number of seconds or minutes.

SECTION 3

Training schedule and record sheet

In this example (Table 3.8) the circuit training, which involves all the activities listed in Section 2, is done twice a week and the repetitions for each circuit increase as the training progresses. In the first week the training uses Progression 1; by the final week it will have gone up to Progression 6.

In between circuit training there are two rest days and one day for a training session of walking and running. So the sequence is: Circuit … Rest day … Walk/run … Rest day … Circuit.

The training schedule, or timetable, has spaces for keeping a progress record, and for noting problems.

SECTION 4

Other comments

1. Advantages of this plan

The rest days prevent over-training, which would risk injury and bring no real benefit. The walking and running will prepare for the shuttle run, and other endurance-testing activities in the fire and rescue service fitness test. Activities such as sit-ups and the triceps press will increase upper body strength, needed for hose-running, ladder raising, and carrying heavy equipment.

Table 3.8 Training Schedule/Record Sheet

Week	Monday Aim	Monday Actual	Tuesday Aim	Tuesday Actual	Wednesday Aim	Wednesday Actual	Thursday Aim	Thursday Actual	Friday Aim	Friday Actual	Saturday Aim	Saturday Actual	Sunday Aim	Sunday Actual
1	10 min walk/run		Rest		Circ. Prog. 1		Rest		15 min walk/run		Rest		Circ. Prog. 1	
2	Rest		15 min run (S)		Rest		Circ. Prog. 2		Rest		20 min run (S)		Circ. Prog. 2	
3	Rest		20 min run (F)		Circ. Prog. 2		Rest		20 min run (S)		Circ. Prog. 2		Rest	
4	20 min run (S)		Circ. Prog. 2		Rest		20 min run (F)		Rest		Circ. Prog. 3		20 min run (F)	
5	Rest		Circ. Prog. 3		25 min run (S)		Rest		Circ. Prog. 3		Rest		30 min run (S)	
6	Rest		Circ. Prog. 4		Rest		30 min run (F)		Circ. Prog. 4		Rest		30 min run (S)	
7	Circ. Prog. 4		Rest		20 min run (S)		Circ. Prog. 4		Rest		30 min run (F)		Circ. Prog. 4	
8	Rest		Circ. Prog. 5		30 min run (F)		Circ. Prog. 5		Rest		20 min run (S)		Circ. Prog. 5	
9	30 min run (S)		Rest		Circ. Prog. 5		Rest		40 min run (S)		Circ. Prog. 5		Rest	
10	40 min run (S)		Circ. Prog. 5		30 min run (F)		Rest		20 min run (S)		Circ. Prog. 6		Rest	
11	40 min run (S)		Circ. Prog. 6		20 min run (F)		Circ. Prog. 6		Rest		40 min run (S)		Circ. Prog. 6	
12	Rest		40 min run (S)		Circ. Prog. 6		30 min run (F)		Circ. Prog. 6		Rest		20 min run (S)	

Running pace: approx. 8–8$\frac{1}{2}$ min/mile for Steady (S); 7–7$\frac{1}{2}$ min/mile for Fast (F)

2. How improvement will be measured.

The best method is to take a Chester Step Test or Harvard Step Test where the heart rate is measured after a fixed period of activity. If the same test is taken a few weeks apart, differences in heart rate, or heart recovery rate, should show that fitness has increased. The other method is to try a shuttle run test and see if you can improve your performance. This is less scientific, since it depends on motivation.

Undertaking the fitness programme

This should be done under the supervision of a tutor or qualified instructor. You should do it at the times you planned and make a genuine effort to improve your fitness. Make notes about your progress, your feelings about the different activities, and any difficulties you encounter. Seek advice from a tutor or instructor if you feel that your fitness programme is not working out in the way that you wanted. If you are ill or injured stop training and see a doctor – and also let your tutor know.

activity
INDIVIDUAL WORK (3.7)

(a) Work out your own fitness training programme. It has to be a programme which would make *you* do better in a public service fitness test.

(b) Carry out the programme.

keyword

Review explain what you did, and why – after you have done it.

Planning your fitness training programme

When planning a programme, whether of fitness training or anything else, follow the stages shown in Figure 3.10.

Reviewing your planning

When you finally **review** your planning and the fitness programme itself, use the records in your log, and ask yourself these questions:

remember

Keep a log or diary of the planning and carrying out of your fitness training programme. Much of this can be done on forms like those shown above.

- How did I decide what activities to include in my fitness programme? (e.g. Were they my personal fitness needs; were they suitable for the test I was going to take? Did I choose them because the facilities were available? Did I target strength of aerobic fitness? Why?)
- What research did I need to do beforehand?
- How did I decide when and where to do my training sessions?
- How did I decide on the length of my training sessions?
- What steps did I take to avoid injury?
- What other health and safety precautions did I take?
- What was the thinking behind the progression of my training?
- How did I record my progress?

Figure 3.10
Stages of planning

Getting the idea

Fact finding

Planning

First step

Evaluate

Next step

Planning

- When and how did I evaluate my training programme?
- What help did I get from other people?
- Did I need to buy any equipment or clothes, or spend any money?
- Did I expect any problems – and how did I plan to overcome them?

activity
GROUP WORK
(3.8)

Prepare a short educational video or leaflet showing and explaining how to plan a fitness training programme.

Evaluating your performance

There are two things you should evaluate:

1. How your fitness improved during your training programme.

2. How good your fitness training programme was.

Evaluating fitness improvement

The best way of doing this is to test your fitness before you started your programme, and re-test your fitness after you have finished it. (If you get the chance, you might find it helpful to test your fitness improvement halfway through the programme as well.)

The most accurate type of fitness test is one that measures your heart rate after a fixed period of activity. The simple test in Case study 3.6 is one that you can do yourself, at home. It is essential to time your stepping accurately, otherwise you may have variations in your heart rate due to different speeds of stepping, rather than differences in your own fitness.

case study 3.6

Step test

This test is designed to measure your cardiovascular endurance. Using a 12 inch high bench (or a similar sized stair in your house), step on and off for 3 minutes. Step up with one foot and then the other. Step down with one foot followed by the other foot. Try to maintain a steady four beat cycle. It's easy to maintain if you say 'up, up, down, down'. Go at a steady and consistent pace.

At the end of 3 minutes, remain standing while you immediately check your heart rate by taking your pulse for one minute.

(*Source*: www.topendsports.com)

activity
INDIVIDUAL WORK

(a) What other ways might there be of testing your fitness?

(b) Why are the steps tests the most accurate?

A slower heart rate, or a faster decrease in heart-rate after the test, shows increased aerobic fitness.

There are other kinds of step test, e.g. the Harvard Step Test and the Chester Step Test which you may be able to do at college, and which will be more accurate than this one.

Evaluating strength improvement

If you want to assess your improvement in strength after a strength-based training programme, you will have to do it by seeing whether you can lift heavier weights at the end of the programme than at the beginning. You should do this form of assessment with the aid of a qualified instructor.

Evaluating the training programme

Evaluating the training programme means answering a few simple questions:

1. Did the programme improve my fitness as much as I wanted it to do?
2. Did I enjoy the programme?
3. Did I suffer any injuries or illness because of it?
4. Did it cost me any money?

Question 1 is important, because the aim of a fitness training programme is to improve your fitness. But the amount of improvement will depend partly on how fit you were when you started the programme. A fit person carrying out a fitness training programme with the aim of improving their aerobic fitness may make only small improvements – because they are fit to begin with. An unfit person, on the other hand, will make big gains simply because they were unfit when the programme started.

If you want to do a strength-based training programme, you should ensure that you are aerobically fit to begin with. It is more difficult to improve strength than improve aerobic fitness: it involves pushing yourself hard by increasing the intensity of your training.

It is worth mentioning that the gains in fitness and strength from training programmes are not permanent. If you stop training, your strength and fitness will fall off. On the other hand, you do need to take rests between training programmes, otherwise you get stale and risk either demotivation or overtraining. For BTEC Firsts, you are required to do only one fitness programme, but if you work in a uniformed public service you will be expected to stay fit – and that will mean starting new fitness programmes from time to time, and varying the activities you do. When evaluating your training programme, you should say something about how you would develop or maintain your fitness in the long term.

Question 2 can be answered by saying what you enjoyed about your exercise programme, and what you didn't. If you didn't enjoy it, suggest changes that could be made to make it more pleasurable.

Question 3 can be a brief review of the risks and how successful you were in dealing with them. If you had any illness or injury resulting from the training programme, you should describe it and say how it could have been avoided. If you suffered any soreness, stiffness, tiredness or discomfort, say whether it was a problem and what, if anything, you did about it. If your programme affected your eating habits, or changed your nutritional needs, you should mention that too.

Question 4 should be mentioned if your training programme cost you money – e.g. if you had to buy clothing or join a gym.

activity
INDIVIDUAL WORK
(3.9)

Record how well your training programme went, how you benefited, and what problems you came across. Then explain what changes you would make to your training programme if you did it again.

progress check

1. Explain why the cardiovascular system is so important for general fitness.

2. (a) What are the two main aims of training and (b) what are the two main effects that training can have on your muscles?

3. Note down five long-term advantages of regular physical activity.

4. Which food group (a) gives a steady supply of energy and which food group (b) is best for building muscles?

5. Name three factors which affect how many calories a person should eat in a day.

6. Name three causes of heart disease in later life.

7. Name two health-related and two skill-related components of fitness.

8. Write down 10 health and safety considerations for someone planning a fitness programme.

9. Give two reasons why circuit training is good for someone wanting to join a uniformed public service.

10. Give three reasons why you should plan your fitness training.

Citizenship, the Individual and Society

This unit covers:

- the terms citizen, citizenship, individual rights and human rights
- the relationship between individuals, society and the public services
- the importance of equal opportunities in society and the public services
- the different roles of statutory and non-statutory public services to the citizen and to a changing society

Public service work is carried out by citizens for citizens. In this unit you will learn what it means to be a citizen, and why citizenship matters.

You will also learn about equal opportunities – an idea which has changed the public services in many ways in the last 20 years.

Finally, the unit will help you to explore the relationship between the uniformed public services and society – the people they work with and for.

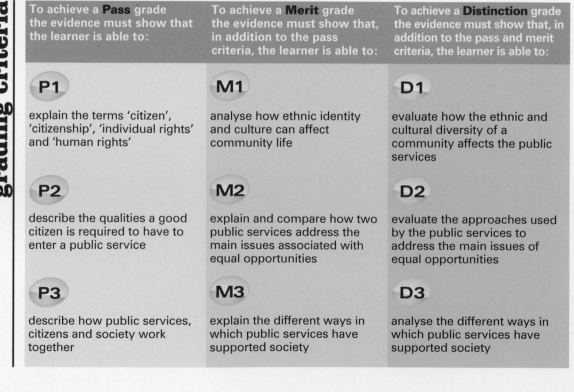

grading criteria

To achieve a **Pass** grade the evidence must show that the learner is able to:	To achieve a **Merit** grade the evidence must show that, in addition to the pass criteria, the learner is able to:	To achieve a **Distinction** grade the evidence must show that, in addition to the pass and merit criteria, the learner is able to:
P1 explain the terms 'citizen', 'citizenship', 'individual rights' and 'human rights'	**M1** analyse how ethnic identity and culture can affect community life	**D1** evaluate how the ethnic and cultural diversity of a community affects the public services
P2 describe the qualities a good citizen is required to have to enter a public service	**M2** explain and compare how two public services address the main issues associated with equal opportunities	**D2** evaluate the approaches used by the public services to address the main issues of equal opportunities
P3 describe how public services, citizens and society work together	**M3** explain the different ways in which public services have supported society	**D3** analyse the different ways in which public services have supported society

grading criteria

To achieve a **Pass** grade the evidence must show that the learner is able to:	To achieve a **Merit** grade the evidence must show that, in addition to the pass criteria, the learner is able to:	To achieve a **Distinction** grade the evidence must show that, in addition to the pass criteria, the learner is able to:
P4 name the legislative documents associated with equal opportunities		
P5 outline the different ways in which public services have affected society		
P6 outline the different ways in which public services have supported society		

Citizen, Citizenship, Individual Rights and Human Rights

keyword

Citizen
a member of a particular political community or state.

Citizen

Citizens have a home and in the place where they live they have the rights and responsibilities listed below.

Rights:

- to vote
- to stand for election (as a councillor or MP)
- to have a passport
- to be able to receive benefits
- to work in the uniformed public services of that country.

Responsibilities:

- to pay tax
- to obey the law.

Citizenship

1. Sometimes citizenship is the same as 'nationality'. 'British citizenship' as defined by the Home Office or the Immigration and Nationality Directorate is the same

as British nationality. It includes the right to live and work in Britain permanently, the right to carry a British passport and the right to vote in British general elections.

2. 'Citizenship' in the phrase 'good citizenship' means behaviour which is responsible and caring towards the community as a whole. Being helpful to neighbours, reporting crimes, and upholding the law are linked to this wider meaning of citizenship.

3. Citizenship is also a school and college subject. It is about the rights and responsibilities of people living in the UK. The government believes that studying citizenship will make people more law-abiding and reduce the amount of crime and disorder in society.

---

case study 4.1 — Citizenship

'We aim at no less than a change in the political culture of this country both nationally and locally: for people to think of themselves as active citizens, willing, able and equipped to have an influence in public life' (Crick report, 1998).

(*Source*: www.dfes.gov.uk)

---

activity
GROUP WORK

(a) Is it possible for a person under 18 to be a citizen?

(b) What are the arguments for and against teaching citizenship in schools?

Individual rights

In the United States this means individual freedoms, of the kind which are written in the US Constitution. Two are given in Case study 4.2.

---

case study 4.2 — Individual freedoms in the US

Amendment I

Congress shall make no law respecting an establishment of religion, or prohibiting the free exercise thereof; or abridging the freedom of speech, or of the press; or the right of the people peaceably to assemble, and to petition the Government for a redress of grievances.

Amendment II

A well regulated Militia, being necessary to the security of a free State, the right of the people to keep and bear Arms, shall not be infringed.

(*Source*: www.archives.gov)

activity

GROUP WORK

(a) What are the limitations on freedom of speech in the UK?

(b) What are the arguments for and against ordinary people having the right to carry guns?

Amendment I means that Americans will have freedom of worship, freedom of speech and freedom to gather together in a peaceful protest. Amendment II means they can carry guns.

'Individual rights' in the US are the freedom to do what you like as long as it doesn't break the law. Sometimes it means the same thing in the UK.

But not always. In the UK 'individual rights' can mean the rights of employees to be treated fairly at their place of work. These individual rights include:

- fair employment contracts
- national minimum wage
- redundancy pay
- unfair dismissal
- maternity/paternity leave
- flexible working hours
- taking time off
- anti-discrimination
- trade union membership
- working hours
- employment tribunals.

(*Source*: www.dti.gov.uk)

Human rights

Human rights

keyword

laws or beliefs which protect people against bad government, bad laws, and cruel, oppressive behaviour by people in power.

The original statement of **human rights** came from the United Nations in 1948. It is called the Universal Declaration of Human Rights. The rights (in brief) include:

- no discrimination
- freedom and security
- no torture
- equality before the law
- no imprisonment without trial
- accused people are seen as innocent until proved guilty
- freedom of movement, inside and outside each country
- the right to seek asylum
- having a nationality

- no forced marriages
- the right to own property
- free thought and worship
- free expression (speech, writing etc.)
- free assembly (peaceful meetings and demonstrations)
- freedom to vote and stand for election
- freedom to do public service
- rights to social security (benefits)
- right to work
- right to have leisure
- right to have a decent standard of living
- right to education and culture
- the freedom to do anything except break the law or interfere with the freedom of others.

Visit www.unhchr.ch

---

activity
INDIVIDUAL WORK
(4.1)

What human rights exist now which did not exist in 1948?

---

keyword

Qualities
ways of behaving or feeling towards other people, e.g. honesty, sympathy, courage etc. Qualities can be either good or bad.

Good citizenship and public service

People who work in a public service should be good citizens. In particular, they should have certain **qualities**.

If you read the recruitment leaflets, websites and job specifications of the public services you will see what qualities they are looking for.

---

case study

4.3

Infantry soldier

Personal qualities

You must be reliable, of good character and of stable personality. We also look for a good level of education, common sense, self-discipline and the ability to stay calm under pressure.

(*Source*: Army website)

activity
INDIVIDUAL WORK

(a) Put the following expressions into your own words: 'reliable'; 'of good character'; 'of stable personality'; 'common sense'; 'self-discipline'.

(b) Visit www.army.mod.uk and compare the qualities needed for an infantry soldier with those needed for an army officer.

Visit relevant websites, e.g.
www.army.mod.uk
www.westyorksfire.gov.uk
www.hmprisonservice.gov.uk
and local authority websites.

www.londonambulance.co.uk
customs.hmrc.gov.uk
www.odpm.gov.uk
www.mcga.gov.uk

Want to find out more on good citizenship and public service? Ask the opinions of people who work in a public service, especially police officers, probation officers, prison officers, officers in the armed forces, priests and religious teachers.

activity
GROUP WORK
(4.2)

Write a leaflet, to be put in the applicants' packs for a public service, outlining the qualities of good citizenship expected of applicants.

The Relationship between Individuals, Society and the Public Services

Different uniformed public services have different relationships with the public. These are summarised in Table 4.1.

Table 4.1 Uniformed public services relationships with public

Public service	Relationships with citizens and society
RAF	Main function: to protect the UK people and UK allies and interests from enemies
	Main relationship with society: indirect, except for people who live near air force bases, or with the relatives of employees
	Responsible to: the government, through the Ministry of Defence
	Praised for: courage and expertise
	Criticised for: low flying in country areas
Police	Main functions: to deter, prevent or solve crime, and keep the peace
	Main relationship with society: dealing with criminals, helping victims, advising and reassuring the general public
	Responsible to: (a) the local public through the Police Authority, (b) the government, through the Home Office and the Chief Constable
	Praised for: courage and professionalism
	Criticised for: occasional errors of judgement, suspected racism, getting involved in politics etc.
HM Revenue and Customs	Main functions: to collect taxes and prevent smuggling and other cross-border crimes
	Main relationship with public: stopping cars and lorries at ferries etc., collecting taxes
	Responsible to: the Treasury (the government department whose job is to collect and give out money)
	Praised for: helping protect the UK against international crime
	Criticised for: collecting taxes!
Fire and rescue service	Main functions: to attend fires and accidents; to prevent fires; to protect the public
	Main relationship with public: rescuing them and their property from fires and accidents
	Responsible to: the local public through the Fire Authority – also to the government through the Office of the Deputy Prime Mininster
	Praised for: courage and expertise
	Criticised for: poor equal opportunities at work (this is being corrected)

activity
PAIR WORK
(4.3)

Interview public service workers to find out how they work together with citizens and society. Present your findings in the form of a short report.

www.ind.homeoffice.gov.uk
www.youth-justice-board.gov.uk
www.metpolicecareers.co.uk

Read the annual reports and policing plans of your local police force, and the reports of your local fire authority. Contact your local crime and disorder reduction partnership. Visit public service websites:

Figure 4.1

The police, citizens and society

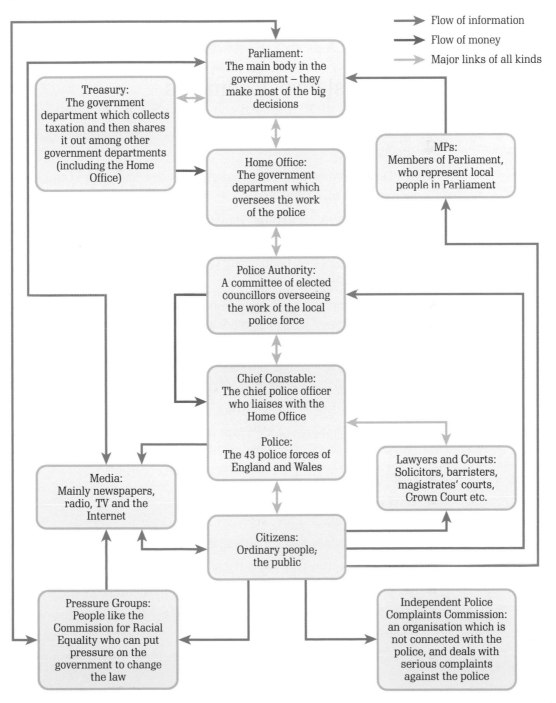

The Importance of Equal Opportunities in Society and Public Services

What are equal opportunities?

'Equal opportunities' refers to fair and equal treatment in the workplace for all sections of the population. There should be no unfair and unlawful discrimination on the grounds of colour, race, nationality, gender, marital status, disability, religion, age, sexual orientation, socio-economic grouping, union activity, politics or any unrelated spent criminal convictions.

> **keyword**
>
> **Legislative documents** laws made by Parliament. The big general laws are called Acts; the small specific ones are called Regulations.

Main legislative documents

- Equal Pay Act 1970 (men and women get equal pay for equal work)
- Rehabilitation of Offenders Act 1974 (reduces discrimination against ex-criminals)
- Sex Discrimination Act 1975 (prevents sex discrimination in employment, recruitment, advertising etc)
- Race Relations Act 1976 (prevents race discrimination in employment, recruitment, advertising etc)
- Safety Representatives and Safety Committees Regulations 1977 (improves health and safety at work)
- Transfer of Undertakings (Protection of Employment) Regulations 1981 (protects workers' jobs when a company is taken over)
- Trade Union and Labour Relations (Consolidation) Act 1992 (clarifies rights and roles of trade unions and their members)
- Criminal Justice and Public Order Act 1994 (outlaws harassment and speech or actions designed to inflame race hatred)
- Disability Discrimination Act 1995 (helps disabled people to get and keep jobs)
- Employment Rights Act 1996
- Working Time Regulations 1998 (protects workers from being forced to work very long hours)
- Human Rights Act 1998 (protects a range of human rights)
- Public Interest Disclosure Act 1998 (protects people's privacy)
- National Minimum Wage Act 1998 (sets a minimum legal wage)
- Maternity and Parental Leave etc. Regulations 1999 (so people with newborn babies can get leave from work)
- Employment Relations Act 1999 (maternity leave, employment tribunals)

- Race Relations (Amendment) Act 2000 (aims to prevent racial discrimination by the police and other public services)
- Part-time Workers (Prevention of Less Favourable Treatment) Regulations 2000 (gives equal conditions of service to part time and full time workers)
- Employment Act 2002 (intimidation of strikers)
- Employment Relations Act 2004 (protection of workers' employment rights)
- Disability Discrimination Act 2005 (more help for disabled people to get jobs)

EU laws

The European Union also makes laws about equal opportunities, which the UK is then expected to pass in Parliament.

For example, the European Parliament passed the Part-time Workers Directive in 1998. This prohibits discrimination against part-time workers. Two years later the UK government brought in the Part-time Workers (Prevention of Less Favourable Treatment) Regulations 2000, bringing UK law into line with European law.

activity
**INDIVIDUAL WORK
(4.4)**

Produce a leaflet for new recruits to a public service outlining the main points in the following laws:

Equal Pay Act 1970

Sex Discrimination Act 1975

Race Relations Act 1976

Human Rights Act 1998

Disability Discrimination Act 2005

www.eoc.org.uk
www.opsi.gov.uk
www.cre.gov.uk

Ethnic identity, culture and community

Ethnic identity is a way of labelling people by their (or their family's) geographical origins. Ethnic identity (ethnicity) is sometimes seen as national (e.g. Pakistani) or regional (e.g. Punjabi). White and Black British are also ethnic identities. If a person's parents come from different ethnic backgrounds, their own ethnicity may be mixed.

Culture is the shared beliefs and lifestyle of a particular group of people. It may be an ethnic group, a religious group, a group based on social class as in 'working class culture' (though class-based definitions are going out of fashion) or a group sharing similar job and/or interests.

> **Norms**
> lifestyle, customs, habits, etc.
>
> *keyword*

> **Values**
> what we think; our beliefs.
>
> *keyword*

Culture is expressed in **norms** and **values**. What we eat, the languages we speak, the way we dress are all norms. What we believe (religious beliefs and ideas of right and wrong) are values.

A *community* is a body of people organised into a political, municipal or social unity. Political means that they have some kind of leadership or power structure. Municipal means that they live within a particular area. Social means that they talk to each other.

If any one of the three points applies, then the body of people is likely to be a community. For example, multiple sclerosis sufferers who communicate through the Internet form a community even if they live in many different countries. They may have no political or municipal unity but they do have a social unity.

Examples of communities in the UK are:

- the nation as a whole
- towns and cities, e.g. Liverpool, Leicester
- suburbs and housing estates which have a clear identity
- streets and villages
- minority ethnic groups
- religious groups both large and small, e.g. Anglicans, Muslims, Quakers, Zoroastrians
- communities which are both ethnic and religious, e.g. Sikhs, Jews
- people with shared interests, e.g. anglers, Millwall football supporters
- groups such as gays and lesbians
- regiments etc. in the armed forces
- occupational groups such as farmers, fisher people, nurses, teachers and police.

> *activity*
> **GROUP WORK (4.5)**   Decide whether the communities listed above have political, municipal or social unity (or more than one of these).

Effects of ethnic identity and culture on communities

Ethnic identity and culture affect all communities, even if everybody in them belongs to the same ethnic group. Having said this, the effects of ethnic identity and culture are most obvious, and of most interest to the public services, in ethnically mixed inner city areas (e.g. Brent and Lewisham in South London, Chapeltown in Leeds, Moss Side in Manchester). Ethnic identity and culture are not bad things in themselves, but they have been linked to social problems in these places. Such communities are affected by:

keyword

Segregation
separateness; living and working apart from other ethnic groups.

■ poverty and inequality

■ cultural and religious differences from 'mainstream' British culture

■ **segregation**

■ hostility between different ethnic groups

■ racism

■ high levels of unemployment

■ high crime rates.

Case study 4.4 comes from a report on the Oldham Riots of 2001 which has a lot to say about these problems.

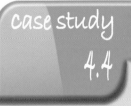

case study 4.4

Community Cohesion: A Report of the Independent Review Team 2003

Large concentrations of population grew up because of proximity to major transport nodes and historical trade links and were further fostered by inappropriate housing and education policies – but it was also recognised that segregation also has behavioural roots. People naturally gravitate toward others who share their values, faith and culture. Also large concentrations of minority ethnic groups make it economic to develop specialist services e.g. specialist shops, cinemas, places of worship etc. which provide further incentives for clustering. However, major supermarkets now supply a wide range of ingredients and ready meals from around the world and Bollywood films can be seen in mainstream cinemas, which indicates the mainstreaming of a number of specialist services. More could be done to mainstream services for minority ethnic groups.

Problems of polarisation seem more likely to arise where there is a concentration of one particular ethnic group. Where there are large mixed ethnic minority populations such as in Brent, a more cosmopolitan ethos results.

(*Source*: 'Cantle Report', www.homeoffice.gov.uk)

activity
GROUP WORK

You are police constables on probation. Make a study of a local community giving information on:

(a) the different ethnic groups (including white British) in that community

(b) the different cultural groups (e.g. occupational, age-based etc.)

(c) the different lifestyles and beliefs of different groups

(d) the effects of these differences on the community.

Talk (or listen) to community workers.

Collect cuttings from your local newspaper on ethnic identity and culture.

Talk about it to people from different ethnic or cultural groups.

Talk to people from your own community.

Collect census information from your local authority or the Office for National Statistics (www.statistics.gov.uk/).

Ethnic diversity

This can be defined as having two or more ethnic groups living in the same community, town or area.

How it came about

The initial cause of ethnic diversity in Britain is the fact that, in the nineteenth and early twentieth century, Britain had an empire. People started coming to Britain from India, Pakistan and the Caribbean (parts of the former empire) around the 1950s. They were welcome because they worked for low pay. At first they intended to send money home and stay for a short time. But it soon became clear that it was better for them and their families – and for the British economy – if they stayed. After 1976 they were protected from open discrimination by the Race Relations Act but remained disadvantaged, tending to live in the poorer areas of the inner cities.

Effects on the police

Ethnic minority groups were regarded as a problem by the police, and matters came to a head with the Brixton Riots, in 1981. Afterwards an inquiry into the riots and their causes was set up, headed by a judge called Lord Scarman. He concluded that they were not race riots, and that poor policing was to blame. Parliament responded by passing the Police and Criminal Evidence Act (PACE) 1984, which defined police powers and discouraged the police from picking unfairly on sections of the community.

Since the 1980s the government and the police have made serious efforts to be **multicultural**.

The police have tried to do this:

1. by treating people from ethnic minorities sensitively and fairly

2. by becoming more diverse themselves.

The police and other public services have a good deal of training in diversity awareness, and working with different communities. The government and independent bodies, such as the Commission for Racial Equality, do what they can to ensure that no public services discriminate against ethnic minorities.

Police recruitment targets have been set with the aim of attracting people from ethnic minority communities. Broadly, these targets aim at a police force of

| keyword | **Multicultural** describing a diverse society where difference is respected and people from all ethnic and cultural backgrounds live together freely and equally. |

which 7 per cent of officers are of ethnic minority background. The figure of 7 per cent comes from the 1991 census which showed that about 7 per cent of Britain's population was non-white.

Similar targets exist now for all the other public services – though some, such as the NHS, have a far higher proportion of ethnic minority staff than the police.

link

Other services, see pages 108–111.

Cultural diversity

Cultural diversity includes things such as:

- changes in family structures
- a changed attitude to 'domestic' violence
- the effects of religious differences
- the decriminalising of homosexuality
- changed attitudes to drugs (the declassification of cannabis).

Changes in attitudes to women and the family mean that the police now have to take problems like child abuse and violence towards spouses (wives or husbands) seriously. Fifty years ago 'an Englishman's home was his castle' and the police kept out of domestic problems. Religion too (especially following the London bombings of July 2005) has raised issues which may threaten public order. There has been a big rise in racial incidents and attacks on Muslims. Homosexuality, on the other hand, is no longer a crime. These changes mean:

- the police workload has increased
- the police need to liaise with communities much more closely than they used to do
- the police are interested in recruiting officers (and special constables) from a wide range of cultural groups.

Evaluation – main points

- The police, and most other public services, have not yet achieved the diversity they are aiming at.
- In 2004 the government figure for the percentage of ethnic minority police officers was 3.3 per cent. They are aiming at 7 per cent, but in fact the 2001 census put the proportion of non-white ethnic minority people in the UK as being 7.9 per cent.
- 'Race Equality: The Home Secretary's Employment Targets – Milestone Report 2004' (available on the Home Office website) states that there is also a problem with retaining ethnic minority police officers (i.e. they leave the job after a short time).
- Police work and the police force is in a state of constant change which tries to reflect the changing needs of a diverse society.

- At the same time the police must remain true to their 'core values' of fighting and preventing crime.

- They have found changing difficult at times, and have been criticised – especially in the Macpherson Report (1999) on the death of Stephen Lawrence – for failing to keep pace with change.

- The police are, however, committed to reflecting and working with a diverse society and are taking steps to progress in this direction (e.g. by testing applicants for racist views and rejecting those who have them).

Other public services

There is increased awareness of cultural diversity by all public services, including the armed forces (which, for example, will now accept gay people). More information about these issues can be found on their websites, or by contacting them.

---

activity
GROUP WORK (4.6)

Hold a debate with the motion: 'The public services fully reflect our ethnic and cultural diversity'. The proposers (supporters) should find evidence that this is true. The opposers should find evidence that this is false. The points should be argued, in an orderly manner, and a vote taken at the end.

Equal opportunities in the public services

This has been a challenge for the uniformed public services. The main reason for this is that all of them except the NHS were traditionally run and staffed by white males.

In the last 40 years there have been big changes, but if we look at the employment statistics for the uniformed public services, we can see that women and people from ethnic minorities are still under-represented.

Equal opportunities in the fire and rescue service

In 1999 a report called *Equality and Fairness in the Fire Service* drew attention to the lack of equal opportunities in the service. The report said that in the treatment of ethnic minority and women firefighters, in dealing with bullying, and in recruitment, huge improvements were needed. It was followed up in 2002 by the *Independent Review of the Fire Service* (Professor Sir George Bain) which strongly criticised the equal opportunities situation in the fire service (as it was then still called). In 2003 the government published a plan for the fire service called *Our Fire and Rescue Service: A White Paper*, setting out ways of making the service more efficient, effective and suited both to the needs of the communities it served and, its employees. The White Paper outlined the main problems: In 2002, women accounted for only 1.74 per cent of the operational workforce, while ethnic minority staff accounted for just 1.8 per cent of the total workforce. The shift system was unsuited to women, and the discipline system was old fashioned and did not fit in with the Human Rights Act of 1998.

Table 4.2 Different roles in the fire and rescue service

Supervisory management	Middle management	Strategic management
Firefighter/control operator	Station management	Area management
Crew management	Group management	Brigade management
Control management		

New roles
Other changes

- Alter the recruitment policy, to attract people with the kinds of skills that are needed for talking to the community, as well as people who are strong, practical and able to fight fires.

- Eliminate bullying and harassment.

- Modernise the discipline system. Under the old system, 'untidiness' was an offence, while bullying and harassment were not.

- Have two-yearly inspections to check progress towards greater diversity.

Equal opportunities in the army

The army is an exception to the Sex Discrimination Act 1975, for women are still not allowed to join certain front-line troops such as the Infantry. Apart from this (and regulations linked to age and disability) the army is now – at least on paper – an 'equal opportunities employer'.

Until recently there was a total ban on homosexuals serving in the army. This ban was lifted with the Employment Equality (Sexual Orientation) Regulations 2003.

Equal opportunities includes banning bullying and harassment. These can be a problem in the army, and are now being taken much more seriously.

case study 4.5   Equality and diversity in the Army

Equality and diversity means:

- Treating every individual fairly, with respect and decency
- Recognising that each of us is different
- Keeping the Army free from unlawful discrimination, including harassment and bullying
- Understanding how you are responsible for your performance and behaviour
- Understanding that you also have a responsibility to act if you see another soldier being treated unfairly
- Valuing the contribution each individual makes to the combat effectiveness of their team and their unit

(*Source*: Basically Fair: Equality and Diversity in the British Army: www.army.mod.uk/)

activity
GROUP WORK

(a) Discuss what difficulties might have led the army to make these statements.

(b) Talk to someone connected with the army about these issues. Do their views agree with the statements in the case study above?

Comparison

Both the army and the fire and rescue service are equal opportunities employers, and both are committed to upholding the law in this field.

But both have had difficulties bringing in equal opportunities, because they have a history and culture of being run by white males. They have felt that it would lower standards if they brought in women and people from ethnic minorities. And in both services (which are famous for their courage and their effectiveness) there has been a problem of bullying, harassment and discrimination which has undermined their reputation. Both the army and the fire and rescue service are trying to change their 'ethos' or 'culture' so that more women, gays and people from ethnic minorities want to work for them.

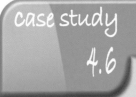

case study

4.6

Recruitment of women and ethnic minorities

Fire and rescue service:

Since 1999, the representation of women and people from ethnic minorities in the operational sector (wholetime and retained combined) year on year, as a percentage of the workforce, has been as follows:

	1999	2000	2001	2002	2003
Women	1.0	1.2	1.4	1.7	2.1
Ethnic minorities	1.2	1.6	1.6	1.8	2.1

(*Source*: Office for the Deputy Prime Minister.)

Progress made on implementing the Ministry of Defence's (MoD's) Race Equality Scheme and introducing our Unified Diversity Strategy:

■ All three Armed Services and the MoD named in the top ten public sector ethnic minority employers.

■ Overall Service ethnic minority strength of 4.9% (including Commonwealth recruits), just short of overall goal of 5% ethnic minority representation. UK ethnic minority intake:

  ▪ 2.1% RN (target 2.5%)
  ▪ 2.8% Army (target 2.9%)
  ▪ 1.8% RAF (target 2.6%).

■ As at 1 April 2004, women comprised 8.9% of UK regular forces (8.7% on 1 April 2003), and 11.6% of the total 2003/04 intake (12.3% in 2002/03).

(*Source*: www.mod.uk)

activity

GROUP WORK

(a) Discuss and comment on the figures above.

(b) What do you think is the ideal proportion of women in the different uniformed services?

(c) Women are not eligible for 30 per cent of jobs in the army, including the infantry. What is your view of this?

Disability

Neither the army nor the fire and rescue service will automatically disqualify disabled applicants. But it must be assumed that the chances of disabled people being recruited as soldiers or firefighters are very slight. However, both services actively recruit disabled people for non-operational posts.

Ways of addressing the main issues of equal opportunities

The approaches used by public services to address the main issues of equal opportunities are outlined in documents called Equal Opportunities Policies. These are usually available in a shortened form (see Case study 4.7).

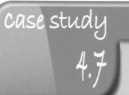

case study 4.7 — Engineers – equality and diversity

Equal Opportunities Policy

1. The Army is fully committed to equality of opportunity. The Army's Equal Opportunities Policy sets out to provide equal opportunities for all personnel within an environment free from all forms of discrimination, harassment and intimidation.

2. The Army welcomes applications from young men and women no matter what their marital status, race, ethnic origin or religious belief. No account is taken of sexual orientation or social background in considering applications. The Army is fully committed to equality of opportunity.

3. The Director of Personal Services (Army) is to provide the focus for Equal Opportunities advice and policy for the Adjutant General. He is to ensure that career policies and management practices have due regard to openness, fairness, clarity and equality of opportunity. He is responsible for updating and auditing the Equal Opportunities Action plan for the Army as required. With the Military Secretary, he is responsible for all aspects of gender and ethnic monitoring of serving Army personnel, including selection, promotion and terms of service.

(*Source*: www.army.mod.uk)

activity
GROUP WORK

Imagine you are in charge of equal opportunities in the Royal Electrical and Mechanical Engineers. The statements listed below all describe things needed to make an equal opportunities policy work. Put them in what you think is their correct order of importance (1–9).

- the army really wants it to work

- officers and others in command understand what equal opportunities means and are committed to it

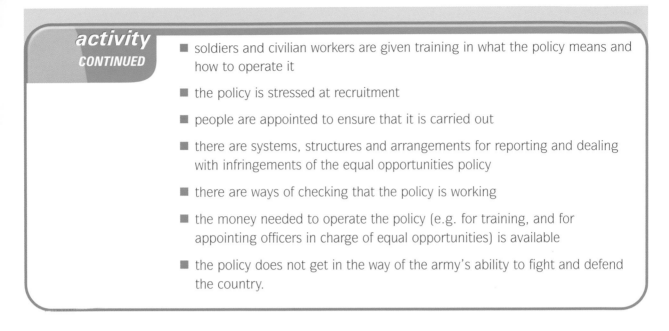

activity
CONTINUED

- soldiers and civilian workers are given training in what the policy means and how to operate it

- the policy is stressed at recruitment

- people are appointed to ensure that it is carried out

- there are systems, structures and arrangements for reporting and dealing with infringements of the equal opportunities policy

- there are ways of checking that the policy is working

- the money needed to operate the policy (e.g. for training, and for appointing officers in charge of equal opportunities) is available

- the policy does not get in the way of the army's ability to fight and defend the country.

How the army deals with bullying

activity
GROUP WORK
(4.7)

(a) Discuss how well you think the anti-bullying policy in Figure 4.2 would work.

(b) Your cousin is joining the armed forces, but is a bit worried about the possibility of being bullied. Note down the advice you would give them to avoid getting bullied – and what you think they should do if they are bullied.

Talk to people who work in public services – especially those who have a special responsibility for equal opportunities.

Collect information about equal opportunities from public service websites.

remember
To 'evaluate' the approaches to equal opportunities, you should ask:
(a) What is being done now?
(b) Does it work?
(c) What improvements could be made?
(d) Are certain minority groups not being treated equally?

Figure 4.2
The army's policy
against bullying

(*Source*: from *Basically Fair:
Equality and Diversity in the
British Army*)

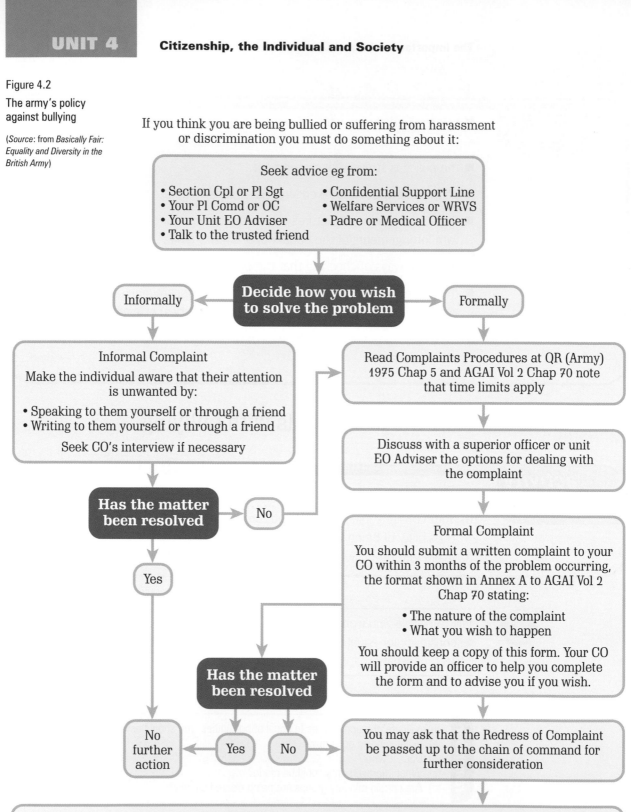

If you think you are being bullied or suffering from harassment
or discrimination you must do something about it:

Seek advice eg from:

- Section Cpl or Pl Sgt
- Your Pl Comd or OC
- Your Unit EO Adviser
- Talk to the trusted friend
- Confidential Support Line
- Welfare Services or WRVS
- Padre or Medical Officer

**Decide how you wish
to solve the problem**

Informally

Formally

Informal Complaint

Make the individual aware that their attention
is unwanted by:

- Speaking to them yourself or through a friend
- Writing to them yourself or through a friend

Seek CO's interview if necessary

Read Complaints Procedures at QR (Army)
1975 Chap 5 and AGAI Vol 2 Chap 70 note
that time limits apply

Discuss with a superior officer or unit
EO Adviser the options for dealing with
the complaint

**Has the matter
been resolved**

No

Yes

Formal Complaint

You should submit a written complaint to your
CO within 3 months of the problem occurring,
the format shown in Annex A to AGAI Vol 2
Chap 70 stating:

- The nature of the complaint
- What you wish to happen

You should keep a copy of this form. Your CO
will provide an officer to help you complete
the form and to advise you if you wish.

**Has the matter
been resolved**

No
further
action

Yes

No

You may ask that the Redress of Complaint
be passed up to the chain of command for
further consideration

Access to Employment Trubunal

Having submitted a formal complaint of harassment or discrimination based on grounds of race, sex,
sexual orientation or relegious beliefs, you may then submit a complaint to an Employment Tribunal by
completing form T1. There is a legal requirement for service personnel to submit an internal redress of
complaint before submitting an application to an employment tribunal. Strict time limits apply to
submitting complaints to Employment Tribunals - See QR (Army) 1975 Chap 5 and AGAI Vol 2 Chap 70.

The Different Roles of Statutory and Non-Statutory Public Services in Relation to the Citizen and to a Changing Society

The public services have a huge influence on us, both as individuals and as a society. Four main effects are given below.

1. *Passing laws*. Some non-uniformed public services, such as the government, affect society very much because they pass laws which influence all our lives. For example, when Ted Heath's Conservative government decided in 1973 that Britain should become part of the EEC (later the EU) it started the process which led to the EU Government influencing our laws on working conditions, human rights, the environment, food standards and so on.

2. *Wars*. Some uniformed services – especially the armed forces – preserved our society and our freedoms by defending Britain in World War II. They did this with great bravery, and at great cost, and saved us from living in a Nazi society where there would have been ethnic cleansing and little freedom. More recently the decision to go to war in Iraq in 2003 has affected society by raising awareness of terrorism, changing attitudes towards Muslims, and increasing the price of oil.

3. *Essential work*. All public services carry out work which at some time or other changes all our lives. Without an education service (schools and colleges), we

Figure 4.3
Police protecting our freedoms

would have DIY education, or none at all. Without the public utilities, water and electricity companies, we might be carrying water from wells and lighting our houses with candles. Without the police and the criminal justice system, ordinary citizens would have to fight crime by setting up roadblocks, or carrying out punishment beatings like the paramilitaries of Northern Ireland. Without the NHS, our lives would be shorter and more fearful ... and so on. Our standard of living and security are maintained by our public services.

4. *Information-gathering*. The public services (including the uniformed public services) affect society by collecting information which then influences Parliament to change the law. For example, without a police investigation it would not have been known how the London bombings of July 2005 came about. Shortly afterwards, a (probable) change in the law was announced, as reported in Case study 4.8.

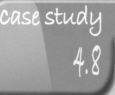

case study 4.8

UK to change deportation laws

5 August 2005, 17:43 IST

British Prime Minister Tony Blair on Friday announced new deportation measures against people who foster hatred and advocate violence following last month's transportation attacks that killed 52 people and four suspected suicide bombers.

Clerics who preach hate and Web sites or book shops that sponsor violence would be targeted. Foreign nationals could be deported under the new measures.

Blair said his government was prepared to amend human rights legislation if necessary if legal challenges arose from the new deportation measures.

Britain's ability to deport foreign nationals has been hampered by human rights legislation. As a signatory to the European Convention on Human Rights, Britain is not allowed to deport people to a country where they may face torture or death.

'Let no one be in any doubt that the rules of the game are changing,' Blair said, promising to crack down on extremists blamed for radicalizing pockets of Muslim youth.

(*Source*: www.rediff.com/news)

---

activity
GROUP WORK

Research and discuss one or more of the following:

(a) How the police tackle crime against women and children, and how their approach has changed over the years.

(b) The arguments for and against the idea that the war in Iraq was linked in some way to the 2005 bombings in London.

(c) Which are better for society – private schools or comprehensive schools?

(d) What are the good and bad features of health care in the UK?

How to find out more:

- talk to people who work in any public service
- visit your local council offices, or their website
- investigate the work of the NHS.

How public services support society

For any problem which people suffer from, there is a public service which tries to deal with the problem and support people (see below).

Table 4.3 Public services dealing with problems

Public services	Problems and support given
Armed forces	Threats: other countries invading, attacking our allies, attacking UK citizens, UK companies or other UK interests (e.g. essential supplies) or the interests of our allies, terrorism; disasters Support: defence, fighting, peace-keeping, deterrence – also some rescue and humanitarian work
Police	Threats: crime and disorder Support: the police patrol, prevent crime, solve crime and fight crime in various ways, reassure the public, and work with other organisations to keep society peaceful and orderly. They also help keep order in disasters and emergencies
Fire and rescue service	Threats: fires, accidents, disasters Support: help prevent or deal with fires, accidents and emergencies, chemical incidents, floods
Ambulance service	Threats: acute illness, disaster; 'routine' illness Support: primary care; transport to hospital; action in disasters and emergencies
NHS	Threats: sickness Support: free medical treatment and care
Her Majesty's Revenue and Customs	Threats: tax evasion, cross-border crime Support: collect taxes and excise duties (petrol, tobacco etc). Fight tax evasion, smuggling and cross-border crime, e.g. drugs, people and weapons trafficking
Prison service	Threat: unpunished criminals Support: deter and punish crime and protect the public by keeping criminals in custody
Immigration and Nationality Directorate	Threat: uncontrolled immigration in the UK Support: control the inflow of people; process asylum seekers and 'economic migrants'
Maritime and Coastguard Agency	Threat: danger at sea, pollution, smuggling Support: ensure safety for all users of the sea in inshore waters; environmental work; help to coordinate rescues; protect the coastline
Probation service	Threat: offenders in society Support: work with offenders to reduce reoffending
Security services	Threat: enemies; terrorism; foreign spies Support: work secretly to gather intelligence and combat the above
Mountain rescue	Threat: injury and death on the mountains Support: advise walkers and climbers; search and rescue

<table>
<tr><td>

keyword

Society
the public, people in
general or 'the
community'.

</td></tr>
</table>

Public services, however, don't simply solve problems. **Society** itself cannot function without the public services. Education, transport, electricity, gas, water, libraries and local government services are all provided through public services. The biggest of these is the civil service, a non-uniformed public service which staffs local and central government offices, jobcentres and many other places.

Public services are not all publicly owned (i.e. by the government). Many have been privatised – e.g. water and electricity companies, some prisons and the railways. But their main function is still to support the public.

The voluntary sector

Charities and voluntary organisations support society. Each one is a public service. Some form partnerships with the police and other uniformed public services in order to deal with problems such as crime and disorder. Others help special groups of people – e.g. people suffering from schizophrenia, or women who have been abused in the home. You will find long lists of these on your local authority's website.

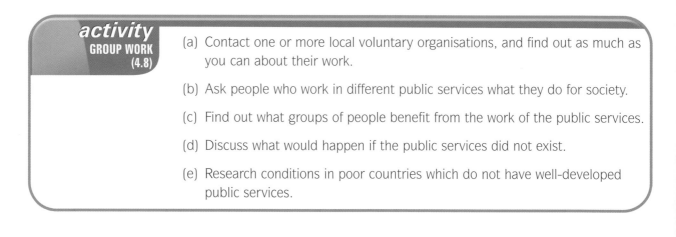

activity
GROUP WORK
(4.8)

(a) Contact one or more local voluntary organisations, and find out as much as you can about their work.

(b) Ask people who work in different public services what they do for society.

(c) Find out what groups of people benefit from the work of the public services.

(d) Discuss what would happen if the public services did not exist.

(e) Research conditions in poor countries which do not have well-developed public services.

Government, public service and society

Public services are part of the 'machinery of government'. If the uniformed public services refused to obey the government, then there would be no workable government.

The bodies shown in Figure 4.4 all have a role in running the country. They are all, in their different ways, public services. And they all support society – some directly, some indirectly.

They are both governmental and non-governmental. The governmental ones include the Prime Minister, the Cabinet, Parliament, the government ministers and the government departments.

Figure 4.4
The machinery of
government

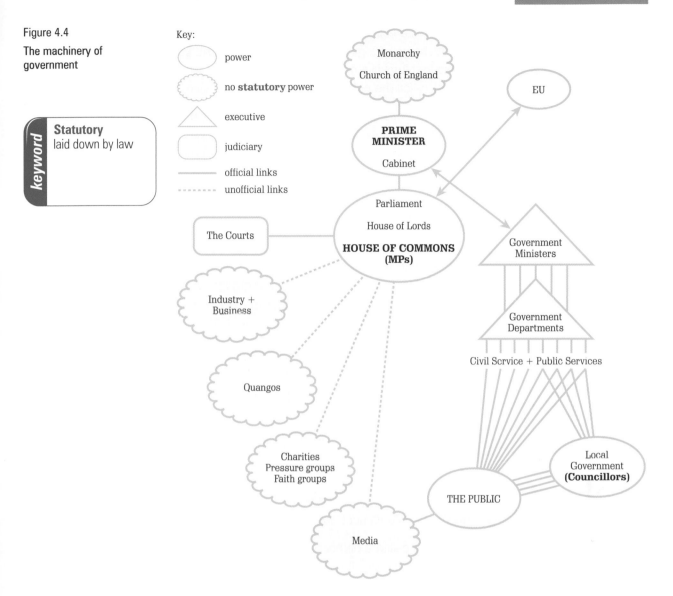

Government bodies are roughly divided into three types:

1. Legislative (they make laws) – e.g. Parliament

2. Judiciary (they test and interpret laws) – e.g. the courts

3. Executive (they do the work) – government ministers and departments.

The most powerful parts of the government are the House of Commons and the Prime Minister.

The Queen is the Head of State but she and the Church of England are ceremonial and have hardly any official power.

There are 659 Members of Parliament (MPs) elected at general elections by the public. Their jobs are to represent their constituents (the people in their voting area) at Parliament (e.g. by telling the government what they want).

The Cabinet is a collection of powerful MPs who are called government ministers. Each is in charge of a government department. The government departments specialise in things like health, defence and so on. The Home Office has responsibility for the police and for the prison service.

The civil servants and the public services carry out the wishes of the government, which itself aims to carry out the wishes of the people. The public services are controlled from a distance by the government, but are rarely told directly what to do.

This 'arm's length' system of control is to avoid accusations that the UK is a police state, or run by the army.

Think-tanks and other organisations which advise the government, and 'regulators' such as the Office for Standards in Education (Ofsted), are also a type of public service. Charities, pressure groups and faith groups (religions) act as public services of a sort, and support society by helping the poor and satisfying spiritual needs.

The media (television, newspapers, the internet etc.) serve the public because most of what we know about the government comes through them. But, unlike most public services, they are run as businesses and can be biased.

Local government has an important role in determining the work of the police, fire and rescue service and the NHS. It also runs other services. All these services carry out the wishes of local people (but under the overall control of central government).

The EU affects the work of the public services by making laws which eventually are debated by Parliament and, usually, passed.

This system is called a democratic system because the people, in theory at any rate, have the final say. If they don't like what the government is doing they can vote it out at the next general election.

activity
GROUP WORK
(4.9)

(a) Visit your local council and find out how it works.

(b) Contact your local emergency planning department and ask them how local public services work together to plan how to protect the public in the event of a disaster.

(c) What are the arguments for and against people having the vote at 16?

Why do we really have public services?

The relationship between the public services and society is a complex one, but we tend to take it for granted because we have grown up with it.

Huge amounts of money are involved – about £28 billion for defence, £15 billion for the police, £2.5 billion for the fire and rescue service, £6 billion for the courts, £3.5 billion for prisons and £1.7 billion for the Immigration and Nationality Directorate (estimated Treasury figures for 2005). £82.6 billion is spent on health. The total amount of money spent in 2005 on all public services was about £466 billion. This is nearly half the GNP (Gross National Product) – the total amount of money that changed hands within the UK, and between the UK and other countries, during that year.

In return for all this money the professional public services:

- protect us from our enemies (armed forces, MI5)
- protect us from crime (police, HM Revenue and Customs, the courts, prison service and probation service)
- protect us from fire, accidents and disasters (fire and rescue service)
- protect us from sickness (NHS, environmental health officers, water and sewerage companies, food standards agency etc.)
- protect us from some of the effects of poverty (civil servants; social security)
- ensure that the country is governed (government departments, civil servants, the police)
- protect the environment (environment agency etc.)
- educate us (education service)

and so on.

One-sided support?

It is often asked whether the public services protect the middle classes, or protect the rich against the poor. Sometimes they seem to support society by limiting individual freedoms. People who believe that society is split between the 'haves' and the 'have nots' believe the public services tend to support the 'haves'.

A matter of survival?

On the other hand, countries without public services (due to poverty or civil war) can be dangerous and unhappy places to live. In such countries, if a house is on fire, people have to watch it burn, if there is no proper water supply and no fire brigade. And if they want to stop crime, they have to pay protection money or set up their own roadblocks.

Good work?

A more positive view of public services is that they ensure the continued well-being of society. And there are many unpaid public service organisations, such as Mountain Rescue or the Citizens' Advice Bureaux, staffed by volunteers. Their work shows the caring nature of people and of society, and reminds us that public service is not just a career – it is something deeper which may have its roots in the moral teachings of the world's great religions. People expect heroism and self-sacrifice from the public services – and sometimes they get it. The public services need billions of pounds a year – but they are not just in it for the money.

---

activity
GROUP WORK
(4.10)

(a) Carry out a survey, using a suitable questionnaire, of what people think about the police, the armed forces and the NHS.

(b) Present your findings, together with your own comments, to the rest of your group.

(c) Talk to someone in public service work about the reasons they do the job – other than for the money.

(d) What is a privatised public service – and what are the advantages and disadvantages of having them?

progress check

1. State four main characteristics of a citizen.

2. Why are human rights important?

3. Give two aspects of bad citizenship which can prevent someone from joining a public service.

4. Name four laws (with dates) which have helped to give workers equal opportunities.

5. What is the difference between 'ethnic identity' and 'culture'?

6. How has the UK's ethnic diversity affected public service recruitment?

7. How far is the army an equal opportunities employer?

8. Under what circumstances can a disabled person get a job in a public service?

9. Give an example of a way in which the police (a) restrict our freedom and (b) protect our freedom.

10. Who polices the police?

Adventurous Activities and Teamwork for the Public Services

This unit covers:

- participating in outdoor pursuits and teamwork
- the benefits of outdoor pursuit residentials and the responsibilities of the organisers
- youth and community projects in our society and their use of outdoor activities
- how the uniformed public services may be involved with outdoor activities and youth and community projects in our society

This unit is about adventurous activities (outdoor pursuits) such as rock climbing, abseiling, hill-walking and camping. It is also about the teamwork you need to use to carry them out. As you do some of these activities yourself you will discover the value they can have for developing the individual

You will also look at outdoor pursuits in a wider context, finding out how society as a whole can benefit from them. And finally you will learn how they are used by different kinds of public service.

grading criteria

To achieve a **Pass** grade the evidence must show that the learner is able to:	To achieve a **Merit** grade the evidence must show that, in addition to the pass criteria, the learner is able to:	To achieve a **Distinction** grade the evidence must show that, in addition to the pass and merit criteria, the learner is able to:
P1 take part in two outdoor pursuits and teamwork recording their participation	**M1** analyse the benefits and the skills that are developed from participating in outdoor pursuits and teamwork	**D1** evaluate the benefits and potential for individual skills development for uniformed public service work
P2 describe the additional potential benefits of participating in an outdoor pursuit residential	**M2** compare youth and community projects that include the use of adventurous activities and teamwork	**D2** evaluate youth and community projects that include the use of outdoor pursuits and teamwork

To achieve a **Pass** grade the evidence must show that the learner is able to:	To achieve a **Merit** grade the evidence must show that, in addition to the pass criteria, the learner is able to:	To achieve a **Distinction** grade the evidence must show that, in addition to the pass criteria, the learner is able to:
P3 outline youth and community projects including their use of outdoor activities		
P4 explain the links one project has with the uniformed public services and explain the purposes of those links		
P5 explain how individuals and teams can benefit from projects and/or activities		
P6 explain how the uniformed public services can be involved in outdoor activities		

Participating in Outdoor Pursuits and Teamwork

keyword
Outdoor pursuits adventurous activities normally done in open country or wild environments e.g. rock climbing, sailing and caving.

Outdoor pursuits include:

Climbing	Watersports	Trekking	Caving
Rock climbing	Canoeing	Hillwalking	Caving
Abseiling	Kayaking	Mountaineering	Pot-holing
Ice climbing	Dragon boating	Fell running	Mine exploration
Gorge walking	Wave skiing	Orienteering	
Gill scrambling	White-water rafting	Pony trekking	
Sea-level traversing	Improvised rafting	Off-road cycling	
	Sailing	Off-piste skiing	
	Sailboarding		
	Windsurfing		

When you take part in outdoor pursuits the aim is to enjoy yourself with minimum risk.

There are four main ways in which group outdoor pursuits for students are normally organised:

1. through the army or some other uniformed public service
2. by the college using the college's staff and equipment
3. using a private provider of outdoor pursuits
4. using a residential centre which organises outdoor pursuits.

Outdoor pursuits are also run by public service organisations such as the Territorial Army and various cadet schemes (including the police). Some fire and rescue services arrange outdoor pursuits, too. In addition, they can be carried out through the Scouts, the Duke of Edinburgh's Award Scheme and other schemes.

Taking part

To get a good grade for your participation you should:

- supply all the information that the organisers want in advance
- take all the clothes and personal equipment you are asked to take with you
- arrive on time for all activities
- follow all instructions
- be enthusiastic
- behave safely and reliably
- be helpful, supportive and considerate towards other people
- play an active, responsible part in all team activities
- look after your own and other people's belongings
- avoid dropping litter and damaging the environment
- tell your tutor or instructor if there are any problems.

No one should ever take part in outdoor pursuits if they are:

- ill
- injured
- under the influence of alcohol or drugs.

If you are taking medication, or have any serious worries about any of the planned activities, let your tutor, instructor or both know in advance.

Recording your participation

The form in which you record your participation in the outdoor pursuits may be decided by your tutor. It could be a written log or diary in which you include:

- a description of what you did
- a description of what you enjoyed about it
- a description of anything you didn't enjoy about it
- an explanation of how you worked with the rest of your team
- what you feel you gained, or learned, from the teamwork
- aspects of your teamwork which need more practice
- an overall assessment of how you feel you did.

---

activity
GROUP WORK
(6.1)

Take part in two outdoor pursuits. Keep a record of what you did and how you did it.

The Benefits of Outdoor Pursuit Residentials and the Responsibilities of the Organisers

What they are

An outdoor pursuit residential is a stay, lasting at least two days and one night, at a centre away from home and college. The centre may be an army camp, a bunkhouse, an outdoor centre, a campsite, a youth hostel etc. During this kind of residential you will take part in activities such as climbing, canoeing and caving.

Their potential benefits

keyword

Potential
possible or likely.

Their **potential benefits** can be either short term or long term. The short-term benefits pass after a few hours or days: the long-term benefits may stay with you all your life.

Potential short-term benefits of a residential include:

keyword

Benefit
advantage; good outcome.

- the enjoyment of doing it
- the sense of achievement of taking part successfully in outdoor pursuits
- the pleasure of being with friends
- the experience of being out of doors, in beautiful countryside
- the excitement of doing something new
- the challenge of doing tough physical activities
- the 'holiday' of being away from college or work for a few days.

remember

In only one residential the development of most skills might not be very great. Skills take time to develop.

Potential long-term benefits of a residential include:

■ development of physical skills (e.g. learning balance and movement on a rock climb)

■ development of intellectual skills (understanding, learning and practising new techniques, such as manoeuvring a kayak)

■ development of social skills (getting on with other people, working with other people, understanding other people)

■ the discovery of things about yourself that you didn't know (e.g. that you are, or are not, afraid of heights; that you are good at rock climbing etc.)

■ an increase in confidence, either with other people or in yourself.

---

activity
INDIVIDUAL WORK
(6.2)

Write a letter to the organisers of a residential you have been on, thanking them for their efforts and telling them what you have gained from each part of the experience.

Outdoor pursuits, skills development and teamwork

The public services believe that the main benefits brought by outdoor pursuits are in developing skills and teamwork. These are outlined in Figure 6.1.

Figure 6.1

Five benefits of adventurous activities and teamwork

Intellectual skills
Understanding, planning, carrying out and reviewing tasks
Learning how things work
Learning about the environment
Anticipation of problems
Awareness of risk

Physical skills
Coordination
Agility
Balance
Dexterity
Awareness of space, weight, speed

Emotional strength
Courage
Confidence
Perseverance
Optimism
Self-belief

Social skills
Team work
Sharing tasks
Getting on with others
Cooperation
Communication
Leadership
Trust

Spiritual insight
Esprit de corps
Self-knowledge
Understanding, and feeling for others
Getting to know other people better
A chance to think about the meaning of life
The beauty of the surroundings

The benefits shown in the diagram come under five headings.

Table 6.1 Types of benefit explained

Skill or benefit and explanation	What it means	How it is developed by outdoor pursuits	Use in public service work
Intellectual skills These might be called 'cognitive' benefits: they are about learning and understanding.	Ability to learn, adapt, understand, think clearly, solve problems, foresee problems, assess risks	By learning to do things we haven't done before; by solving problems – e.g. in rock climbing	Helps people to learn the job; improves study skills and problem solving – e.g. firefighting in confined spaces
Emotional strength This is a mixture of toughness, courage, determination, patience and compassion	It helps to make you confident, and gives other people confidence in you It enables you to stick at a task, and work on a problem, longer than other people	By working under cold, wet, difficult conditions – e.g. walking long distances; pitching tents in bad weather. Also by helping others who are in difficulty	Needed in any difficult testing job – e.g. policing on a Saturday night, peacekeeping in Iraq, rescuing people in a motorway pile-up
Social skills The ability to relate to other people and work with them	Includes communication skills, teamwork and leadership	By working closely with other people; by leading, organising, listening and learning	Essential in public service work – especially policing, the prison service; any job involving working with people
Physical skills Using our bodies so that they do what we want (or need) them to do	Agility, speed and efficiency in movement; good coordination; dexterity	By many activities: paddling a kayak, climbing a rope ladder, cross-country skiing, riding a horse	Needed in the armed forces – e.g. handling weapons; setting up equipment; essential for firefighters
Spiritual insight Feelings about the meaning of life, the beauty of nature and a deeper understanding of other people	Includes loyalty, sympathy, compassion, a desire to help others, a deep understanding of other people, generosity, love of nature	By being out in the country and by working with others as equals in a caring and supportive manner	The sense of responsibility for the well-being of other people is what makes many join the public services

activity
GROUP WORK
(6.3)

To gain a better understanding of the 'skills or benefits' discuss occasions when each of you showed intellectual skills, emotional strength, social skills, physical skills and spiritual insight. Each member of the group should give an example of each, in relation to something they have done, said or thought.

Outdoor pursuits, individual skills and public service work

Figure 6.2
Individual skills

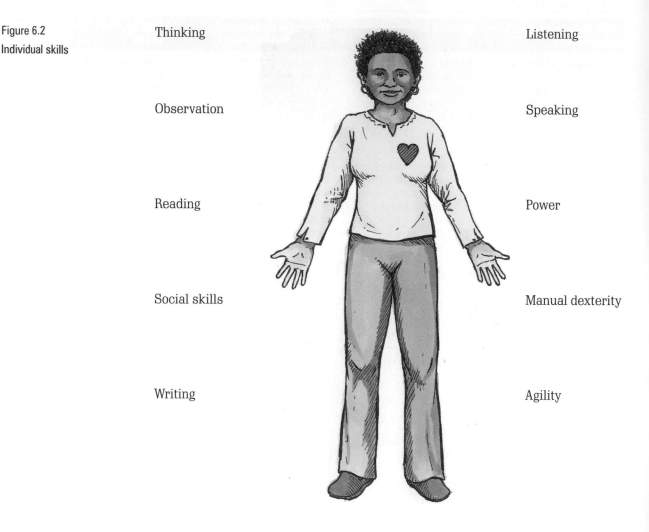

Thinking

Listening

Observation

Speaking

Reading

Power

Social skills

Manual dexterity

Writing

Agility

Table 6.2 shows some outdoor pursuits, the individual skills they develop and examples of where those skills are relevant to uniformed public service.

The benefits of outdoor pursuits and their **potential** for developing people's individual skills are not easy to demonstrate scientifically. The activities are variable and complex, and mental benefits cannot be measured as accurately as strength, fitness or weight.

But the public services themselves believe strongly in the value of outdoor pursuits.

keyword

Potential
usefulness (in this example).

Table 6.2 Adventurous activities

Outdoor pursuit	Skill(s) used	Uniformed public service work linked to skill
Rock climbing	Thinking (planning/following the route) Listening (instructions for belay) Speaking (giving warnings e.g. falling stones) Agility (balance and nimbleness needed in climbing)	Firefighting (planning how to tackle a blaze; listening and shouting instructions; agility needed on ladders and in hose-running) Army exercises (e.g. assault course)
Sea-level traversing	Numeracy (calculating tides) Thinking (route-planning) Listening, speaking, agility (all as for rock climbing)	Gunners etc. in the army (calculating trajectory of shells) Rescue work in the ambulance service (thinking, listening, speaking and agility)
Kayaking	Thinking (planning route) Observation (watching the water) Power, manual dexterity (handling the paddle and the boat)	Work in the armed forces, fire service, coastguard work (all these services might use kayaks in rescue work)
Improvised rafting	Social skills (teamwork) Thinking (problem solving) Manual dexterity (building the raft)	Teamwork and problem solving are used in the police and all other uniformed public services

case study 6.1 — Adventurous training

1. Officer training, Sandhurst

Adventurous training expeditions, including climbing, sailing, caving, kayaking, diving, trekking and many other activities, are among the most stimulating and popular activities at Sandhurst. Advice is given during the planning stages, but the success or failure of each expedition depends entirely upon the initiative, resourcefulness and courage of the officer cadets themselves.

(*Source*: Army website)

2. Mountain Leader – Royal Marines

The highly skilled job of the Mountain and Arctic Warfare Cadre (the other Special Forces Unit of the Royal Marines) involves all aspects of mountaineering, reconnaissance, route-finding, climbing and survival in cold temperatures. As Mountain Leader, you are guide and instructor to Companies on mountain exercises or leader of the reconnaissance troop in a Commando.

(*Source*: www.royal-navy.mod.uk)

activity
GROUP WORK

(a) Why is Sandhurst so interested in outdoor pursuits as a way of developing intellectual and social skills?

(b) Discuss the skills the Royal Marines are developing. What differences are there between their approach and the army approach at Sandhurst?

Teamwork benefits

Teamwork is used in all public services, military and civilian, but the work in the police, customs, and prison service is much less physical than the work in the armed forces and the fire and rescue service. The teamwork aspect of outdoor pursuits is more useful for these 'civilian' public services than any of the physical skills practised.

Basic aspects of teamwork – especially team spirit, or 'esprit de corps' – are developed through outdoor pursuits. But the more complex teamwork needed in some forms of public service work – for example where teams are set up to develop long-term planning and strategy in the police – may need more specific training, using theory, lectures and classroom study. The kinds of leadership skills outlined in Case study 6.2, for example, might be best developed using a mixture of outdoor and other activities.

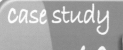
case study
6.2

Leadership skills

Planning – seeking information, defining tasks, setting aims

Initiating – briefing, task allocation, setting standards

Controlling – maintaining standards, ensuring progress, ongoing decision-making

Supporting – individuals' contributions, encouraging, team spirit, reconciling, morale

Informing – clarifying tasks and plans, updating, receiving feedback and interpreting

Evaluating – feasibility of ideas, performance, enabling self assessment
(*Source*: John Adair, www.businessballs.com)

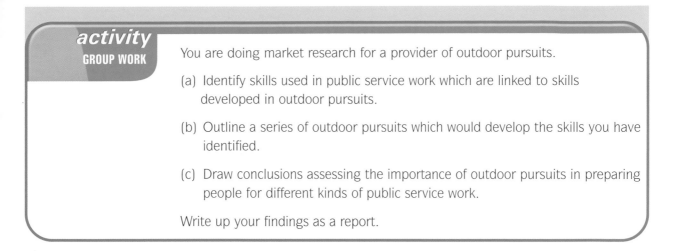

activity

GROUP WORK

You are doing market research for a provider of outdoor pursuits.

(a) Identify skills used in public service work which are linked to skills developed in outdoor pursuits.

(b) Outline a series of outdoor pursuits which would develop the skills you have identified.

(c) Draw conclusions assessing the importance of outdoor pursuits in preparing people for different kinds of public service work.

Write up your findings as a report.

Youth and Community Projects in Our Society and Their Use of Outdoor Activities

keyword

Project
a group, organisation or plan.

Youth and community **projects** which use **outdoor activities** come in all shapes and sizes. They include:

- charities
- uniformed public services
- independent providers
- clubs and societies
- the Youth Service.

Charities

keyword

Outdoor activities
almost any recreation which is done out of doors. It includes outdoor pursuits, but can also include less energetic activities such as angling or gentle walks.

Charities are mainly non-profit-making organisations which offer something 'good' to people who would not otherwise have it. They get their money from users of the charity, public donations, fundraising activities or from the government (through local authority and central government grants).

Duke of Edinburgh's Award (charity)

The Duke of Edinburgh's Award, which is supported by a number of uniformed public services such as the Metropolitan Police, caters for individuals rather than groups.

The award itself is free, but the activities which make up the award may cost something. In each area of the UK there are local representatives of the Duke of Edinburgh's Award Scheme who will give you more information if you are interested.

case study 6.3

Duke of Edinburgh's Award

What is the award?

The Award is a four-section programme with three levels:

- Bronze (for those aged 14 and over)
- Silver (for those aged 15 and over) and
- Gold (for those aged 16 and over).

The sections involve:

- Service (helping people in the community)
- Skills (covering almost any hobby, skill or interest)
- Physical recreation (sport, dance and fitness)
- Expeditions (training for, planning and completing a journey on foot or horseback, by boat or cycle)
- Residential project (gold level only)

(*Source*: www.theaward.org/)

activity
GROUP WORK

(a) Discuss (i) the advantages and (ii) the drawbacks of the Duke of Edinburgh's Award as compared with Outward Bound.

(b) What is the attitude of the uniformed public services to the Duke of Edinburgh's Award?

www.met.police.uk
www.theaward.org
www.scouts.org.uk

Bendrigg Trust (charity)

'The Bendrigg Trust was established in 1978 to specialise in courses and activities for disabled and disadvantaged young people. During this period we have developed a reputation as one of the most versatile and forward thinking residential centres in the country. Groups enjoy a wide range of indoor and outdoor activities and, at the same time learn a great deal about themselves and others. This is especially true when group members from different backgrounds share activities and facilities at the lodge.'

(*Source*: www.bendrigg.org.uk)

The Scout Association (charity)

This is possibly the most well-known youth project using outdoor pursuits.

> 'The Scout Association provides outdoor pursuits and personal development opportunities for 400,000 young people aged 6–25. Internationally, we have over 28 million young people enjoying the benefits of Scouting across 216 countries.
>
> 'Personal development means promoting the physical, intellectual, social and spiritual well-being of the individual, helping them achieve their full potential. In Scouting, we believe that young people develop most when they are 'learning by doing,' when they are given responsibility, work in teams, take acceptable risks and think for themselves.'
>
> (*Source*: www.scouts.org.uk/)

Scouting has a long tradition of involving young people. For many years it was for boys or young men only, but now, in the UK, about 10 per cent of the members are female. People join on an individual basis. It is staffed mainly by volunteers.

Uniformed public services

The job of the uniformed public services is to serve the country, but they also organise outdoor activities for young people. These are carried out by:

- cadet schemes
- Army Youth Teams and Look at Life days
- the Territorial Army
- some police forces, as part of their youth diversionary schemes
- the fire and rescue service (occasionally).

The armed forces carry out outdoor activities in order to encourage recruitment. However, *there is no compulsion to join up*.

These organisations get their money from the government, and they either charge nothing, or very little.

Cadet schemes

Cadets are young people who join an organisation connected to a uniformed public service. They carry out outdoor pursuits which are linked to the work of the public service itself.

Some police forces have cadets; others haven't. The aims of the Metropolitan Police cadets are given in Case study 6.5.

Armed forces cadets offer plenty of adventurous training, some of it in a military setting. The cadets are an organisation, rather like the Scouts in some ways, which you can attend on a weekly basis. Cadet schemes are subsidised, so members pay much less than the cost of the activities.

Information about the Army Cadet Force is given in Case study 6.5. There are similar schemes in the RAF and the Royal Navy.

Independent providers (businesses)

There are many people who want outdoor pursuits, but for one reason or another they don't want to do it through the armed forces. Such 'customers' include:

- family groups wanting an adventure holiday
- business organisations who want to give their staff team-building activities in order to build up the morale and team spirit of the company
- some school and college groups who want adventure that is not 'military' in tone.

Independent providers run their operations as businesses, and therefore need to pay staff, and make a profit, out of their operations.

---

case study 6.4

Discover more with PGL

More centres: PGL has 28 owned and managed residential adventure centres across England, Scotland, Wales, France and Spain

Better staff: Your group's experience at each of our centres depends on the calibre of our staff, which is why we invest so much in ensuring the highest standards

More educational courses: PGL's acquisition of 3D Education and Adventure and our partnership with the teaching profession means that we deliver the widest range of educational courses

More adventure: PGL offers the widest range of activities at exceptional value for money

More care: We manage your PGL experience from start to finish, taking pressure off you, because we know what you need

More experience: After nearly 50 years of experience, you can be sure that your educational experience will be safe, secure, friendly, exciting, challenging and FUN

(*Source*:www.pgl.co.uk)

---

activity
INDIVIDUAL WORK

(a) Research the cost of outdoor activity weeks with private providers.

(b) In what ways would you expect them to be more or less fun than a week with the army?

Private providers of outdoor pursuits often specialise in particular activities or particular 'client groups' (types of customers). In the example given the client group are school students and their teachers, and the outdoor pursuits provided are designed to be both educational and enjoyable.

Clubs and societies

Throughout the country there are clubs and societies which offer all kinds of outdoor pursuits. In some cases there is a membership fee; for some of the smaller and more local activities you just turn up on the day.

Outdoor pursuit clubs such as climbing and potholing clubs may charge a membership fee, to pay for premises (e.g. 'club huts' in mountainous areas) and for equipment. Very often they have a social function, which means they look for members of a certain type – people who are likely to get on well together.

The Youth Service (local government provision)

This is a local government service which 'manages, supports and promotes effective youth work'.

The Youth Service supports many schemes which aim to give interesting, enjoyable and purposeful activities to young people, so that they:

- fulfil their potential
- keep away from crime.

The service works through partnerships with the police, providers of outdoor pursuits, social workers, schools and so on.

activity
GROUP WORK
(6.4)

Research your local Youth Service to find out what it does and why.

www.outwardbound-uk.org/adventures

Comparison of youth and community projects that include the use of outdoor pursuits and teamwork

When you compare two outdoor pursuit projects, centres or whatever, you should think about what it is you are going to compare. There are some things that you can't compare, such as the quality of the instruction, unless you have been to them both. But as long as you have the *same type of information* for two centres you can make a comparison based on the information you've got.

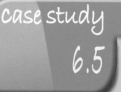

case study 6.5

Look at Life courses

The Princess of Wales's Royal Regiment conduct Look at Life (Work Experience) courses throughout the year at the following locations:

- Folkestone, Kent with the Tigers Youth Team (TYT)

- Longmoor, Hampshire with the Regimental Youth Team (RYT)

Our courses are *one week* long and cater for MALES who are between 14–16 yrs of age. Students need to be free from injury, not on medication or suffering from asthma. Students will be taught and practised in some of the following:

- Team building (more gets done together than alone)

- Command tasks (fun with planks, barrels, boxes and ropes)

- Fitness (swimming, gymnasium and assault course)

- Self-confidence awareness

- Introduction to PWRR military equipment and army way of life

- Laser rifle shooting (as used to train PWRR marksmen)

- Overnight survival exercise (make a shelter and live in it with army survival rations)

- plus lots of other activities.

There are lots of prizes to be won and every student leaves with a certificate and other Regimental gifts. Each student will receive (by post) a written report that covers how he participated in the key elements of the course. These make good additions to Record of Achievement or Personal Development files.

Course prices

- Accommodation – FREE

- Food (3 meals a day) – FREE

- Equipment – FREE

- Transport to and from local train station – FREE

These courses tend to fill up very quickly. Don't miss out get your bid in NOW.

(*Source*: The Princess of Wales's Royal Regiment)

Figure 6.3

Put to the test – a young person doing an assault course

case study 6.6

Outward Bound courses

Purpose and objectives: Personal development and adventure

Activity days: 21

Age groups: 14–15; 16–18; 19–24

Locations: Wales, the Lake District and Scotland

Suitable for: Developing skills and qualities such as communication, leadership and self confidence. Enhancing a personal curriculum vitae. A gap year project. Learning many new outdoor activities. A cultural experience for those wishing to develop English as a second language. The Duke of Edinburgh's Gold Award Residential.

Special features: Available as both a centre based and an expedition course. An eco-service project. A final unaccompanied expedition. An extensive personal development report. The Outward Bound Badge and Diploma.

The most exciting, rewarding, heart-beating, and downright satisfying experience Outward Bound has on offer!

The instructors operate to a simple formula. Week one is dedicated to the teaching of both new outdoor skills and developing the essentials of teamwork and leadership. Week two is when the instructor invites course members to begin making their own decisions and plans, and week three is dominated by the final Adventure Journey where new skills are applied and tested. The Classic Outward Bound Course is special because of its length – seventeen activity days and full-on enjoyment gives time to have a fundamental influence on all those who take part. The achievements are greater, the satisfaction more fulfilling and the levels of personal confidence the course generates are unsurpassed.

The Classic Outward Bound Course contains more outdoor activities such as the trapeze, high ropes course, and rafting than any other Outward Bound experience.

...

Classic Expedition Courses are tougher than centre-based courses and require higher standards of personal organisation and enthusiasm. Activities may also be used in a different order. They undertake a journey through West Scotland or West Wales. These courses are supported by the Outward Bound centres at Loch Eil and Aberdovey at regular intervals. Accommodation is in tents, mountain huts and log cabins.

Activities:

Week 1 Group Dynamics, First Aid Training, Navigation Training, Gorge Walking, Raft Construction, Sailing, Camp Craft.

Week 2 Rock Climbing, Flat Water Canoeing, Canoe and Kayak Journeys, High Ropes Course, Trapeze, Orienteering.

Week 3 Final Adventure Journey, Final Personal Interviews, Diploma and Badge Presentations.

Cost: £1075 (2005)

(*Source*: Outward Bound)

Comparison

activity
GROUP WORK
(6.5)

On the basis of the case studies 6.5 and 6.6 and the comparison provided in Table 6.3, discuss

(a) why the Outward Bound programme is able to run successfully at £1075, when there are army programmes which are free of charge.

(b) which of the two programmes you would rather go on and why.

Individual work

Research other projects and make similar comparisons.

Table 6.3 Case study comparison

Features to compare	Army Youth Teams (Case study 6.5)	Outward Bound (Case study 6.6)
Who is it meant for?	Males, 14–16	Both sexes, 14–15; 16–18; 19–24

Comparison: The army takes only males from 14–16; Outward Bound has three projects – divided by age group – and takes both males and females. The army's gender discrimination reflects the fact that some army units only take men. It suggests too that they are short of women's toilet facilities etc., and that there may be no women in their army youth teams. Outward Bound is not limited in this way – they can be expected to have some women staff, and women's facilities.

How long does it last?	One week	Three weeks (21 days)

Comparison: The army programme lasts one week (probably five days but it doesn't say). This may avoid homesickness and won't rob the clients of their weekends! The Outward Bound programme lasts three weeks, and might not be suitable for young people who are likely to feel homesick. On the other hand, a longer programme will have a greater effect than a one-week programme, and the clients will learn more than they would in one week. It may be difficult if the young people find they don't get on with each other: Outward Bound might need to choose its clients with care, otherwise there could be problems.

Where is it?	Folkestone, Kent, or Longmoor, Hampshire	Wales, Lake District and Scotland

Comparison: For people who like impressive scenery, the Outward Bound destinations are more beautiful and challenging (though the weather can't be trusted!). The people on the Outward Bound course may come from all over the UK (and beyond), so they'll need money and time to travel to the centres. On the other hand, most people who go on the army programme will probably come from south-east England, which will save them the time, hassle and expense of travelling a long way.

Accommodation	Not stated	Tents, mountain huts and log cabins
Activities	The Army Youth Teams do team-building, command tasks, fitness, self-confidence awareness, and introduction to military equipment and the army way of life, laser rifle shooting and an overnight survival exercise.	Outward Bound does group dynamics, first aid, navigation, gorge walking, raft construction, sailing, camp craft, rock climbing, flat-water canoeing, canoe and kayak journeys, high ropes, trapeze, orienteering, an adventure journey and a personal interview

Comparison: Both organisations combine physical activities with character-building activities. The military equipment and the laser-rifle shooting show that the army programme is slanted towards young people who might well want to make the army their career. They also do team-building and command tasks – both ideas linked to army work. In the army programme there is a stress on fitness (some of it indoors); Outward Bound does entirely outdoor activities which may demand fitness but are not intended to build fitness. Outward Bound makes use of gorge walking, outdoor rock climbing and kayak journeys: things which are not widely available in Kent and Hampshire. Most of what the army offers could be done in and around an army camp.

Educational aspects	Team building, leadership, self-confidence, problem solving	Communication, leadership, self-confidence, language skills, organising, solving problems, making decisions

Comparison: The character-building side of the programmes is similar. Leadership, problem solving and self-confidence are developed in both – and team building (the army) has a lot to do with organising and making decisions (Outward Bound). Language skills, for people who have English as a second language, refers to spoken English: there is no sign that there is any formal English teaching. It suggests that some clients for Outward Bound courses come from outside the UK.

Certificates etc.	Prizes. Certificates, regimental gifts, written report by post	Extensive personal development report, Outward Bound badge and diploma

Comparison: The two programmes are similar in that they offer a report which could be used in a record of achievement and in applications for jobs and courses at a later date. The Outward Bound material suggests that the report is longer and more detailed – this is what you would expect, since the instructors will have known the young people for three weeks, rather than five days. The army sounds generous with its prizes, certificates and regimental gifts, but Outward Bound also offers a badge and a diploma.

Talk to:
– people who provide outdoor pursuits to the public, or to students
– people who work with young people and organise outdoor pursuits
– people who have taken part in outdoor pursuits in different places
– people in the local authority or the local Youth Service.

Visit some of these websites:

www.ngfl.gov.uk   www.theama.org.uk

www.army.mod.uk   www.trinitysailing.co.uk

www.outdoor-learning.org   www.youth-justice-board.gov.uk

www.mike.gerrish.care4free.net   www.yha.org.uk

www.ramblers.org.uk   www.connexions.gov.uk

www.oytscotland.org.uk   www.dfes.gov.uk

www.aircadets.org

Also check out your own local authority!

Evaluating youth and community projects that include outdoor pursuits and teamwork

| keyword | **Evaluate** to decide, by research and careful thought, how good something is. |

To **evaluate** a project you should try to find out what it is supposed to achieve, whether it achieves it, and whether it is good value for money. If the project is run by a commercial organisation, you need to know whether it (a) makes a profit for the provider and (b) is good value for money for the customer. If the project is run by a public service, does it benefit the public service as well as the user? If the aim is to rehabilitate young offenders, does it succeed?

Other points
Safety

The more adventurous an activity is, the less safe it is likely to be. Over the years there have been a number of high-profile deaths in outdoor pursuits for young people. Examples are the deaths of four canoeists in Lyme Bay in 1993 and the drowning of two girls in Stainforth Beck, Yorkshire in 2000. The total number of deaths associated with school/college outdoor pursuits between 1985 and 2001 was 46, of whom 42 were young people.

Outdoor centres and projects are now inspected by the Adventure Activities Licensing Authority, and staff have to be qualified and experienced. Activities are given a thorough risk assessment. Nevertheless, there will always be a small, but real, danger of injury, sickness or death.

Questions to ask include:

■ Who set up the project?

■ Who is the project intended for?

- Who really benefits from the programme?
- What are the aims of the project or programme?
- Is it likely to fulfil its aims?
- Who pays for the project?
- Is it good value for money?
- Is the project enjoyable?
- Is the project safe?
- Is it discriminatory – and if so, how and why?
- Does it cause any environmental problems?
- Could the programme be made better – and if so, how?

Environmental issues

Adventurous and outdoor activities are sometimes criticised because they tend to damage the environment. Gorge walking, gill scrambling, hill-walking and off-road cycling can destroy rare plants and leave the hills scarred with huge footpaths. On the other hand, young people may gain a respect and love for nature if they are taken out into the countryside on outdoor pursuits.

Economic aspects

Activity centres benefit:

Economic
to do with money,
business and trade.

keyword

- the people who run them
- other people who live in the countryside because they bring work.

Projects to help young offenders

A number of projects use outdoor pursuits (especially the Duke of Edinburgh's Award) to help young offenders change their attitudes so that they are less likely to offend in the future. One such project is run by the Probation Board of Northern Ireland (PBNI).

The above is explained more on pages 145–46.

In the late 1990s there were some highly publicised 'boot camps' which aimed to help young offenders by putting them through a tough course of intensive discipline, work, physical training and assault courses. The HIT regime and the Colchester regime were evaluated as follows (see Case study 6.7).

case study

6.7

The HIT regime and the Colchester regime

The HIT regime at Thorn Cross was successful in significantly reducing reconviction offences in the two years following release. Its monetary benefits, in terms of crime savings, greatly exceeded its costs.

A fundamental difficulty in determining the reasons for this success is that the HIT regime is (as its name suggests) an intensive programme and pays as much attention to the throughcare and resettlement elements of a sentence as to its offending behaviour and education elements. All of these may be important in reducing reoffending and it would be unwise to ascribe the success of the regime to any one particular element. Nevertheless, the fact that the Colchester regime had no significant effect on reconviction offences suggests that the drilling and physical training elements of the HIT regime were not crucial to its success.

(*Source*: www.homeoffice.gov.uk)

activity

INDIVIDUAL WORK

As quickly as you can, note down all the possible advantages and disadvantages of running tough 'boot camps' using outdoor pursuits for young offenders.

How the Uniformed Public Services May Be Involved with Outdoor Activities and Youth and Community Projects in our Society

Why such links exist

Projects linked to the uniformed public services are of two main types:

1. Connected with recruitment for that service.
2. Connected with helping at-risk young people to avoid crime by giving them challenging activities and raising their self-esteem.

Recruitment-related outdoor pursuits

These include 'Look at Life' days and weeks.

link

See Case Study 6.5 on page 138; also page 141.

Helping young offenders

The uniformed public services sometimes run projects to help young offenders, or young people who may be at risk of offending in the future.

They may do this because of the success the armed forces have had in the past, in recruiting people with (minor) criminal records, training them as soldiers etc., and so 'turning them round' and making them into good citizens. The police have also experimented with this in some of their 'youth diversion schemes'.

The Probation Board of Northern Ireland (PBNI) runs the Duke of Edinburgh's Award Scheme.

Case Study 6.3 on page 134 describes the Duke of Edinburgh's Award Scheme.

The PBNI believes that the structured Award scheme is very effective in changing the attitudes of young offenders, and giving them a more responsible and constructive approach to life (see Case study 6.12).

The scheme run by the PBNI costs nothing for the young offender. The money comes from the taxpayer. The project is non-discriminatory (the Award is sometimes called the International Award because young Catholics or republicans might reject a scheme which is connected with British royalty). The probation service has close links with the prison service and the police.

case study 6.8

Benefits to the offender

Table 6.4 Changing attitudes

What are the indicators of risk of re-offending?	What can the award offer?
Anti-social attitudes	Pro-social ethos
Pro-criminal friends	New friends, positive role models
Tendency to act impulsively	A progressive process/planning tasks
Low self-esteem	Self-esteem through achievement – positive affirmation
Egocentricity	Service to others
Rigid thinking	Opportunities to show enterprise and creativity
Aggressive attitude	Non-competitive participation
Inefficacy in problem solving	Practice in problem solving
Unable to handle conflict	Handling conflict as part of a team
Unemployment	A recognised qualification/new skills/practical service
Poor decision making	Make decisions and accept consequences

(a) Explain:
- pro-social ethos
- positive role models
- positive affirmation
- handling conflict.

(b) Why are all these considered good by the PBNI?

(c) List all the reasons you can think of to explain why getting the Duke of Edinburgh's Award increases an offender's chances of getting work, training or education.

Take part in an activity for young people run by a public service (e.g. the army) and find out why they do it.

Purpose of public service links

1. The Award is being used to help the PBNI to achieve its aims of reducing the chance of offenders re-offending.

2. It enables the PBNI to use methods which reward offenders who don't re-offend, by giving them interesting, valuable experiences. A carrot-and-stick system of discouraging re-offending is more effective than using simply punishment (the stick) through the courts.

3. The Duke of Edinburgh's Award is accepted by employers and colleges – and increases the offender's chances of getting work, training or education.

How individuals and teams benefit from outdoor pursuit projects and activities
Youth Offending Teams

In the case of other projects the relationship between the uniformed public services and the outdoor pursuits is less direct. An example of this is a youth offending team (YOT).

Youth offending teams are partnerships set up between a number of public services and other agencies, with the aim of cutting down on youth crime and supervising the non-custodial sentences and rehabilitation of young offenders. Like most such groups they use a 'carrot and stick' approach – a mixture of punishments and rewards – to try to make young offenders stop offending.

In Figure 6.5 the Duke of Edinburgh's Award plays a part in the overall organisation of a youth offending team.

Figure 6.4

Benefits from links with an
Army Youth Team

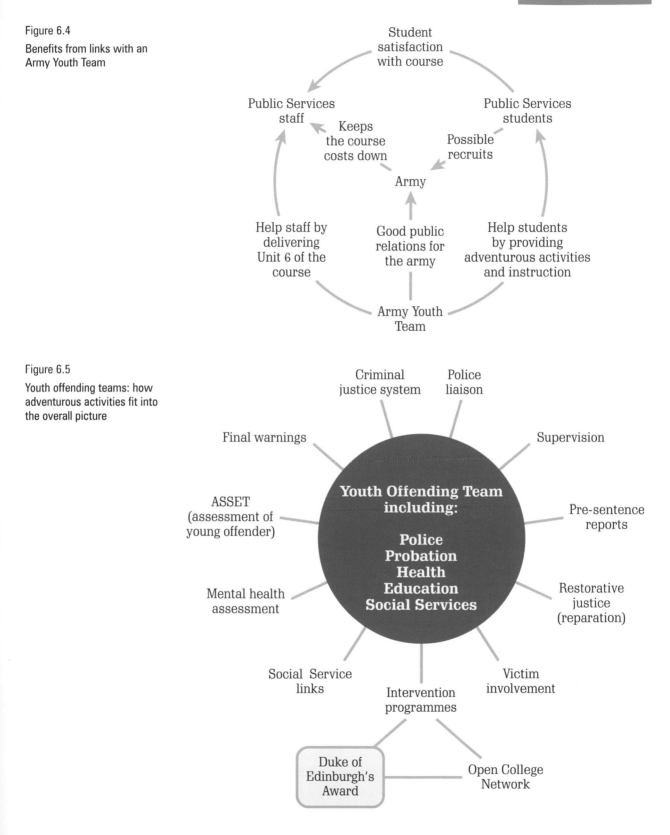

Figure 6.5

Youth offending teams: how
adventurous activities fit into
the overall picture

The Duke of Edinburgh's Award Scheme gives a lot of useful information about their partnerships with both public services and diverse groups in the population in their Annual Review (a book which can be downloaded from their website). There is a brief example in Case study 6.9.

---

case study **6.9**

The Northern Rock Foundation

The Northern Rock Foundation has enabled us to increase the numbers of special needs and excluded young people having access to the benefits of the Award in the North East of England. The work has concentrated on young people with mental health problems; with learning disabilities and those at risk of offending. Three pupil referral units, a secure unit, two mental health units and three Youth Offending Teams are looking to introduce the Award.

(*Source*: www.theaward.org)

---

activity
INDIVIDUAL WORK

Contact your local authority and find out if local Youth Offending Teams are involved in such activities and how they work.

---

remember

When doing outdoor pursuits or residentials, keep a log!

Outdoor activities in the uniformed public services

Most uniformed public services occasionally do work which includes outdoor activities but the armed forces are the most heavily involved, by a long way.

Adventurous training plays a big role in the armed forces. A scheme which involves Army, RAF and Royal Navy personnel is JSAT (see Case study 6.10).

In the army there are four levels of adventurous training, ranging from the level which is done in initial (basic) training through to special expeditions and training for instructors.

The units which do most outdoor pursuits are the Royal Marines commandos (they are part of the Royal Navy, not the army). They exercise in northern Norway, sometimes in temperatures as low as −40°C, practising manoeuvres and fighting. But they also have to train in desert conditions, and have been fighting in Iraq.

The armed forces encourage outdoor pursuits on a recreational basis. They also take part in expeditions to major mountain ranges in distant parts of the world. For example, the Army Mountaineering Association is planning an expedition to the Himalayas (Shishi Pangma) for 2007.

case study 6.10 — Joint Service Adventurous Training

The soldierly qualities of leadership, courage, determination, team spirit, loyalty etc. are deemed to be essential by our Commanders. The use of the adventurous training activities sanctioned under the Joint Service Adventurous Training (JSAT) scheme is an effective means of developing these qualities.

Whatever reason you may see as the principal purpose for officers and soldiers participating in adventurous training, the aim that encapsulates such training is:

'To develop through participation in authorised pursuits, leadership and necessary qualities that enhance the soldier's ability to withstand the shocks and strains of war and operations'.

(*Source*: www.army.mod.uk/)

activity
GROUP WORK

Discuss how adventurous training can 'enhance the soldier's ability to withstand the shocks and strains of war and operations'.

The rescue services sometimes need to use outdoor pursuit skills when carrying out rescues in mountains or at sea. And although most mountain rescue teams are volunteers, they get help from the uniformed services if they need it, as Case study 6.11 shows.

Figure 6.6
Adventure with attitude

case study 6.11 — Mountain rescue

Mountain Rescue in the whole of the United Kingdom is free of charge both to the person rescued and to any organisation to which he may belong. Except for incidents on sea cliffs where HM Coastguard are responsible, the overall responsibility for search and rescue in the UK rests with the Chief Constable of the Police for the area in which the incident occurs. It may request the assistance of voluntary rescue teams, National Park Rangers, RAF Mountain Rescue Teams, RAF or Royal Navy search and rescue helicopters.

(*Source*: www.bluedome.co.uk)

activity
GROUP WORK

Make a collection of news stories where the uniformed public services have used outdoor pursuit skills to carry out rescues. Use them as the basis of a presentation showing how the skills developed in outdoor pursuits can save lives.

progress check

1. Name 10 'outdoor pursuits'.
2. Give three short-term and three long-term benefits of residentials.
3. Outdoor pursuits develop intellectual, social and physical skills. Name three of each.
4. State four different types of organisation providing outdoor activities.
5. Outline two benefits of cadet schemes (a) for the armed forces and (b) for the cadets.
6. What is the Youth Service and what are its main aims?
7. What can be done to ensure that outdoor activities for young people are safe?
8. What are 'diversionary schemes'?
9. What are the aims of the Duke of Edinburgh's Award?
10. Why does the army organise expeditions to the Himalayas?

UNIT 7

The Value of Sport and Recreation in the Public Services

This unit covers:

- the importance of sport and recreation to the public services
- the safety issues that need to be taken into consideration when the public services organise sports and recreational activities
- planning and organising activities and events
- regular participation in a sporting or recreational activity

Sport and the public services go well together. In this unit you will find out why sport and recreation are good both for people who work in public services, and for the public services themselves.

Then you will look at safety in relation to sport and recreation, and the planning and organisation that goes into a sport or recreational activity.

You will be expected to take part regularly in a sport or recreational activity and explain how you have benefited from this. And finally you will explain how individuals in general can benefit from sport and recreation.

grading criteria

To achieve a **Pass** grade the evidence must show that the learner is able to:	To achieve a **Merit** grade the evidence must show that, in addition to the pass criteria, the learner is able to:	To achieve a **Distinction** grade the evidence must show that, in addition to the pass and merit criteria, the learner is able to:
P1 describe the benefits of sport and recreational activities to the public services	**M1** explain how sport and recreational activity contributes to the development of members of a named public service	**D1** justify the uses of sport and recreational activities by two named public services
P2 describe the benefits of sport and recreational activities to the individual	**M2** analyse the safety practices applied to a named sport activity or a named recreational activity	**D2** evaluate the differences between safety practices that the public services are required to apply and those that individuals should consider when participating in two named sports activities

grading criteria

To achieve a **Pass** grade the evidence must show that the learner is able to:	To achieve a **Merit** grade the evidence must show that, in addition to the pass criteria, the learner is able to:	To achieve a **Distinction** grade the evidence must show that, in addition to the pass and merit criteria, the learner is able to:
P3 identify the safety issues to be taken into consideration by the public services when organising a sporting or recreational activity	**M3** analyse the need for good planning and in the organisation of sport and recreational activities	**D3** evaluate the long and short term benefits to the individual from regular participation in sport or recreational activities
P4 explain what needs to be taken into consideration when planning, preparing and organising a sport or recreational activity	**M4** explain the long and short term benefits to the individual of participating regularly in sport or recreational activities.	
P5 plan and participate in regular sport or recreational activities		
P6 identify the personal benefits from participation in regular sport or recreational activity		

The Importance of Sport and Recreation to the Public Services

keyword

Sport
physical activity that is done to improve fitness and may be competitive.

Recreation
any activity which is done for pleasure.

The dividing line between **sport** and **recreation** is not always clear. Amateur sport is also recreation, but not all recreation is sport. Recreations include angling, playing chess, rock climbing, watercolour painting, disco dancing, playing a muscial instrument, reading books and collecting antiques.

Sport has been defined as – 'all forms of physical activity which, through casual or organised participation, aim at expressing or improving physical fitness and mental well-being, forming social relationships or obtaining results in competitions at all levels' (*Source*: Council of Europe, Europe Sports Charter, 1993).

Table 7.1 shows that there are plenty of similarities between sport and recreation.

Table 7.1 The similarities between sport and recreation

Types of sport and recreation	Physical activity?	Teams?	Pleasure?	Competition?	Mental activity?	Social activity?
Team sports e.g. football	Yes	Yes	Yes	Yes	Yes	Yes
Individual sports e.g. fell-running	Yes	Yes, but not essential	Yes	Yes	Yes	Yes, when you meet or train with other runners
Non-physical games – e.g. chess	No	Yes, but not essential	Yes	Yes	Yes	Yes, in chess clubs and teams
Physical recreation e.g. potholing	Yes	Yes; it would be dangerous and very difficult to do it alone	Yes	No (though there are records to be be broken – e.g. deepest pothole)	Yes	Yes – potholers form clubs
Semi-physical recreation – e.g. playing the piano	Needs coordination, but does not use as many calories as most sports	Not necessary, but a band or orchestra is a team	Yes	Yes – but it's fairly rare	Yes	If there is a band, audience or teacher, it is social
Non-physical recreation – e.g. reading	No	No	Yes	No	Yes	Yes – if you talk about what you read, or join a 'reading group'

Benefits of sport and recreational activities to the public services

For many years the public services, and private industry, have encouraged their employees to get involved in sport and recreational activities in their spare time. This is because they believe it benefits their organisations.

case study

7.1

Benefits of sport

The benefits of sport to a workplace, according to the supporting evidence of the Carter Report 2005, include:

- Enhanced productivity

- Improved staff loyalty

- Reduced staff absenteeism

■ Healthier, more alert workforce

■ Happier office environment

■ Transfer of 'team ethic'.

(*Source*: Appendix 8, Supporting Evidence, Carter Report: *Review of National Sport Effort and Resources*, 2005, www.culture.gov.uk)

activity

GROUP WORK

(a) How do these benefits help an employer?

(b) How do these benefits help the workers themselves?

(c) How do these benefits apply to a public service?

Enhanced productivity

In the public services this means getting more work done, or better work done, in the time available.

A 'typical day' for a firefighter includes:

■ appliance and equipment checks

■ physical training

■ practical training

■ a lecture session

■ hydrant or fire safety inspections

■ emergency calls or 'stand bys' in other station areas

■ community fire safety issues.

(*Source*: West Yorkshire Fire and Rescue Service)

keyword

Fitness
the ability to exercise for a long time without getting tired.

Physical **fitness** is developed, or used, in most of these activities. Practical training, hydrant and fire safety inspections, and call-outs themselves, will all be handled faster and better if firefighters are fit.

Sport during leisure time adds to firefighters' fitness and coordination skills. This tends to make them more productive, because they work faster, and to a higher standard.

Improved staff loyalty

Sport creates a feeling of belonging. If staff are loyal they don't like to let down their colleagues or the public service they work for. In the words of an army regiment, the Royal Artillery:

A passion for sport is a vital part of the Royal Artillery's culture. We run teams and clubs playing any number of sports – mainstream and specialist, team and individual. The list is endless.

Sport is an excellent way of developing your leadership and tactical skills – crucial elements in any winning team. What's more, the spirit that bonds you and your team mates is as important on the field of play as it is on the field of battle.

(Source: www.army.mod.uk)

Reduced staff absenteeism

case study 7.2

Staff absenteeism

Staff absenteeism costs UK business over £10bn a year in direct costs alone. Conservative estimates suggest at least 1% (or £100m p.a.) can be saved through active workplace programmes. Additional costs to business include poor staff retention, lower service levels and reduced organisational efficiency. (Evidence in CBI 2004: FIA 'Get Fit for Business')

(Source: Appendix 8, Supporting Evidence, Carter Report: *Review of National Sport Effort and Resources*, 2005)

activity
GROUP WORK

(a) Discuss the times you were absent in your last year at school. What were the real reasons?

(b) Why do many public services have high rates of absenteeism?

(c) Why might sport and recreation for a workforce reduce absenteeism?

Healthier, more alert workforce

There is evidence that sport is good for health, so if workers in the public services take part in sports they should be healthier than if they don't.

link See Unit 3 Uniformed Public Service Fitness, pages 69–71.

And since sport is good for self-esteem (making you feel good about yourself) and involves quick thinking, playing recreational sport should make workers more alert as well.

www.culture.gov.uk (Carter Report)
www.dh.gov.uk
Department of Health White Paper 2004: *Choosing Health: Making Healthy Choices Easier*.

Happier office environment

Active sport and recreation have been shown to reduce mild depression. As it says in Dietary Guidelines for Americans 2005, 'Overall, mortality rates from all causes of death are lower in physically active people than in sedentary people. Also, physical activity can aid in managing mild to moderate depression and anxiety.'

US Department of Health and Human Services; US Department of Agriculture; www.healthierus.gov/dietaryguidelines

Transfer of 'team ethic'

The idea here is that acting as a team in recreational sport will help employees to act as a team in the workplace. So public service workers who play sport will be good at teamwork, and will make the public service more effective.

Recreation (but not sport)

Less is known about the benefits of non-sporting recreation for workers than the benefits of sports. But recreations such as theatre, music and the arts might have similar effects:

- enhance productivity by improving the communication skills of public service workers, giving them a better understanding of human behaviour, and giving them a boost in **morale**

- improve staff loyalty through the teamwork involved in, say, putting on a play or concert with other members of staff

- reduce staff absenteeism by reducing stress; taking part in recreational activities is an excellent way to relax and forget the pressures of work

- improve the health and alertness of those in the workforce who take part – because of the mental stimulation and thinking skills needed for many creative recreational activities

- create a happier office environment because, like sport, other recreations may reduce some kinds of depression

- transfer the team ethic because many non-sporting recreations still involve working as teams, cooperating unselfishly to bring about the aims of the group.

The government views theatre as similar to sport in the ways it can benefit society (though of course many more people take part in sport than in drama). Since theatre can benefit the community, and since a public service workplace is a community, theatre could benefit a public service.

> **keyword**
>
> **Morale**
> confidence, team spirit and the will to succeed.

How sport and recreational activity can help develop members of a public service

Sport and recreation can help develop (improve) a public service workforce – both as individuals and as teams. Some reasons are given below.

Social cohesion

Sport and recreation provide social cohesion – that is, binding people together as friends or team-mates. If public service workers play sport with other people in their own service, friendship and understanding will develop. They will communicate better (and thus become more efficient) in their work, and morale should be higher.

Public visibility

If a public service has a sports team, it is good for public relations. They mix with other people, and gain respect. Sport therefore helps public service workers by improving their standing in the community.

Public service sport can go beyond the local community. For example, the police take part in international competitions through the USPE (European Police Sports Union) championships.

case study 7.3 Police Sport UK

'The Police Sport UK website www.policesportuk continues to grow. The biggest number of hits recorded [was] over 11,000 in November 2004. This is a wonderful tool for advertising and reporting sporting events.'

(*Source*: www.policesport.com)

activity
INDIVIDUAL WORK

Find out how many local sports teams are attached to local public services.

At the highest level the gold medals for Kelly Holmes in the 2004 Athens Olympics brought attention to the fact that she had been in the army and had developed her skills with them.

Morale

Morale is the level of confidence, enthusiasm and positive attitudes in a team or group of workers. Although morale is hard to measure, it is believed that sport and recreation are good for morale. High morale is linked to high quality and efficient work – and to courage in the armed forces.

Stress

Workplace stress is a problem in the public services, because the work is hard and sometimes there seems to be little to show for it. There can also be stress caused by dealing with tragic cases and major disasters. Stress lowers morale, and the quality and quantity of work done. Stress 'may show up as an increase in absenteeism (especially frequent short spells of sickness), lateness, disciplinary problems or staff turnover, or a reduction in output or quality of product or service.' (HSE: *Work-related Stress: A Short Guide*). The HSE advises managers to: 'encourage a healthy work-life balance'. In other words, more sport and recreation equals less stress.

Personal satisfaction

It is hard to have a happy work life if you don't have a happy personal life. Sport can bring satisfaction through a sense of achievement, the pleasure of expressing physical strength, endurance and skill, and the sense of challenge and competition.

Sport is also a controlled outlet for aggression. There are times in public service work – for example in the police, the prison service, and the armed forces – where officers might be tempted into unprofessional aggressive acts (e.g. beating up a suspect in the back of a police van). Having an outlet for natural aggression in sport helps public service employees not to take out their aggression on other people.

Personal development

Sport builds character. It teaches quick thinking, problem solving, leadership and teamwork in a fun way (and it is easier for all of us to learn if we are enjoying ourselves). It helps us to understand our own motivation, the way we tick, and this knowledge can then be applied to work. Sport teaches empathy – understanding the other person's point of view (another vital skill in public service work). Team sports, and sports like rock climbing and potholing, where communication is carried out in difficult conditions, are excellent for developing listening and speaking skills – which themselves are used so much in public service work.

Organisational skills

Sport needs planning. You have to obtain the right gear, learn the skills, train, learn about health and safety and then put all this knowledge into practice. This is much the same as the process of learning the job in the uniformed public services. Planning team strategy in, say, football, requires some of the same skills and abilities as those used in public service planning – e.g. planning how to deal with a motorway pile-up. Sport is a painless way of learning valuable organisational skills.

activity
GROUP WORK
(7.1)

Question members of the public services about the sport and recreational activities they do, and the benefits they feel they get from them. Present your findings to the rest of your class.

Further reasons why public services use sport and recreational activities

1. *A general need for more sport and recreation.* People do not spend enough time in sporting and recreational activities. Lack of sport and recreation has become a public health problem for the UK as a whole (see Tables 7.2 and 7.3).

Table 7.2 Top ten sports, games and physical activities[1] among adults in Great Britain, by sex, 2002–2003

Males	(%)	Females	(%)
Walking[2]	36	Walking[2]	34
Snooker/pool/billiards	15	Keep fit/yoga	16
Cycling	12	Swimming	15
Swimming	12	Cycling	6
Soccer	10	Snooker/pool/billiards	4
Golf	9	Weight training	3
Weight training	9	Running	3
Keep fit/yoga	7	Tenpin bowling	3
Running	7	Horse riding	2
Tenpin bowling	4	Tennis	2

[1] Participation in the four weeks before interview.
[2] Walking two miles or more for recreational purposes.
Source: *General Household Survey*, © Office for National Statistics.

Table 7.3 Time spent on main activities[1] in the United Kingdom, by sex, 2000–2001

United Kingdom	Hours and minutes per day	
	Males	**Females**
Sleep	8:23	8:33
Leisure		
Watching TV and Video/DVD	2:41	2:17
Social life and entertainment	1:16	1:33
Reading and listening to radio and music	0:36	0:35
Hobbies and games	0:26	0:16
Sport	0:18	0:11
All leisure	5:17	4:52
Employment and study[2]	4:17	2:42
Housework and childcare	2:17	4:03
Personal care[3]	2:07	2:19
Travel	1:28	1:21
Other	0:09	0:10

1 Adults aged 16 and over.
2 Includes voluntary work and meetings.
3 Includes eating, drinking, washing and dressing.
Source: *Time Use Survey*, © Office for National Statistics

Stamina
the ability to work for a long time without getting tired; endurance or 'staying power'.

keyword

2. *The need for public service workers to be fit*. The public services require fit and active people to work for them. This is true not only of the armed forces and the fire service: nurses, for example, need to have plenty of energy and **stamina** to do their job.

Sport and recreation are good for health, and the public services, as responsible employers, have a duty of care for their employees. They have occupational health schemes, and encouraging sport and recreational activities is good for the health and well-being of their workers – and cuts absenteeism.

3. *Recruiting and retention*. The armed forces have a special need to be fit and strong. The Army Sports Control Board, which supervises sports in the army, justifies army sport in the case study below.

case study 7.4   Sport in the army

The importance of Sport in the Army and Army Sport goes far further than physical development, self esteem, esprit de corps etc as it also has a significant impact on recruiting and retention, the Continuous Attitude Survey returns confirm such. We at the ASCB know from first hand experience that recruits have been encouraged to join the Army by our Martial Arts, Basketball, Canoeing and Cycling teams playing against and associating with civilian clubs. Although not being objective in these matters we firmly believe that as a by-product, the Army receives excellent value for money from the privilege of being paid to play sport.

(*Source*: www.army.mod.uk)

activity

INDIVIDUAL WORK

(a) Define 'recruiting' and 'retention'

(b) Why should sport improve both of these in the army?

(c) Give four reasons why retention is important in a public service.

4. *Social benefits*. Sport and recreation are social activities. Social benefits include the pleasure of mixing and interacting with other people, and the teamwork and communication skills which come from this. Public service sports clubs stress the social benefits to be gained by their members.

case study

7.5

The Lancashire Constabulary Sports and Social Club

Current formation

The Club is divided into eight separate bodies each governed by a similar constitution.

There are seven Divisional Clubs (including Headquarters) and a County Club that operates across the whole force.

The objects of the Club shall be to encourage and promote all forms of sport, social and recreational activities for all its members.

(*Source*: www.slateman.co.uk)

activity

GROUP WORK

(a) Why is the Lancashire Constabulary Sports and Social Club organised into divisions?

(b) Who do you think the various sports teams compete against?

(c) Discuss why the club should be good for public relations.

(d) (Individual) You are interested in a sport and wish to join a public service. You read in a newspaper that the government is intending to cut back on sport and recreation in the public services, on the grounds that it is 'a waste of time and money'. Write a letter to an MP explaining how important sports and recreational activities are for two public services, and giving reasons why there should be no cut-backs.

How sport and recreational activities benefit individuals

Sport and physical recreation can lengthen life, improve health and fitness and increase happiness and well-being.

General health benefits include:

- increased health and efficiency for the main body systems, especially the
  - cardiovascular system (heart and blood circulation)
  - musculoskeletal system (muscles, bones and joints)
  - metabolic system (digestion and absorption of food, and converting that food into energy)
  - endocrine system (glands of all kinds)
  - immune system (protection from illness)

- protection from major illnesses – people who exercise or do sport regularly are less likely to suffer from:
  - cardiovascular disease (heart disease, including heart attacks; high blood pressure, which can lead to heart attacks; clogged arteries, which can lead to high blood pressure)
  - bowel cancer
  - non-insulin-dependent diabetes mellitus (a kind of diabetes suffered by older people)
  - osteoarthritis (causes painful joints and, sometimes, disability)
  - falling in old age
  - obesity
  - depression (mild or moderate forms).

Non-physical recreation

Recreation which is non-physical, such as reading or listening to music, can benefit the mind enormously. But it will not improve your physical fitness and health.

The main risks from sport and physical recreation are of injury, which is why health and safety are so important – as we shall see below.

---

activity
GROUP WORK
(7.2)

Design a poster to encourage more participation in sports and recreational activities, stressing the benefits of these to the individual.

Talk to sports teachers, instructors and enthusiasts.
Find books and visit websites which deal with this subject.
www.middevon.gov.uk (quick information)
www.fitness.gov (US government site, with the low-down)

The Safety Issues that Need to be Taken into Consideration when the Public Services Organise Sports and Recreational Activities

In planning and organising any activity there is a rule which states, 'What can go wrong, will go wrong'. When the public services organise sports and recreations, they must make those activities as safe as possible.

Figure 7.1 shows that there are six main issues to be taken into consideration:

- the activity itself
- the venue
- the participants
- staff and officials
- paper work
- emergency arrangements.

All of these have to be considered by the organisers.

activity
INDIVIDUAL WORK
(7.3)

(a) Choose a sport which you know about.

(b) Using the six headings above, list as many safety factors as you can think of in relation to arranging an event in your chosen sport.

There is more on this in Unit 3 Uniformed Public Service Fitness, on page 83.

Safety practices

All sports and physical recreational activities have an element of danger in them. The aim is to make them as safe as possible, without losing the excitement.

In some potentially dangerous sports, such as diving, this means having carefully thought out rules, which have to be followed both for the sake of the diver and of the other people using the pool.

Figure 7.1
Organising a safe activity

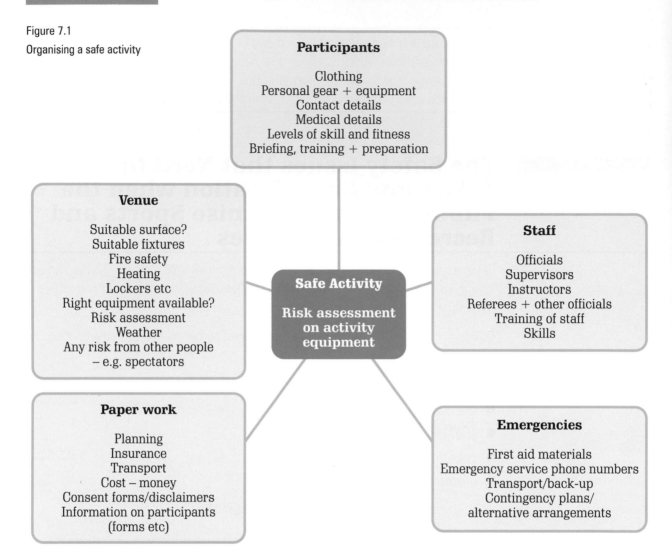

Participants

Clothing
Personal gear + equipment
Contact details
Medical details
Levels of skill and fitness
Briefing, training + preparation

Venue

Suitable surface?
Suitable fixtures
Fire safety
Heating
Lockers etc
Right equipment available?
Risk assessment
Weather
Any risk from other people
– e.g. spectators

Safe Activity

Risk assessment on activity equipment

Staff

Officials
Supervisors
Instructors
Referees + other officials
Training of staff
Skills

Paper work

Planning
Insurance
Transport
Cost – money
Consent forms/disclaimers
Information on participants
(forms etc)

Emergencies

First aid materials
Emergency service phone numbers
Transport/back-up
Contingency plans/
alternative arrangements

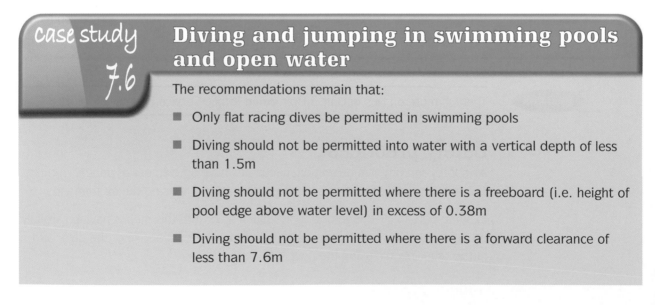

case study 7.6 Diving and jumping in swimming pools and open water

The recommendations remain that:

- Only flat racing dives be permitted in swimming pools

- Diving should not be permitted into water with a vertical depth of less than 1.5m

- Diving should not be permitted where there is a freeboard (i.e. height of pool edge above water level) in excess of 0.38m

- Diving should not be permitted where there is a forward clearance of less than 7.6m

- Running dives should not be permitted

- Diving should not be permitted in leisure pools, unless they comply with the above. Diving should not be permitted when waves are in operation.

- Every reasonable effort should be taken to prevent diving from elevated design features

- 'No diving' signs that comply with the Safety Signs Regulations should be prominently sited

- Signs should be displayed at all vantage points and where they might be obscured by bathers at a height of 1.8m or more

...

- Jumping in should only be taught by someone with an appropriate qualification and experience and should be taught from a crouching position with the pupil being taught how to bend the knees and use the arms to minimise impact and retain balance.

activity
GROUP WORK

(a) What are the main risks associated with diving?

(b) Of the items in the case study, which are rules and which are other safety practices?

(c) Draw up a list of sanctions (penalties) which could be applied to people who broke the safety rules or failed to follow safety practices.

The guidance in Case study 7.6 was originally written for children but now applies to adults as well. Dangers are caused (a) by the style of dive which might injure the diver or someone else in the pool, (b) by shallow water, (c) by lack of space in front of the diver, (d) by running before diving or jumping into the pool, (e) by diving or jumping into leisure pools, which are unsuitable and (f) by jumping or diving from too great a height. The safety practices have been designed to limit each of these dangers.

The people in charge of the pool, teachers or instructors and the jumpers or divers themselves all have a responsibility to follow these safety rules.

<blockquote>
activity
GROUP WORK
(7.4)

(a) Choose a sport or recreation, find out the rules which must be followed to make it as safe as possible, and explain why they are needed.

(b) Put your findings together to make a guidance booklet suitable for public service personnel who are involved in sports and recreations.
</blockquote>

Talk to someone who knows your chosen sport or activity.
Consult books on sport or sports safety.
Use your own knowledge of a sport or activity.
Visit useful websites such as www.brianmac.demon.co.uk/

Who is responsible for safety?

Public service safety responsibilities

If public services organise a sport or recreational activity, they have a 'duty of care'. This means that they must do what is 'reasonably practicable' to make the activity safe. Their legal responsibilities are, most of the time, the same as those of other employers.

The way in which safety responsibilities are divided between the public service organising the event and the people taking part is shown in Case study 7.7.

Evaluation of differences

The responsibility of the Army Youth Team is to organise the activity and make sure that it is carried out safely and enjoyably. They need to be firm and clear in their instructions and must insist on good discipline. At the same time they must be sensitive to the students and their concerns.

The responsibility of the students is to make sure that they are dressed suitably, have eaten properly, are in good health and ready to do the activity. They must be there on time and must follow the instructions of the Army Youth Team all the time the activity is going on. While in the cave they must take reasonable care of their own safety and that of their companions.

<blockquote>
activity
INDIVIDUAL WORK
(7.5)

Write health and safety guidance for two sports or activities carried out or organised by public service members. State the safety measures which are the responsibility of the public service, and those which are the responsibility of the individual. Explain the differences between the two, and why it is necessary to understand them.
</blockquote>

case study 7.7 — Army Youth Team

An army youth team (AYT) is taking a group of 10 students down a cave.

Public service (AYT) responsibility	*Student responsibility*
1. To carry out a risk assessment of the cave (a) *What are the risks?* Possible dangers (e.g. deep pools, tight passages) must be identified (b) *Who might be harmed?* Inexperienced or badly equipped students *How?* By falling into pools or getting stuck in narrow gaps (c) *What precautions should be taken?* Students should wear proper wetsuits etc.; they should be warned of the dangers; good lighting should be supplied (d) *A written record should be kept of the risk assessment*	To follow instructions and take proper care of their own safety
2. The AYT must know what kind of weather conditions are needed for the cave to be safe. E.g. is there a risk of flooding?	Students not involved in this
3. The AYT must know what the capabilities of the students are. How fit are they? How motivated are they? Have they been down caves before? Are they all well? Do any have phobias about going down holes in the ground?	Students must inform AYT of any difficulties they might have. If they are unwell and do not say so they put everybody at risk; if they have phobias they could spoil the caving for the others
4. The AYT must provide specialised clothing and equipment	Students must follow all instructions about clothing and equipment – for the sake of their own safety and well-being
5. The AYT must provide food, drinks, first aid, safe transport	Students must eat enough, drink enough and behave themselves on the transport
6. The AYT's own instructors must be suitably trained, skilled and qualified for running the activity	Students must follow all instructions
7. The AYT must check that the weather will be suitable all the time they and the students are in the cave	Students not concerned
8. There must be contingency plans in case anything goes wrong	Students must understand and follow these plans if necessary

activity

INDIVIDUAL WORK

(a) How would an AYT carry out a risk assessment of a cave?

(b) How would the AYT find out what the students were capable of down a cave?

(c) Why are students not concerned with some of the checks?

Talk to an army PT instructor or games teacher.

Visit your local sports centre and find out what their safety responsibilities are – and why.

Visit a useful website, such as www.policesportuk.com

Planning and Organising Activities and Events

Thinking ahead

Detailed planning is needed for a recreational or sporting activity involving a number of people. If, on the other hand, you are planning activities for yourself – or for yourself and a couple of friends – the planning is more straightforward.

Figure 7.2 shows some of the things to be taken into consideration before climbing Ben Nevis, the highest mountain in Britain.

The diagram does not include everything you would need to take into consideration before climbing Ben Nevis. You would need to think about your clothes, socks, boots, the exact food you wanted to take, whether you wanted to take a map, compass, whistle or mobile phone, the first aid items that you might want to take – and so on. You would also want to consider your own fitness. For a fit young person climbing the mountain is an easy walk, but if you were injured, or you thought your boots weren't going to fit you, or if you didn't have much time, or if you were going with someone else who was less fit than you, you might rethink your plans.

If your plans for a sport or recreational activity involve other people, they get much more complicated. This is particularly the case if the plans involve a team – or teams – and if they involve spectators (see below).

activity

GROUP WORK
(7.6)

Produce a wallchart, suitable for young people, showing the thinking that goes into setting up a sporting or recreational activity.

Figure 7.2
Climbing Ben Nevis – some considerations

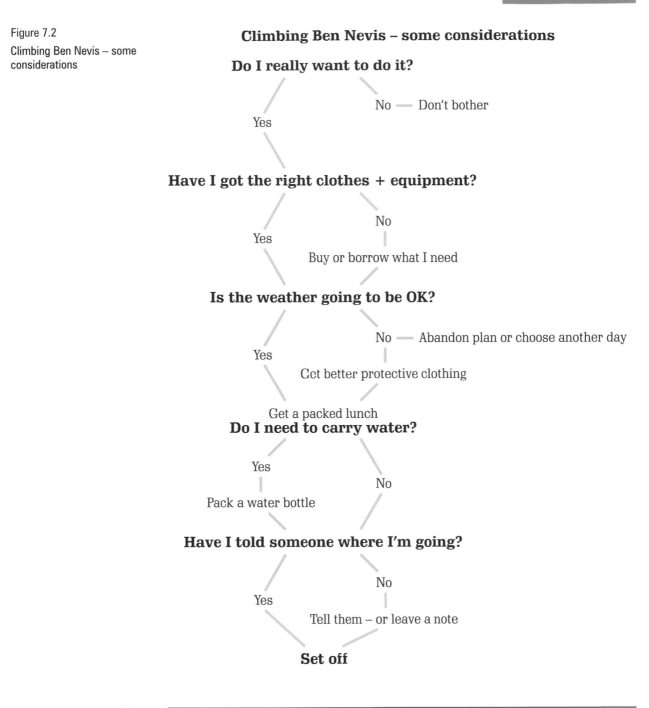

Climbing Ben Nevis – some considerations

Do I really want to do it?

No — Don't bother

Yes

Have I got the right clothes + equipment?

No

Yes

Buy or borrow what I need

Is the weather going to be OK?

No — Abandon plan or choose another day

Yes

Get better protective clothing

Get a packed lunch

Do I need to carry water?

Yes

No

Pack a water bottle

Have I told someone where I'm going?

No

Yes

Tell them – or leave a note

Set off

Talk with:
- people who organise sport, training etc. in one of the uniformed services
- sports teachers in your college
- voluntary youth leaders such as scout leaders, or the captains and organisers of amateur sports teams.

Large-scale planning and organisation

The planning for even a medium-sized sports competition is a big job. The main stages are shown in the flowchart in Figure 7.3.

The main aspects of planning here are:

1. Somebody needs to be in charge – the Event Coordinator.
2. The Event Coordinator is usually chosen by a committee that already exists (e.g. the committee of a police sports club).
3. Subcommittees are appointed to help with different aspects of the planning and organisation of the event.
4. The Coordinator decides who does what, how much money there is, and how the event is going to be publicised.
5. The subcommittees get to work organising finance, security, volunteers etc.
6. The Event Coordinator and the Event Committee keep an eye on the planning process, and make sure everything is going well. Meetings are held, and problems are solved.
7. The event takes place.
8. There is a review of the event. People decide if it was a success, how much money has been made, learn any lessons that need to be learned for next time and thank the volunteers and participants.

Figure 7.3

Stages in organising a sporting event

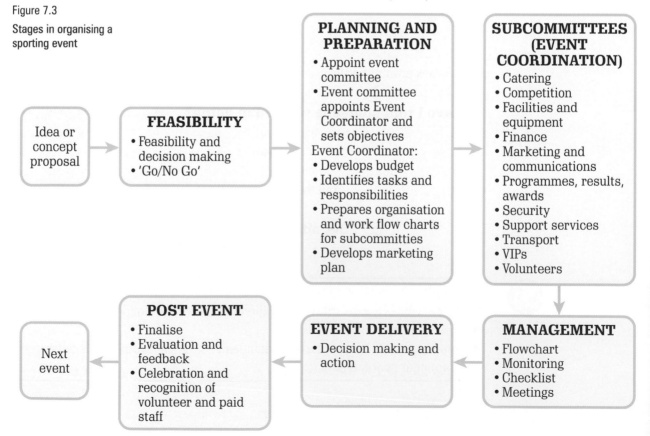

**GROUP WORK
(7.7)**

(a) Decide what the difference is between (a) planning and (b) organisation.

(b) Why is it necessary to involve a number of people in these processes? Note down as many reasons as you can.

Why planning and organisation matter

There are lots of reasons why an event involving many people has to be well planned and organised. Indeed, the quality of the whole experience depends on it.

A well-planned and organised activity is:

- enjoyable, because people know what they are doing, and when they are supposed to do it. Competitors and spectators feel they are valued, because proper arrangements have been made for them. If the spectators have paid, they feel they have got good value for money, and go away feeling happy. The sportspeople too go away feeling that they have had a good experience, and that the event was worth taking part in (even if they didn't win!). Everybody hopes that a similar event will be run again in the future.

- profitable, if money is to be made, because the costs have been worked out in advance, and the event has not gone over budget. Entrance charges etc. have been set at a realistic level – high enough to make a profit, but not so high that people are put off coming. There is good accounting, so everybody knows where the money has been spent, and what is happening to the money that has been made. There are no accusations of mismanagement or dishonesty.

- safe, because safety has been planned into the event and the activities. Facilities have been good, and well maintained: stewarding and officiating has been by skilled people who know what they are doing and why. If anybody has got hurt, there have been good arrangements to treat them or take them to hospital. If crowds have attended, crowd management has been good, and spectators have watched in safety and comfort. If the weather has been bad, it has been planned for and no one has suffered unnecessarily because of it.

A badly planned activity is:

- boring (because people hang about too long and nobody knows what's happening)

- depressing, because it seems nobody has bothered to organise it properly. This devalues the efforts of the sportspeople taking part, and the spectators who took the trouble to come

- likely to lose money, because it has been badly costed or publicised

- potentially unsafe, because safety arrangements have been neglected, or are shambolic

- likely to put people off doing anything similar in future.

activity
GROUP WORK
(7.8)

(a) Prepare and deliver a talk suitable for youth club organisers showing clearly and in detail why sport and recreational activities need to be well planned.

(b) Research the Hillsborough Disaster or another sporting disaster, and find out how failures in planning or organisation led to loss of life.

---

i

Talk to someone in your college who organises sports events or residentials.
Visit some useful websites – e.g.
www.ausport.gov.au
www.hse.gov.uk
www.dfes.gov.uk

Regular Participation in a Sporting or Recreational Activity

One of the things you need to do in this unit is plan and participate in regular sport or recreational activities. This means you must choose a sport or activity that you like, arrange how you are going to do it, who you are going to do it with, what equipment and money you need, where you're going to do it, and when you're going to do it. You are strongly advised to keep a diary or record of what you do.

There is a fitness training requirement in Unit 3: Uniformed Public Service Fitness, pages 83–91, which is very similar to this.

---

remember

The planning should be done on paper.

Criterion P5 in the Specification does not say that the activities *have* to be sporting, or physically testing. It should be possible to achieve this criterion not only by taking part in sports or (say) outdoor activities, but in other ways as well – for example, by playing in a brass band, fishing, helping out at a recreational youth club, or recording the scores in a cricket match or athletic competition. If in doubt, talk with your tutor about it.

Planning tennis practice

Suppose you and some friends decide to plan a few weeks' tennis practice. You could book (or go to) a court in the local park, and organise it like this:

Planning

1. Try to make sure that you are all at a roughly similar level in your tennis. This will prevent the best people from getting bored and the worst from feeling discouraged.

2. Check that you are all free to turn up at the time arranged.

3. Check that the clothes and equipment that you need are available.

4. Check that the court will be available.

5. Arrange to have someone to verify (sign) that you have done the activity so that it can be counted towards your BTEC qualification.

6. Do a quick risk assessment on the court (checking each week that there is no broken glass etc.).

Activity outline

Each member of the group should have a copy of the activity outline (an example is given in Table 7.4).

Table 7.4 Activity outline

Names	Activity: Weekly tennis practice	Comments	Signature of staff member/ instructor
.... Coach	Aims: To improve tennis skills; to improve general fitness Times: Friday mornings, 10.30–12.00 Place: Crow's Nest Park Kit needed: Tennis clothes; rackets, balls, soft drinks		
Week 1	Main coaching topic: returning the ball Warm-up – 10 mins. Coaching – 20 minutes. Games – 1 hour with breaks.		
Week 2	Main coaching topic: serving Warm-up – 10 mins. Coaching – 20 minutes. Games – 1 hour with breaks.		
Week 3	Main coaching topic: forehands Warm-up – 10 mins. Coaching – 20 minutes. Games – 1 hour with breaks.		
Week 4	Main coaching topic: backhands Warm-up – 10 mins. Coaching – 20 minutes. Games – 1 hour with breaks.		
Week 5	Main coaching topic: hitting from baseline Warm-up – 10 mins. Coaching – 20 minutes. Games – 1 hour with breaks.		
Week 6	Main coaching topic: coming to net Warm-up – 10 mins. Coaching – 20 minutes. Games – 1 hour with breaks.		
Week 7	Main coaching topic: competition Mini-tournament Assessment from coach		

In the comments column you should note down your own observations of how each session went, and what you learned. In the signature column your activity should be witnessed, so that assessors and verifiers of your work have proof that you have actually done it. (Check with your tutor about this.)

Coaching

Participation could take the form of coaching other people. If you choose to do this, the following advice may be useful:

- Create a positive environment
  - Learn names quickly
  - Smile, praise and encourage
  - Be patient and supportive
- Set achievable goals
  - Keep the player's maturation in mind
  - Make sessions challenging
  - Ensure skill development is progressive
- Vary your sessions
  - Change format and activities regularly
  - Ensure equal opportunity for all players
  - Avoid elimination games where players sit out
  - Include non-competitive team work
  - Include supervised play with minimal guided instruction
  - Use different teaching/coaching methods (tabloids/cards)
- Teach skills
  - Plan skills for sessions and introduce easiest ones first
  - Teach one skill, or one part at a time
  - Regularly revise skills from previous weeks
- Demonstrate
  - Remember 'a picture paints a thousand words'
  - If you can't demonstrate a skill, choose someone who can
  - Demonstrate what to do, not what not to do
  - Make sure all players can see the demonstration
- Involve all players
  - Have ample equipment available
  - Use several small groups rather than one large one
  - Aim to have every player practising the skill each 30 seconds at least
- Provide instant feedback
  - Use lots of praise
  - Be supportive – shouting and criticising won't achieve anything

■ Use your voice well

  ▪ Don't shout or talk too much

  ▪ Try to have as much one-to-one as possible

(*Source*: www.ausport.gov.au/junior)

activity

**INDIVIDUAL WORK
(7.9)**

(a) Draw up a timetable for regular sport or recreational activities lasting at least one month.

(b) Follow that plan.

Personal benefits from participation in regular sport or recreational activity

link

There is more information on this topic in Unit 3: Uniformed Public Service Fitness, pages 69–71.

remember

'Participate in' can mean do the activity, coach the activity or officiate (e.g. by being a referee).

Personal benefits concern your own happiness, health and well-being. They come under three main headings.

Your feelings

The most personal benefits are your own feelings. They might include:

■ your enjoyment of the activity itself

■ a feeling of achievement

■ a feeling of physical fitness and health

■ the pleasure of doing things with other people

■ the pleasure of being praised for doing well

■ the feeling of having done something you didn't think you could do

■ enjoying the movement, using your strength, skill, speed etc.

■ making friends.

Fitness and strength

There may be some measurable improvements in fitness or strength – e.g. 'I can now lift heavier weights than I could two months ago'.

Character and skills

You may also feel that your character has benefited in some way – that, for example, your confidence has increased, or your understanding of other people. You may communicate or organise yourself better.

Figure 7.4

A feeling of achievement

 **activity**

INDIVIDUAL WORK (7.10)

Keep a diary of your own sport and recreation, noting what you have got out of it.

Long- and short-term benefits to the individual of participating regularly in sport or recreational activities

Explanations of how the individual can benefit from three contrasting types of recreation are given in Table 7.5.

activity

GROUP WORK (7.11)

Discuss the benefits of the sport and recreational activities that you do. Note them down under the following headings:

(a) Physical

(b) Emotional

(c) Intellectual

(d) Social.

Compare your findings with those of other people.

Table 7.5 The short- and long-term benefits of three contrasting types of recreation

Activity	Short-term benefits	Long-term benefits	Explanation
Step aerobics (Other social and active recreations and sports have similar benefits to step aerobics)	*About 1 hour* The enjoyment of doing step aerobics with your friends, the pleasure of having a good workout, of feeling tired and knowing you can now have a good rest. *About 2 days* A slight but noticeable increase in fitness. You may feel you can dance better, and that you don't get so out of breath when running for the bus. You might feel your appearance has benefited and you have burned up calories.	*About 6 months* If you do aerobics for, say, 4 months, and then stop taking exercise, your fitness will start to go down. After about 6 months you will be back where you were before you started your step aerobics programme. But you have still benefited for those 6 months. If you continue long term the fitness benefit will last indefinitely, and even get greater. You will have the long-term health benefits mentioned on page 177 above.	Regular physical activity such as step aerobics has short- and long-term effects on the body, making heart, lungs, muscles, digestion, skin, glands and brain all work better. There are added psychological benefits in meeting people and sharing exercise sessions with them. By making friends through a shared enjoyable activity we increase our personal confidence, our communication skills, our knowledge of life and our ability to think.
Hill-walking by yourself (This is an active but non-social activity)	*About 5 hours* Like step aerobics hill-walking is good for aerobic endurance and brings the same fitness and health benefits. *About 2 days* As with aerobics there is a slight but noticeable increase in fitness. Unlike aerobics, which improves dancing skills, hill-walking does not improve any social skills. But many older people in the public services enjoy it because it relieves stress and gives them a rest from being with other people.	Regular hill-walking over months and years brings similar long-term health and fitness benefits as step aerobics. It is very good for both long-term health and fitness. It brings no real social advantages, but it relieves stress. It doesn't build confidence with other people, but it can make you self-reliant because you have to find your way in fog, plan your time, and so on. It has psychological benefits, and can give people time to think and solve problems.	Individuals who like hill-walking may not like step aerobics – and vice versa – because the two activities suit different personalities and age groups. Furthermore, step aerobics is mainly done by women, while solitary hill-walking is mainly done by men. Both activities are very beneficial to people who enjoy them, because they are good for aerobic fitness, relieve stress, and bring mental benefits.
Watercolour painting This is an activity which is not a sport and which, on the whole, is not social. Many hobbies and crafts are like this.	This is not an activity which will improve your aerobic fitness, or your general health. While doing it, and for a few hours afterwards, you may feel pleasure at the activity and the results. The activity is not social, but if other people look at your work they may praise it, and this may give pleasure. Like many 'hobbies' it gives mental stimulation and practice in problem solving.	Over months and years, with increasing practice, some coordination skills will be improved. If you meet other people with the same pastime you will make friends and this may develop social skills. Recreations like watercolour painting are popular with older people in the public services, because they relieve stress. Watercolour painting helps you to appreciate beauty, so it has some 'spiritual' value.	Recreations such as watercolour painting do not demand strength or fitness, and some very good painters have been disabled. This type of recreation demands self-discipline and thought if done to a good standard. It can give peace and tranquillity, which may be good for people with busy, demanding jobs where they work with many other people.

Can sport and recreation be bad for you?

There are many benefits for the individual in doing regular sporting or recreational activity. But a full evaluation should mention possible drawbacks as well.

1. *Risk of injury*. This is the biggest single drawback to active participation in sport and physical recreations. Some of the main types are given below:

   ■ Strains, tears and fractures: these come from sudden movements, collisions etc. The danger is greatest with children and teenagers, who may be permanently damaged if the growth plates of their long bones are damaged

   ■ Hyperthermia and dehydration: these happen if people get overheated and don't take enough fluid while exercising hard. They can kill if not treated quickly

   ■ Hypothermia: the effects of cold, in skiing, swimming, mountaineering etc. This can be fatal

   ■ Hypoglycaemia: low blood sugar following strong exercise (can lead to fainting etc.)

   ■ Amenorrhea: lack of periods in women athletes who overtrain

   ■ Bladder injuries from long-distance running

   ■ Kidney failure following muscle injuries caused by weightlifting

   ■ Infections from swimming baths, or swimming in unclean lakes etc.

   ■ Drowning

   ■ Asthma attacks

   ■ Heart attacks (more common for unfit people taking strenuous exercise).

2. *Harmful recreations*. There are activities described as recreations, such as binge-drinking and the taking of 'recreational' drugs, which are harmful either to a person's health, career prospects or long-term happiness. They bring no advantage to people wishing to work in the public services, other than by increasing the need for police and prison officers.

Sport and diversity

If we look at the different sports, and different track and field events in athletics, we can see that there are ethnic differences in the make-up of teams. There has been concern for some time that there are not enough people of Indian or Pakistani background playing in British football. Over the years there has been a history of racial abuse from some football and other sports fans. It appears that there is still a risk that individuals might be discriminated against if they take part in sport and similar recreations.

Nevertheless, it is generally felt that sport is a force against discrimination, not for it, and great sportspeople become role models not only for their own ethnic groups, but for others too. Individuals of all races benefit from taking part in sport and active recreations because they do so in an environment which is increasingly non-racist. This improvement should continue – especially with the prospect of the Olympic Games in London in 2012.

---

activity
GROUP WORK
(7.12)

(a) Is it possible to get too interested in sports and recreational activities?

(b) What are the financial costs of your sport or recreation?

(c) How much is your own social life linked to sport and recreation?

(d) The other potential drawback of sport and recreational activities is that they can sometimes distract from work or study because they are too interesting or enjoyable. But is this a drawback?

Ask different people what they get out of their regular sporting and recreational activities. Ask them to go into some depth, analysing their own feelings and experiences. It may be useful to take notes so you can quote their exact words.

---

progress check

1. State five ways in which sport and recreational activities can benefit a public service.

2. List five benefits of sport and recreation for people who work in the public services.

3. Outline two main ways in which sport and recreation can benefit health.

4. What are the six main safety aspects to be considered when planning a sports event?

5. If the army takes people rock climbing, what are the army's safety responsibilities, and what are the climber's?

6. What is the difference between planning and organisation?

7. Give five pieces of advice for good sports coaching.

8. What are the three main personal benefits from regular participation in sport?

9. If a person does regular exercise, then stops, how long will it take them to become as unfit as someone who had never exercised in the first place?

10. State five possible health risks of sport.

UNIT 8

Land Navigation by Map and Compass

This unit covers:

- map reading skills
- using a compass
- developing route planning skills whilst considering environmental issues
- safety issues, including how to treat potential medical conditions

And it will get you out of the classroom.

You will use a map and compass, and plan long walks in open country. You will make route cards and work out how long a planned walk will take.

In addition you will learn how to get back to safety if there is an emergency.

Then you will find out how to take care of yourself on mountains and moorland, and how to take care of the environment when you are there. And you will find out what the law says about going on other people's land.

Finally, you will study some basic first aid that could come in useful if you are 'off the beaten track'.

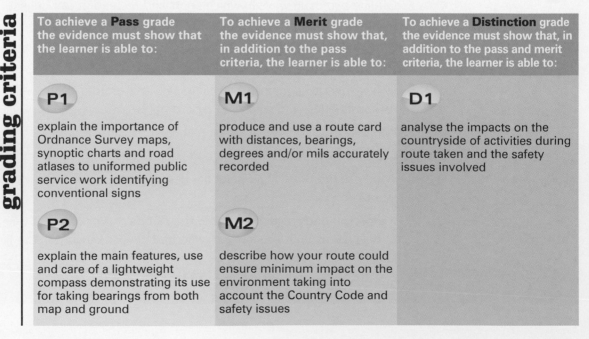

grading criteria

To achieve a **Pass** grade the evidence must show that the learner is able to:	To achieve a **Merit** grade the evidence must show that, in addition to the pass criteria, the learner is able to:	To achieve a **Distinction** grade the evidence must show that, in addition to the pass and merit criteria, the learner is able to:
P1 explain the importance of Ordnance Survey maps, synoptic charts and road atlases to uniformed public service work identifying conventional signs	**M1** produce and use a route card with distances, bearings, degrees and/or mils accurately recorded	**D1** analyse the impacts on the countryside of activities during route taken and the safety issues involved
P2 explain the main features, use and care of a lightweight compass demonstrating its use for taking bearings from both map and ground	**M2** describe how your route could ensure minimum impact on the environment taking into account the Country Code and safety issues	

grading criteria

To achieve a **Pass** grade the evidence must show that the learner is able to:	To achieve a **Merit** grade the evidence must show that, in addition to the pass criteria, the learner is able to:	To achieve a **Distinction** grade the evidence must show that, in addition to the pass and merit criteria, the learner is able to:
P3 explain and demonstrate the use of magnetic bearings and variation and ways of determining direction without a compass	**M3** explain the symptoms of, and how you would treat two, potential medical conditions that may be encountered whilst navigating	
P4 produce and use a route card with a minimum of three legs and an emergency escape route included		
P5 explain safety considerations required for planning and undertaking a route, using route cards		
P6 describe the actions to be taken to minimise the effects of land navigation as protected by laws, regulations and agreements		
P7 explain the safety issues to be taken into consideration		
P8 describe the medical conditions that could occur during an activity and how to deal with them		

Map Reading Skills

keyword

Map
a plan of an area showing the main features of interest and the distances between them.

keyword

Road atlas
a book of maps for drivers.

Ordnance Survey maps, road atlases and synoptic charts

Ordnance Survey **maps** are the basis of all UK maps, whatever forms those maps actually take. Even maps produced by other companies (such as Harvey, and A–Z street maps) use information that comes from the Ordnance Survey.

Ordnance Survey maps have an important role to play in planning, local government and uniformed public service work in the UK (see Case study 8.1).

---

case study
8.1

Ordnance Survey

Ordnance Survey is a vital player in delivering my Office's key objective – to create sustainable communities. These are places in which homes, infrastructure, public services and private enterprise are planned together – so that we promote economic prosperity, as well as cleaner, safer and greener living environments.

Ordnance Survey's products help to create sustainable communities by giving business, communities and the Government the information they need to make key decisions – such as where to site new development and how to protect our countryside and open spaces.

It also plays an important role in the success of cross-Government initiatives such as the Planning Portal and Transport Direct. And, of course, the quality and detail of its maps are appreciated by members of public who want to enjoy Britain, learn about our heritage or simply find their way around.

(*Source*: Ordnance Survey Framework Document 2004 – from the introduction by John Prescott; www.ordnancesurvey.co.uk)

---

activity
GROUP WORK

(a) List all the ways you can think of that maps would be used by the police.

(b) Why do you think the Ordnance Survey is linked to the government?

For many years Ordnance Survey (OS) maps were paper maps – the kinds of maps you will use when doing this unit. But since the 1970s, with computerisation, there has been a revolution in mapmaking. The old maps were made by people walking up and down the whole country using surveying equipment. They were amazingly good, but not perfect. Modern OS maps are made using satellite, radar, computers and digital technology and are 100 per cent accurate.

Importance of Ordnance Survey maps to uniformed public services

Ordnance Survey map information is included in electronic, high-tech GPS and other navigation systems, and it is in this form that Ordnance Survey maps are used by the uniformed public services. Case study 8.2 describes an electronic navigating system used by the Royal Navy.

case study 8.2 — WECDIS

WECDIS is a state-of-the-art system that will provide the Royal Navy and Royal Fleet Auxiliary with electronic charts and information to enhance situational awareness. It will greatly increase navigational accuracy and improve ships' safety.

WECDIS will improve the maritime picture through features that can overlay military data, such as prohibited areas of minefields, beach profiles for amphibious landings and dived navigation facilities for submarines. The technology for each ship will be composed of two operator control stations together with a laptop and remote station for route planning.

(*Source*: www.mod.uk)

activity
GROUP WORK

Contact the armed forces and ask them:

(a) when they normally use digital mapping and

(b) when they normally use paper maps.

keyword

Digital mapping a system of map-making using computers to survey, store, transmit and present the information.

The police, fire and ambulance services also use **digital mapping** technology.

case study 8.3 — Digital technology and mapping

In the Metropolitan Police
Examples of these technologies include in-car computers that provide police officers with the ability to share information with the control room and offer direct access to the national police information database, address databases and electronic mapping. Through a global positioning system (GPS), these computers will also allow control room staff to see the location and availability of all police response vehicles at any time.

(*Source*: www.unisys.co.uk/clients)

In the Fire and Rescue Service (Firelink)
Firelink will provide a number of features essential to the operation of the new RCCs.

Control staff will communicate with appliances over a whole region (and even nationally) from any single RCC. They will be able to send and receive data to and from mobile data terminals. A number of Fire and Rescue Services already use mobile data: Firelink will make this available nationwide. Control staff will be able to see on their screens where resources are in real time at all times, and will be able to send the best resource to deal with the type of incident every time.

(*Source*: Improving Resilience 01 – The FireControl Project ODPM)

activity
GROUP WORK

(a) What are the advantages to the police of having in-car computers?

(b) What are the advantages to the fire and rescue service of having regional control centres (RCCs) instead of local control centres?

The fact that public services use GPS and other systems does not mean that they do not read or see maps. In fire and rescue service control centres, for example, the maps appear on computer screens, so the operatives in control centres still need to know how to read them.

The importance of OS mapping in the work of the uniformed public services is very great – in fact they can't do without it. They use it for planning strategies, exercises and operations.

Though the Ordnance Survey specialises in maps of the UK, it has a wider aim of collecting other geographical information and (through partnerships) mapping other parts of the world which are of importance to the UK, including places where the armed forces operate.

Kinds of map

The Ordnance Survey produces a range of maps, most of which are important to the uniformed public services in one way or another.

Table 8.1 Kinds of map

Type of map	Scale	Importance to uniformed public services
Landplan	1:10,000 (very large-scale)	This is like a street map. It would be useful to the police, fire and ambulance services. It gives detailed information for a small area (e.g. one town).
Explorer	1: 25,000 (large-scale)	This is a walker's map. The army use it for training purposes and in navigation exercises. It gives good information for country areas, and is also very useful to mountain rescue. It would be useful to the Coastguard (for giving detailed information about the shoreline).
Landranger	1: 50,000 (medium-scale)	This is an all-purpose map covering a 25 miles by 25 miles area – i.e. 40km by 40km. It can be used for local motoring or walking, but it gives walkers less information than the Explorer map because the scale is smaller.
Road	1: 250,000 (small-scale)	This small-scale map is good for motoring. It gives a clear picture of all the main roads and features, but misses out small details, footpaths etc. It is useless for walkers. The main use for the public services is to find the way from one town to another, and it could be used by any of the uniformed public services for this purpose.
Route	1: 625,000 (very small-scale)	This map is suitable for long distance and motorway driving. It would be useful for the armed forces, who might be based in the south and want to do exercises in, say, the Scottish Highlands. Main roads are clearly marked, but there are few small details.

Examples of each of these five main kinds of Ordnance Survey map are given below.

Figure 8.1

Landplan map

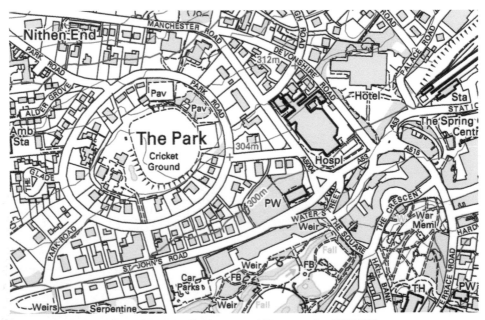

keyword

Scale
the size of a feature on a map, in relation to its real size, expressed as a ratio, e.g. 1:25,000.

Figure 8.2
Explorer map

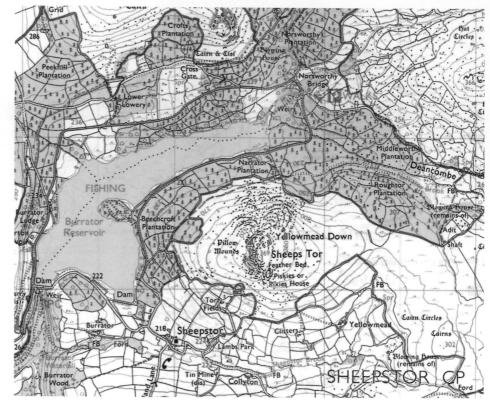

Figure 8.3
Landranger map

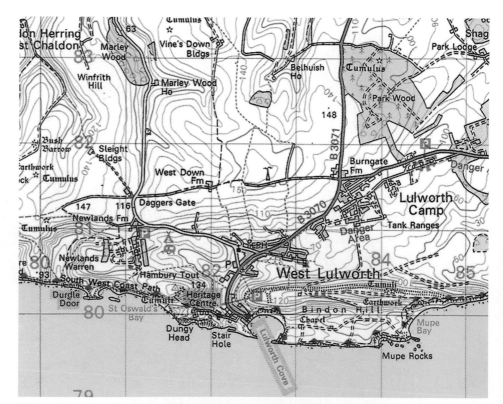

Figure 8.4
OS road map

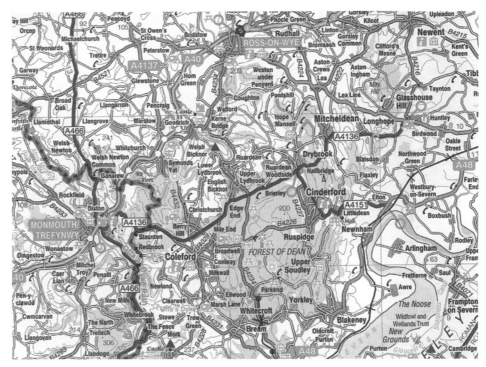

Figure 8.5
Route map

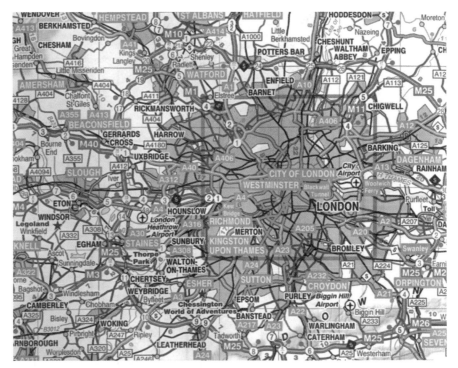

The type of map you are most likely to use for this unit is an Explorer map (1:25,000), though the Landranger can also be used for land navigation by map and compass.

Grid references

Grid references are groups of six figures which are used to identify a position on a map. They are based on the blue squares on your map, and the numbers that run along each side of the map.

Figure 8.6 is a simplified map of a place called Maggie's Farm.

To give a six-figure grid reference for the farm:

1. Read *along* the line numbers from left to right ('eastings') and put down the number of the line to the left of the farm. This is 05.

2. Estimate tenths of the distance across the square from left to right, starting at line 05. These are shown on the bottom of the square in the simplified map. Maggie's Farm is six-tenths of the way across the square, so the next figure in the grid reference is 6.

3. You have now done the first half of your grid reference, and it is 056. Write this down.

4. Read *up* the line numbers from bottom to top ('northings') and put down the number of the line below the farm. This is 17.

Figure 8.6

Maggie's Farm

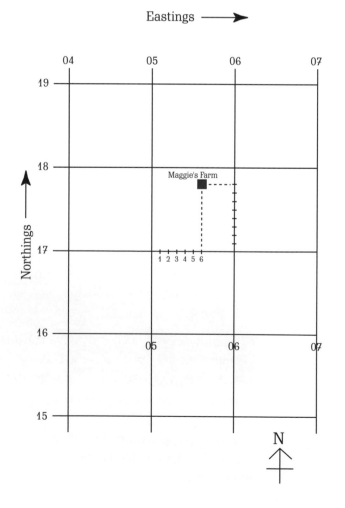

5. Estimate tenths of the distance up the square from bottom to top, starting at line 17. These are shown to the right of the square on the simplified map. Maggie's Farm is eight-tenths of the way up the square, so the next figure in the grid reference is 8.

6. You have now done the second half of your grid reference, and it is 178.

7. Put the two halves of your grid reference together and you have the 6-figure grid reference for Maggie's Farm, which is 056178.

The method is exactly the same whether the OS map is 1:25,000 or 1:50,000.

The squares are 1km in size, so a six-figure grid reference gives the position of the place you have pinpointed to the nearest 100m.

Always read eastings before northings.

remember

Distances

One of the things you will need to do in this unit is to use your map to work out distances.

For this, you need to know the scale of your map. It will be either 1:50,000 or 1:25,000.

1. Distances on the OS 1:50,000 map

This map is covered with blue squares – and the side of each square is 2cm in length. On the ground, this is 1km.

If you put a ruler down between two places on a map, and discover that the distance is 13cm, you know that the real distance on the ground is 6.5km – in a straight line.

2. Distances on the OS 1:25,000 map

The OS 1:25,000 map also has blue squares on, but they are much bigger – 4cm each side. But on the ground these squares are still 1km. If you put a ruler on the map and find that two places are 13cm apart, the real distance on the ground is 3.25km.

Conventional signs

These are small symbols, shapes or signs on a map which have a specific meaning. They are usually listed down the right-hand side of a paper map. It is worth making an effort to learn these – or most of them – because, if you do, it will make map reading much easier.

Different types of map use different conventional signs. In Figure 8.1 above, for example, the yellow oblongs are buildings, and the single thin black lines are fences, hedges or walls. This is a large-scale map where every building is shown.

In Figure 8.5 individual buildings are not shown at all, but the conventional sign for built-up areas is a patch of pale brown. This lack of detail is because the map is a small-scale one.

Figure 8.7 Map signs

52 – Ground survey height
284 – Air survey height

Surface heights are to the nearest metre above mean area level. Heights shown close to a triangulation pillar refer to the ground level height at the pillar and not necessarily at the summit

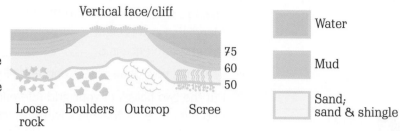

Vertical face/cliff

75
60
50

Loose rock Boulders Outcrop Scree

Water

Mud

Sand; sand & shingle

Synoptic charts

A **synoptic chart** is a weather map. These are of great importance to the army, Royal Navy and RAF. Occasionally they appear on the television weather forecast, but the best place to see them is the Meteorological Office (Met Office) website.

i   www.met-office.gov.uk

Figure 8.8

A synoptic chart/weather map

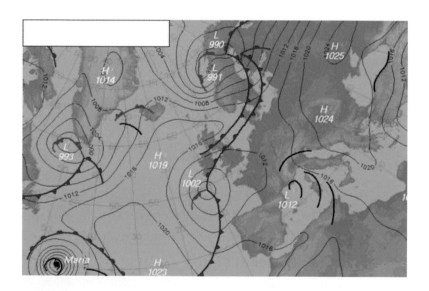

activity
GROUP WORK
(8.1)

(a) With the help of an atlas, locate London, Stockholm, Paris, Marseilles and Athens on this map.

(b) State the wind direction and probable weather at those places at the time and date the map was valid for.

A weather map like this is only valid for a particular time on a particular day. The weather will never be exactly the same again. This one gives information about the weather at midnight between 8 and 9 September 2005.

The thin black lines are called *isobars* and join places which have equal air pressure. Where they are close together the winds are strong, and where they are wide apart the winds are slight or non-existent. The white letters label areas of high and low pressure. The weather is fine and still (but possibly foggy) in areas of high pressure, but windy and wet near areas of low pressure. The wind blows clockwise round areas of high pressure and anticlockwise round areas of low pressure. The direction of the wind roughly follows the isobars, but spirals in slightly towards the centres of areas of low pressure. On the night this synoptic chart refers to, there was a light easterly wind over most of Britain.

The coloured lines with teeth on are called *fronts* and the thick black lines without teeth are called *troughs*.

The fronts are lines of rain and cloud which move in the direction shown by the teeth. They mark the boundary between warm and cold air. Usually there is about 5°C between the two. The red ones with curved teeth are warm fronts, and the blue ones with pointed teeth are cold fronts. Warm fronts bring a period of light rain; cold fronts bring heavier rain, but it does not last as long. Behind a warm front the weather is usually cloudy and mild. Behind a cold front the weather is bright, showery and cool. Fronts bring more rain if they are nearer to the centre of areas of low pressure. The purple fronts, called 'occluded fronts', and the troughs also bring rain, but the air temperature does not change much when they pass.

An active front can bring several hours of heavy rain, especially in places like Scotland, Wales or the Lake District. A weak front may bring no rain at all, just cloud.

The armed forces need to know the weather, since flying conditions, sea conditions, and land conditions all vary with the weather. This applies not only to the UK, but to other countries as well. For example, in Iraq, fronts and troughs may bring thunderstorms or sandstorms, and a southerly wind may bring intense heat, all of which can affect the army's capability.

Nearer to home, periods of dry weather bring grass or woodland fires; heavy snow disrupts traffic; heavy rain can bring floods, and any kind of bad weather is of interest to Coastguard and mountain rescue. Bad weather, and the risks it brings, can be forecast fairly accurately using modern synoptic charts.

activity
GROUP WORK
(8.2)

Produce an exhibition on the subject 'How the Uniformed Public Services Use Maps'. Include a section on 'Useful Symbols'.

Practise reading and using OS maps, weather maps and road maps.
Talk to people in public services about how they use maps.

Using a Compass

A compass is an instrument which shows directions.

Main features

It consists of a balanced steel needle which has been magnetised so that the red end points north and the black end points south. The reason why the needle always points north and south is that the earth itself is a giant magnet.

The needle is contained in a case called a housing. Under the needle is a face or dial on which directions and bearings are marked.

The compass is light and portable.

The most important features are the magnetised needle, the housing, the red arrow under the housing pointing to N, the index line, the direction of travel arrow and the long straight edges.

Describing direction

Cardinal points

The cardinal points are the main directions: North, East, South and West. Then there are intermediate directions: North-east, South-east, South-west and North-west. These can be further divided into directions such as North-north-east or East-north-east.

Describing direction in this way is easy to do, and everybody understands it. But it is not very accurate.

Bearings

The second method is by taking **bearings**. This is the one you will normally use.

If you look at the housing of a compass you will see that it has 360 tiny divisions on it. They are numbered clockwise round the dial, starting at 0 with N, reaching 90 at E, 180 at S and 270 at W. It is these divisions and numbers that you look at when you are using bearings.

Bearings are an accurate and useful way of describing direction. They are always given as three figures, so they should have 0 as the first figure if they are less than 100.

Mils

Mils are a measurement of angles rather like degrees, only even more accurate. They are used mainly by the armed forces for aiming guns and missiles. There are 6400 mils in a full circle. This means there are roughly 17.8 mils to a degree. This kind of angle measurement is much more accurate than the degrees system. Mils are shown only on expensive compasses and are counted, like degrees, in a clockwork direction. Special instruments are needed to read them accurately.

keyword

Bearing
a direction measured in degrees counted clockwise round the face of the compass, from 000 to 359. Degrees are given in three figures.

Figure 8.9

Diagram of a compass face showing all directions

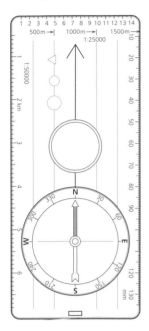

Using the compass

The compass can be used:

- with a map, when planning a route. Here you use the map and compass beforehand to find the direction(s) you want to walk in. These are then written down on your route card (see below). This process is called 'taking compass directions from the map'.

- if you are lost, or want to check directions during a walk. Here you take the compass reading (direction or bearing) of a landmark before checking with your map. This is called 'taking compass directions on the ground'.

- in fog or darkness, to make sure you keep walking in the same direction.

Taking compass directions from the map

This is best done in two stages:

1. 'Setting the map'. You do this so that you know the top of the map is facing north.

   (a) Hold or lay the map flat.

   (b) Turn the compass housing so that N points toward the direction of travel arrow.

   (c) Put the compass on the map.

   (d) Line up the long edge of the compass with a vertical grid line.

   (e) Holding the compass on the map, turn compass and map together, keeping the compass's long edge in line with the vertical grid line, until the magnetic needle points to N in the housing.

   (f) The vertical gridlines, and the top of the map, now point north.

2. 'Taking bearings from the map'.

   (a) First find where you are on the map, and also find the place you wish to go to.

   (b) Set the map so that the vertical gridlines are pointing due north.

   (c) *Without moving the map*, place your compass on the map so that one of the long straight sides passes exactly over where you are now, and where you want to go to, on your map.

   (d) Turn the compass housing until the north (red) end of the magnetic needle and N in the housing meet.

   (e) The bearing showing at the index line is the bearing (direction) you need to travel in.

Taking bearings on the ground

If you want to find the bearing of a landmark (e.g. a hill) that you can see:

(a) Face in that direction.

(b) Hold the compass level in front of your chest, and point the direction of travel arrow towards the landmark.

(c) Turn the compass housing until the north end of the magnetised needle is pointing to N on the housing.

(d) Read the bearing at the index line (the rim of the housing nearest the direction of travel arrow).

Taking bearings in fog

The purpose of this is to make sure you keep walking in the same direction in thick fog.

(a) Hold the compass level, in front of your chest, with the direction of travel arrow pointing the way you are going.

(b) Turn the compass housing until the N in the housing meets the north end of the magnetised needle.

(c) Read the bearing at the index line.

For accurate readings:

(a) Do not take compass readings if the compass is near objects containing iron, steel or nickel as these magnetic metals may affect the direction of the needle.

(b) When using a lightweight compass, give time for the needle to settle properly.

(c) Make sure you have a torch with you, if you are using a compass at night.

(d) If you use a compass outside the UK, check the magnetic variation in the region first. Compass needles do not point north in all parts of the world (see 'magnetic variation' below).

Care of a lightweight compass

(a) Keep it in a safe place – either on a cord round your neck, or in a plastic bag in a rucksack side pocket.

(b) Since it is made of plastic, make sure it does not get knocked or scratched against rocks, walls etc.

(c) Don't shake it violently.

(d) Protect it from heat.

(e) Keep the compass away from magnets (they may affect the magnetism of the needle so that it doesn't work properly).

activity
GROUP WORK
(8.3)

Take part in a training exercise, in open country, using map and compass. You must take bearings from map and ground, explain how the compass works, and show that you can look after it.

Magnetic variation

There are three kinds of north:

1. True north – this is the shortest distance to the North Pole.

2. Grid north – shown by the vertical gridlines on an OS map. It is almost exactly the same as true north.

3. Magnetic north – the direction the compass needle points to. In the UK this is about 4 degrees to the west of true north.

The difference between true north and magnetic north is called magnetic variation.

When we use a compass we get magnetic bearings. To convert these bearings into true bearings we have to follow a rule:

Grid to mag(netic) – ADD (i.e. add 4 degrees to the grid bearing)

Mag to grid – GET RID (i.e. subtract 4 degrees from the magnetic bearing)

NB. These figures only apply to the UK.

This gets a bit more complicated when we are talking about bearings very close to true north. The differences between magnetic bearings and true bearings within a few degrees of true north is shown in Table 8.2.

Table 8.2 Magnetic variation differences

Bearings based on magnetic north (i.e. taken from the compass)	Bearings based on true north (the direction of the North Pole) or grid north (north on the map)
358	354
359	355
000	356
001	357
002	358
003	359
004	000
005	001
006	002

All magnetic bearings are 4 degrees more than bearings based on true north. But note the relationship between magnetic bearings 000–003 and true bearings 356–359.

Determining direction without a compass

There are several ways of determining direction without a compass. Not all of them are accurate.

Using the sun

If you have a watch, and the sun is shining, you should be able to tell the direction using the sun. In British Summer Time the sun is at its highest at about 1.30pm. So at 1.30 it is due south. Six hours before this – i.e. at 7.30am – the sun is due east, and six hours later, at 7.30pm, the sun is due west. The sun moves about 15 degrees every hour, so at 4.30pm in summer it is south west, or at a bearing of 225. In winter, because the clocks change, the sun is at its highest at 12.30pm.

This doesn't work when it's cloudy – or at night.

Using a watch and the sun

If you hold a watch so that the hour hand is pointing towards the sun, and you bisect (halve) the angle between the hour hand and the 12, the line forming the bisection points south.

This does not work with a digital watch.

Using the stars

On a clear night the stars will give you an accurate pointer towards north, at any time of the year. This is because the Pole Star ('Polaris') is always due north. The Pole Star is quite bright and can be found by following the last two stars of an easily recognisable star group, the Great Bear (sometimes called 'The Plough'), as in Figure 8.10.

This does not work south of the Equator.

Figure 8.10

How to find the Pole Star, using the Great Bear as a signpost

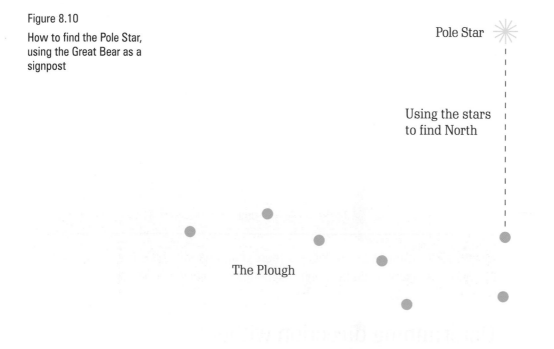

Pole Star

Using the stars to find North

The Plough

Using the wind

If you have watched a weather forecast and know which way the wind is blowing, this can be useful – especially if you can see which way the clouds are moving.

This method is not reliable, because wind directions can change rapidly, especially in bad weather.

Looking at the ground

Experienced walkers can tell directions by looking at grass or snow on the ground. In the UK, mountain and moorland grass is usually beaten down by the west wind, so the stems and blades tend to point eastwards. Snow comes from the north or the east, and drifts usually form on the southern or western sides of stones etc. But when it starts to melt, it melts on the south sides of stones and trees first. Trees often bend towards the east because of the prevailing wind.

This method is dodgy, but it is better than nothing.

Moss and lichen on trees

It is said that trees are greener on the north side, because this side stays damp away from the sun. Unreliable.

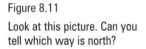

activity
GROUP WORK
(8.4)

Go with a compass to an area of open land and

(a) take bearings of landmarks

(b) look for and note down any features of weather, sun, plants etc. which seem to show the direction.

Figure 8.11

Look at this picture. Can you tell which way is north?

Developing Route Planning Skills Whilst Considering Environmental Issues

When professionals, such as the army, are planning routes in open country, they prepare a route card and leave a copy at their base, in case they need to be rescued. You should do the same.

Route cards

A route card is a piece of paper which outlines, in table form, the route of a walk. It gives all the information which the walkers need, and which rescuers would need if they had to set out, even in darkness and fog, to find them. Here is a specimen route card, followed by explanation. It is based on the extract from the OS 1:25,000 map on page 200.

When you plan a route you need to work out how long it will take, and put times on your route card. This means taking into account the steepness of slopes (going uphill or downhill). You also need to think about terrain (see page 201).

Gradient and contours

Contours are brown lines drawn on a map connecting points of equal height above sea level. They are labelled with the height, with the tops of the figures uphill. A contour labelled '500' is 500m above sea level, and every place on that contour is exactly 500m above sea level. On a 1:25,000 map, contours are usually 10m apart.

If contours are close together the hill is steep. If they are wide apart, it has a gentle **gradient**.

Timing a route card

To work out the times for each leg on your route card you need to know the speed at which your party is likely to walk. Fast walkers on a flat road or path may go as fast as 4 miles an hour (i.e. 6km an hour). But 2 miles an hour (3km per hour) is an average speed for most walkers.

On the specimen route card on page 199, the timing is based on the speed of a party which walks on the flat at 3km an hour.

People walk more slowly when they are going up and down hill (especially uphill). The steeper the hill, the slower they walk. On the specimen card, about half an hour has been added for every 300m rise. Where the hill is less steep, or where the leg is shorter, or where people are walking downhill, the addition to the time is less.

Accurate calculations of timing are difficult because walkers are human and hills vary in steepness.

See Case study 8.4 for further guidelines.

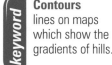

keyword

Contours
lines on maps which show the gradients of hills.

keyword

Gradient
the steepness of a hill.

Figure 8.12 Specimen route card

Route Card Date .... Expedition members ....

Telephone numbers ....

Start + grid reference: Ford, Brockstones 466053. Starting time 9.30 am ....

Leg	To + grid reference	Details of route	Direction and bearing	Distance	Height	Walking time	Rests	Total time	Estimated time of arrival	Escape
1	Overend 464058	Follow walled lane, turn right at Overend	N 350 (6230)	0.5 km	Level	10 mins	none	10	9.40am	Go back same way
2	Ullstone Gill 457071	Wide track follows valley side to where it crosses a big stream	NNW 330 (5874)	1.5	+ 50m	40 mins	10 mins	50	10.30am	Go back same way
3	Smallthwaite Knott 451081	Track climbs long, stony hillside. View of Kentmere Reservoir to left at top	NNW 330 (5874)	1 km	+180m	50 mins	none	50	11.20am	Follow path back
4	Shelter 452096	Track continues rising. Keep high ground on right. Shelter is on a pass between 2 mountains: Harter Fell and Mardale Ill Bell	N 008 (142.4)	1.6 km	+ 150m	1hr 5 mins	10 mins	1hr 15 mins	12.35pm	Go down to Kentmere Reservoir SW – follow stream
5	Mardale Ill Bell 448101	Follow track up steep stony slope to cairn and top of hill. Small Water (lake) down on right	NW 310 (5518)	0.7 km	+ 100m	35 mins	30 mins lunch	1hr 5 mins	13.40pm	Kentmere Reservoir S
6	Posts 433095	Walk west, then south west, to High Street Roman road, keeping steep slope and Kentmere Reservoir down to left	WSW 260 (4628)	1.5 km	No change	45 mins	10	55	14.35pm	Kentmere Reservoir SE
7	438065	Walk south along ridge path over Froswick and Ill Bell, then over Yoke and down hill till path levels out	S 175 (3115)	4 km	+ 170 – 320	2 hrs 25 mins	20	2 hrs 45 mins	17.20pm	Left (east) down steep slopes
8	Tongue House ruins 452069	Turn left and follow stream down into valley past waterfalls and sheepfold. Ford River Kent. Meet track at Tongue House	NE 055 (979)	2.2 km	– 330	1 hr 10 mins	10	1 hr 20 mins	18.40pm	Follow path SE back
9	Overend 464058	Follow track along flat fields, down the valley	SE 170 (3026)	2km	– 10m	40 mins	10	50	19.10pm	Follow path
10	Brockstones 466053	Follow same path we started on.	S 180 (3204)	0.5km	Level	10 mins	10	10	19.20pm	Follow path

NB. (a) A 'leg' is a section of a route. There are therefore 10 legs in this example. (b) Because bearings are accurate they do not correspond exactly to directions. (c) The figures in brackets are mils.

Figure 8.13

Map no. 7, South East Lakeland

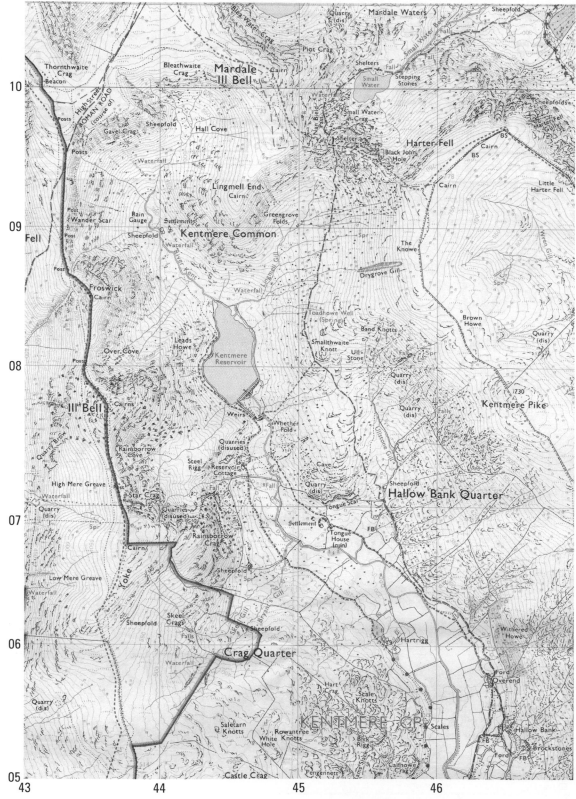

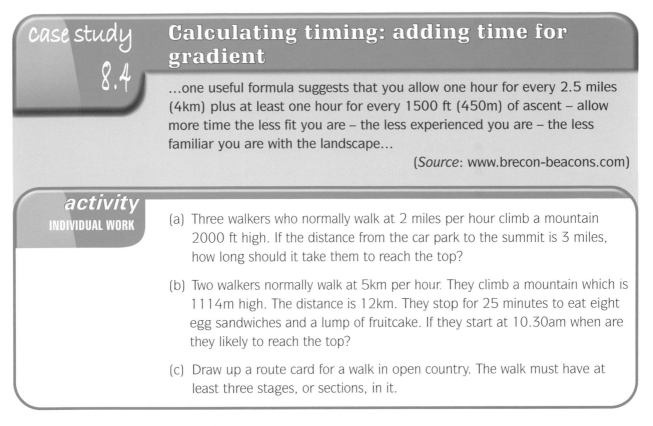

case study 8.4

Calculating timing: adding time for gradient

...one useful formula suggests that you allow one hour for every 2.5 miles (4km) plus at least one hour for every 1500 ft (450m) of ascent – allow more time the less fit you are – the less experienced you are – the less familiar you are with the landscape...

(*Source*: www.brecon-beacons.com)

activity
INDIVIDUAL WORK

(a) Three walkers who normally walk at 2 miles per hour climb a mountain 2000 ft high. If the distance from the car park to the summit is 3 miles, how long should it take them to reach the top?

(b) Two walkers normally walk at 5km per hour. They climb a mountain which is 1114m high. The distance is 12km. They stop for 25 minutes to eat eight egg sandwiches and a lump of fruitcake. If they start at 10.30am when are they likely to reach the top?

(c) Draw up a route card for a walk in open country. The walk must have at least three stages, or sections, in it.

Terrain

remember

A route card must include accurate details of the distances and bearings (in 'degrees and mils').

Terrain is the nature of the ground. It can be rough, smooth, stony, wooded, rocky, steep, uneven, boggy or snow-covered. (Many of these are marked with conventional signs on the OS 1:25,000 'Explorer' maps.) It is easier and quicker walking over smooth, flat, firm terrain than over rocky, boggy or snowy terrain. If the terrain looks difficult, add about 10 minutes per kilometre to the planned times on your route card.

activity
GROUP WORK
(8.5)

Convert the bearings in degrees which you have worked out for your route card into bearings in mils.

Limiting environmental damage

Visit most parts of upland Britain – especially places such as the Lake District and Snowdonia – and you will see the environmental damage caused by hill walkers.

Land navigation involves walking and can therefore:

■ damage vegetation

■ enlarge footpaths until they become eyesores and erode the soil

■ cause the dropping of litter

■ disturb the habitats of wild animals, birds and plants

■ pollute water.

This damage can be limited by:

■ the walkers themselves

■ landowners and private citizens such as farmers

■ local government and statutory authorities such as national parks

■ the government, when it passes laws which affect access to and use of the countryside.

The walkers

Walkers should follow a set of rules called 'the Countryside Code'. Many of these rules are now law (see Case Study 8.6).

Landowners and farmers

Landowners and farmers sometimes try to minimise the effects of land navigation by stopping people from going onto their land. They might do this by:

---

case study
8.5

Countryside Code

Enjoy the countryside and respect its life and work

Guard against all risk of fire

Fasten all gates

Keep your dogs under close control

Keep to public paths across farmland

Use gates and stiles to cross fences, hedges and walls

Leave livestock, crops and machinery alone

Take your litter home

Help keep all water clean

Protect wildlife, plants and trees

Take special care on country roads

Make no unnecessary noise

activity
GROUP WORK   Examine each rule in turn, and explain why it is necessary.

- closing footpaths or allowing them to become overgrown
- putting up notices telling people to keep off
- strengthening fences and walls
- closing the land temporarily for things such as shooting or lambing
- putting dangerous animals such as bulls in fields where a public footpath goes.

Some of these are illegal. If footpaths are designated as a 'right of way' it means that the public have a legal right to walk along them. Farmers are breaking the law if they close a right of way without good reason.

Strengthening fences and walls and prohibiting access at certain times of the year, for reasonable purposes, are both legal. But putting bulls near public footpaths is not.

case study 8.6 — Access laws

The chief law dealing with access to the open countryside is The Countryside and Rights of Way (CRoW) Act 2000. Here are the main points:

The Countryside and Rights of Way (CRoW) Act creates a new legal right of access on foot to areas of open, uncultivated countryside allowing walkers to explore away from paths on approximately four million acres of mountain, moor, heath, down, and common land in England and Wales. It includes safeguards to protect the environment and landowners' interests and will NOT allow people to walk through private gardens or over crops.

...

The new right of access is restricted in several ways. For instance, it does not allow walkers to drop litter, light fires, cause damage to plant or animal life and bathe in non-tidal water. It does not allow camping and organised games. The Act does not distinguish between access during the day and at night, although local restrictions could affect access at night. Walkers are responsible for their own safety at all times. Anyone breaking a restriction will be treated as a trespasser and barred from entering the land for the next 72 hours. The Act does not confer additional rights for cyclists or horse-riders but existing rights are not affected.

...

The Act allows land to be closed for nature or heritage conservation. It also includes measures to protect Sites of Special Scientific Interest and Areas of Outstanding Natural Beauty.

...

The new access arrangements will not restrict the way the land is used as long as landowners do not endanger, obstruct, or discourage visitors. Landowners may close or restrict access to their land for up to 28 days per year (including some Saturdays and Sundays) for any reason. Landowners may apply to the countryside bodies for further closures or restrictions for reasons of land management, fire risk or danger to the public.

(*Source*: The Ramblers Association)

activity
GROUP WORK

(a) Why does the law prohibit camping, and bathing in rivers and streams?

(b) How many reasons can you think of for a farmer to prohibit access to land?

Government and authorities

Local and national government, and the National Park Authorities which run national parks can minimise the effects of land navigation by controlling access to open countryside.

Areas of land where people have a 'right to roam' as designated under CRoW are now shown on Ordnance Survey 'Explorer' maps (1:25,000).

Other action taken to minimise the effects of land navigation

Besides laws and bye-laws (small local laws), national parks and 'countryside bodies' (the Countryside Agency; the Countryside Council for Wales) and other organisations such as National Park Authorities and the Forestry Commission, can take action to minimise the effects of land navigation. The Lake District National Park has experimented with closing car parks, or making them smaller, to reduce the number of visitors to some upland areas. Many national park authorities have built strengthened footpaths over peat bogs and other fragile areas to protect them from erosion caused by too many walkers.

activity
GROUP WORK
(8.6)

Produce a poster showing what walkers can do to limit the environmental damage they cause, and what they should know about walking on private land.

Talk to a farmer or landowner, if you can.
Talk to an experienced walker.
Visit these websites:
www.defra.gov.uk
www.countryside.gov.uk
www.ramblers.org.uk
www.brecon-beacons.com

Route planning to limit environmental damage

Farmland

The Country Code says 'Keep to public paths across farmland'. Farmland is land enclosed either for growing crops or for keeping animals on specially planted grass. On the Explorer maps, farmland is left white, without any conventional signs indicating the type of vegetation.

Figure 8.14

Conventional signs on Explorer maps – vegetation

🌲🌲🌲	Coniferous trees	〰️	Scrub	° ° ° ° °	Orchard
🌳🌳🌳	Non-coniferous trees	〰️〰️	Bracken, heath or rough grassland		
🌾🌾	Coppice	〰️〰️	Marsh, reeds or saltings		

If you keep to footpaths and bridle paths (i.e. narrow lanes) while going through farmland you will not damage crops or frighten animals (provided you move quietly). These paths are marked on the Explorer maps and can be mentioned on your route card. Gates should always be shut by walkers once they have been through them. Where a path appears to cross a fence or wall, there should be a gate or stile.

Open land

Open land is not farmland, even though it is often grazed by sheep and cattle. On the Explorer maps open land is marked with groups of small grey-green lines indicating 'bracken, heath or rough grassland'.

When you are on open land you will cause less damage to the environment by keeping on paths. If your planned route leaves the paths, take care not to leave litter, trample on wild flowers or frighten sheep.

www.countrysideaccess.gov.uk

activity
**INDIVIDUAL WORK
(8.7)**

As if you were talking to a national park ranger, explain how your route card demonstrates that you have done as much as you reasonably can to choose a route which will not damage the environment.

Safety Issues, Including How to Treat Potential Medical Conditions

Safety must always be considered when navigating in open country. Figure 8.15 outlines the main things you need to think about.

List all the things that could go wrong on a walk up a mountain in Britain in summer.

Below is an explanation of some of the main safety issues shown in Figure 8.15.

1. *Distance and terrain*. When planning a route you may want one which is difficult and challenging. But be aware of the risks. Don't plan a route which is too long and difficult for your party. Plan it so that you won't get lost, especially in fog or bad weather. Dangerous terrain includes:

   - *Steep slopes*. Avoid these unless you have good walking boots. Don't run down them – you could break an ankle, or run over a cliff. Don't try to climb them too fast – it can be exhausting. Don't dislodge stones – people may be below you – and watch out for stones coming down from above.

   - *Cliffs*. Keep away from the tops of cliffs – the ground may be loose, and the wind could blow you off.

   - *Screes*. These are steep slopes covered with stones. They are unsafe for inexperienced walkers.

   - *Soft peat or floating bogs*. People have got stuck in them.

2. *The weather*. Always check the weather forecast before you set off. Always expect the weather to be worse than it looks. Rain, wind and snow can be dangerous. They make the ground slippery underfoot, and it is easy to get cold and tired in bad weather. If the weather is bad, don't go up a mountain at all unless you are fit, experienced and well equipped. If you do go out in bad weather you need waterproof, warm clothing, good boots, and a **contingency plan** in case the weather gets even worse.

3. *The team*. Any group of walkers must know their own capabilities – and those of everybody else in the group. It is best to walk with people who have the same level of fitness and motivation as yourself. Groups of three or more are safer: if someone is injured one person can stay with them, and the other can go for help. Normally *a group should never split up*.

4. *Time of year*. In winter the days are short and the weather is worse. Most accidents happen in winter. Special care is needed in planning, so that you don't have to stay out after dark. In summer, take sun-block and something to drink.

5. *Equipment*. The basic needs are walking boots, warm clothes, a waterproof anorak, a woolly hat, good socks, a spare pullover in your rucksack, waterproof leggings if it is wet or snowy, a rucksack, first aid, map, compass, torch and whistle. Get advice from tutors or organisers.

6. *Food and drink*. A good packed lunch with sandwiches and (say) chocolate will do. Fruit is refreshing but heavy. Take something to drink unless you are sure you can drink from streams (some are polluted, so don't take risks). Never take alcohol.

keyword

Contingency plan
a way of getting to safety.

Figure 8.15 Safety considerations for route planning

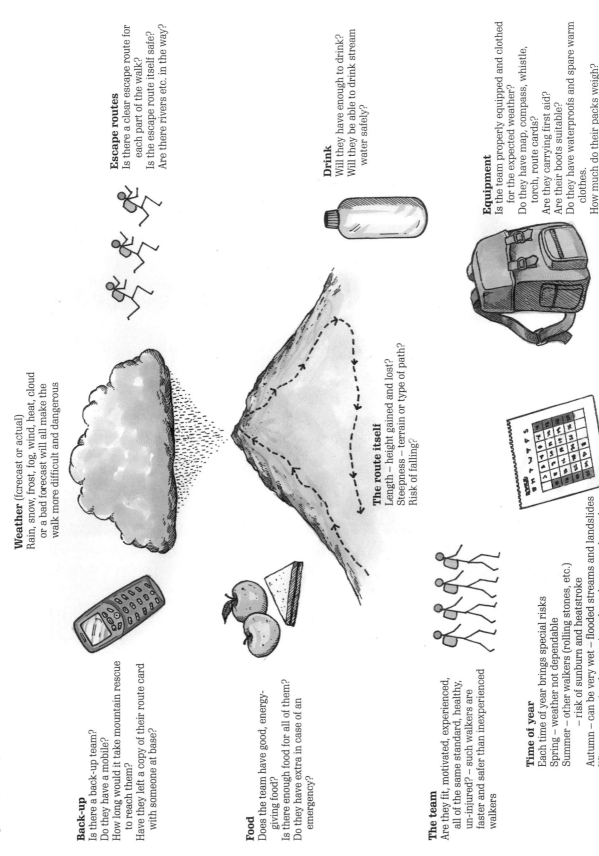

Weather (forecast or actual)
Rain, snow, frost, fog, wind, heat, cloud or a bad forecast will all make the walk more difficult and dangerous

Escape routes
Is there a clear escape route for each part of the walk?
Is the escape route itself safe?
Are there rivers etc. in the way?

Drink
Will they have enough to drink?
Will they be able to drink stream water safely?

Equipment
Is the team properly equipped and clothed for the expected weather?
Do they have map, compass, whistle, torch, route cards?
Are they carrying first aid?
Are their boots suitable?
Do they have waterproofs and spare warm clothes.
How much do their packs weigh?

The route itself
Length – height gained and lost?
Steepness – terrain or type of path?
Risk of falling?

Back-up
Is there a back-up team?
Do they have a mobile?
How long would it take mountain rescue to reach them?
Have they left a copy of their route card with someone at base?

Food
Does the team have good, energy-giving food?
Is there enough food for all of them?
Do they have extra in case of an emergency?

The team
Are they fit, motivated, experienced, all of the same standard, healthy, un-injured? – such walkers are faster and safer than inexperienced walkers

Time of year
Each time of year brings special risks
Spring – weather not dependable
Summer – other walkers (rolling stones, etc.) – risk of sunburn and heatstroke
Autumn – can be very wet – flooded streams and landslides
Winter – snow, ice, heavy rain – short days are a hazard

Figure 8.16

British mountains can be tough

7. *Contingency plans*. Plan an escape route and make it as easy as possible. Leave a route card or message at base so that people will know where to search for you, if you don't turn up at the end of the day.

8. *Back-up*. If you are late and have a mobile, ring your back-up team (instructors or whatever). If you are in trouble, ring 999 (police). If you haven't got a phone, and are trapped out at night, huddle together in the warmest possible place and blow a whistle (or flash a torch if the weather is clear) about six times a minute. Only split up if someone is badly injured and you have to get help.

activity
**GROUP WORK
(8.9)**

Using your route card, draw up contingency plans saying what you would do if:

(a) one of your party broke a leg

(b) one of your party was suddenly taken ill

(c) a violent thunderstorm broke out

(d) you were lost in thick fog

(e) you were caught out after dark.

Simple first aid for walkers

Outdoor navigation is not the most dangerous activity in the world, but there are risks. You should know what they are, and you should be able to carry out certain types of first aid. Common problems and simple treatments are given below.

case study 8.7 — Advice from the Mountaineering Council of Scotland

If one of your party has an accident and cannot be moved:

- treat any injuries as best you can

- calculate your exact position on the map

- if possible, leave somebody to care for the casualty whilst others descend with a map to get help

- on reaching a telephone, dial 999 and ask for the police

- report the map grid reference where you left the casualty and details of the casualty's condition.

(*Source*: www.mountaineering-scotland.org.uk)

activity — INDIVIDUAL WORK

Using the internet, research mountaineering accidents which have happened in the UK, and note down the cause of each accident.

Blisters

As soon as you feel a blister coming, take off your boot and socks and put a sticky plaster over it.

Grazes

Wash the graze in clean water. Dry the graze and put a clean dressing over it.

Ticks

Check for these after your walk if you have been out in thick vegetation in summer. They can get onto any part of the body. Pull them out with tweezers. Although they normally have no long-lasting effects they can carry a serious illness called Lyme's disease. If you get a skin rash and feel tired, and have swollen lymph nodes, flu-like symptoms (headache, muscle and joint pain) within a month of being bitten, *see a doctor*. The illness will be cured if it is treated, but can lead to serious problems if it isn't.

Sunstroke (mild)

Get into a shady place, rest, and have cool drinks.

activity — GROUP WORK (8.10)

(a) Discuss what should go in a first aid pack for walkers – then show your ideas to your tutor.

(b) Produce a wall chart suitable for an outdoor centre showing injuries or illnesses that can happen in open country and what to do about them.

Ask an expert walker about mountain first aid.

Look in the library for books on hill-walking.

Check out websites on mountain first aid:

www.bcadventure.com

www.yhagroup.org.uk

More serious problems

Young people are unlikely to become seriously ill when navigating on land. The main life-threatening risks are probably falls, being hit by falling stones, drowning and hypothermia.

Older people are most likely to die of heart attacks.

A few serious conditions are outlined below. If anybody seems seriously ill or injured call the emergency services using 999 (or 112).

Hypothermia (extreme cold)

Get the sufferer out of the wind. Replace wet clothes with dry clothes. Give warm drinks. Don't let the sufferer lose consciousness. Call 999 if it looks serious.

If someone has stopped breathing

Place the patient on his/her back and follow these steps:

1. To open the airway lift the patient's neck and tilt the head back.

2. Keeping the neck elevated, pinch the nostrils to prevent air leakage.

3. Place your mouth completely around the victim's mouth and blow, watching for chest expansion.

4. After removing your mouth, listen for air leaving the patient's lungs and watch for the chest to fall. Check for an airway blockage if the chest does not rise.

Repeat these steps approximately 12 to 15 times per minute.

Get help!

Shock

Treat bleeding, raise legs, lower head, loosen clothing, insulate from cold, check pulse and breathing, get help. Do not move patient or give food and drink.

Spinal injuries

Do not move patient, get help immediately.

Fractures

Do not move patient until the broken part is secured and immobilised (splint, sling), dial 999. Do not give food or drink.

Hyperthermia

case study 8.8

Hyperthermia is a result of the body being overheated due to increased air temperature, solar or reflected radiation, poorly ventilated clothing, a low fitness level or excess bulk.

Symptoms include:

1. Heat cramps may occur and should be treated by moving the victim to a shady area and supplying water and salt tablets.

2. Heat exhaustion is a mild form of hyperthermia and includes symptoms such as headache, dizziness, fainting, clammy skin, blurred vision, nausea and vomiting. Treatment is the same as heat cramps.

3. Heat stroke is the most serious degree of hyperthermia. The victim will have little or no perspiration, a hot and flushed face, full pulse, and become either apathetic or aggressive. Cool the victim as quickly as possible paying extra attention to the head, neck and chest. If the body's temperature continues to rise, unconsciousness, delirium, convulsions and ultimately death may occur.

To avoid hyperthermia, avoid strenuous activity on hot days, wear loose clothing and a hat, drink plenty of fluids and take salt tablets.

(*Source*: www.bcadventure.com)

activity
INDIVIDUAL WORK

Give a short presentation, suitable for a cadet group, about the symptoms and treatment for two medical problems/injuries that walkers can suffer from.

Find a first-aider who will explain the first aid problems that can happen on mountains or hills.

Ask the St John's Ambulance or Red Cross to give advice.

Find books on first aid which deal with the subject.

Scottish Sports Council and the Scottish Mountain Safety Group, *Enjoy the Scottish Hills in Safety*. Copies of the leaflet may be obtained from the Mountaineering Council of Scotland, The Old Granary, West Mill Street, Perth, PH1 5QP or www.mountaineering-scotland.org.uk

Steve Bollen, *First Aid on Mountains*, London: British Mountaineering Council, 1990; 3rd edn, 1998.

Peter Steele, *Medical Handbook for Walkers and Climbers*, London: Constable, 1999.

www.scoutbase.org.uk

www.mountaineering-scotland.org.uk

www.thebmc.co.uk

progress check

1. What are the two main kinds of OS map used for land navigation in the UK?

2. How do you work out a grid reference for a point on a map?

3. What is a weather front?

4. What do isobars tell us about wind speed and direction?

5. How do you set a map?

6. How do you take bearings from a map?

7. How do you take bearings from the ground?

8. What is the present figure for magnetic variation?

9. List five ways in which walkers can damage the environment.

10. What are the main dangers for people navigating in open country in the UK?

Law and its Impact on the Individual

This unit covers:

- communities' consensus of opinion on what is acceptable behaviour and how criminal law has evolved
- the powers given and the points to prove to support a successful prosecution
- the codes of practice set out by the Police and Criminal Evidence Act 1984 and subsequent amendments which apply to the rights of offenders throughout the judicial process
- the role of the prosecution, the defence and the courts

The police, the prison service and the probation service are all part of the criminal justice system, working to put the rule of law into practice. But all public service employees should be good citizens, and one of the rules of good citizenship is upholding the law.

This unit will introduce you to some of the main points of English criminal law. You will begin with common law, which deals with crimes such as murder, robbery and rape. And you will discover how legal decisions in the past affect the cases of today.

Then you will study the powers of the police when dealing with suspects, and the rights of suspects when being questioned, or charged with a crime. You will find out what happens to suspects after they have been charged.

Finally, you will examine the legal system in the criminal courts, and the roles of the different people who work in them.

To achieve a **Pass** grade the evidence must show that the learner is able to:	To achieve a **Merit** grade the evidence must show that, in addition to the pass criteria, the learner is able to:	To achieve a **Distinction** grade the evidence must show that, in addition to the pass and merit criteria, the learner is able to:
P1 describe how common law has evolved from community norms and customs to present-day legislation	**M1** analyse the powers available to police dealing with a suspect	**D1** justify the use of police powers when dealing with suspects

grading criteria

To achieve a **Pass** grade the evidence must show that the learner is able to:	To achieve a **Merit** grade the evidence must show that, in addition to the pass criteria, the learner is able to:	To achieve a **Distinction** grade the evidence must show that, in addition to the pass and merit criteria, the learner is able to:
P2 explain how decided cases and stated cases may give direction to current cases being tried in court	**M2** explain when bail can be refused after charge for both adult and juvenile offenders	
P3 explain the powers available to the police to deal with suspects	**M3** describe the process of disclosure and the role of the disclosure officer using a case study to produce the necessary documentation	
P4 research a selected piece of legislation and identify the points to prove beyond all reasonable doubt		
P5 describe the rights afforded to a person held in police custody before and after charge		
P6 explain the role of the Crown Prosecution Service, the Defence and the Courts		

Communities' Consensus of Opinion on What Is Acceptable Behaviour and How Criminal Law Has Evolved

A short history of common law

Before 1066 Britain was mainly inhabited by Anglo-Saxons, and the **laws** they operated were basically village customs, and differed from place to place.

> **keyword**
>
> **A law**
> a rule which can be enforced by the courts.

In 1066 Britain was invaded by William the Conqueror and started to become a united country. William the Conqueror's people, the Normans, set up feudal courts run by local barons (big landowners), and these started to develop a system of laws which was the same for most of England and Wales. This system came to be called **common law**. To try to make **the law** fairer and more reliable they used a system of 'precedents' which is one of the main features of common law. What this means is that, when a case comes to court, the judge looks for other cases similar to it which have been heard before. The case is then decided in the same way as those earlier, similar cases.

After about 1400, a new aspect of common law called 'equity' was developed. 'Equity', which means 'fairness', still exists. It is linked to common law, but it is concerned less with following the exact letter of the law and more with doing what is fair to people, or is 'in the public interest'.

The case below shows the difference between common law and equity.

Miller v *Jackson* [1977] QB 966

The facts: The plaintiffs owned a house by a cricket ground. Cricket had been played on the ground long before the house had been built. The plaintiffs complained of damage caused by cricket balls and loss of enjoyment of their property. They took the cricket club to court seeking damages (based on common law) and an injunction (based on equity) to stop cricket being played on the ground. The cricket club argued that it had done everything possible to prevent balls coming into the plaintiff's garden, including putting up a 15-foot high fence.

Lord Denning was the judge on this case. He decided that the cricket club had to pay the plaintiffs some money because of the annoyance they had caused. (This is in line with common law.) But Lord Denning refused to stop people playing cricket on the ground altogether – since it had been going on for 70 years and cricket was a part of local community life. (This judgment is based on equity.)

Statute law

Statute law can only be made by Parliament. The first English Parliament passed the Magna Carta in 1215 – a set of laws designed to limit the power of King John's followers. Laws were passed controlling fines, land usage, legacies, measures of corn and wine, rents, witnesses at trials and freedom of travel for traders.

In the 1600s Parliament became much more important and by the Act of Settlement 1701 it took over most real power from the monarchy. From then on all new laws were statute laws. However, statute laws have always relied to some extent on the ideas of common law. Even laws such as the Data Protection Act 1998 are designed to protect privacy, an idea which was important in common law as well.

keyword

Common law
old laws on basic crimes like murder, robbery, rape etc. based on old traditions.

keyword

The law
a system of rules which can be enforced by the courts.

keyword

Statute law
written laws made by Parliament, e.g. the Road Traffic Act 1988.

 link

There is more on the courts and the legal system on pages 236–40.

activity
**INDIVIDUAL WORK
(9.1)**
Produce a flow chart showing the main dates and stages in the development of the English legal system, and explaining in simple terms how common law changed into the present system.

The Powers Given and the Points to Prove to Support a Successful Prosecution

What is a case?

A case is a situation in which a disagreement or accusations of wrongdoing are settled through the law, in front of a judge (or magistrates). The judge or magistrates make sure the arguments follow the rules, and *may* decide who is right and who is wrong – in other words, make a judgment.

In criminal courts the Crown (i.e. the state) brings the prosecution (using police evidence and the Crown Prosecution Service). Criminal cases are named (for example) *R* v *Grant* [2005] where R stands for 'Regina' (the Queen) and Grant is the accused person; v means 'versus' (against) and 2005 is the year.

In a civil court where an ordinary citizen (or company or other organisation) has brought the case against another ordinary citizen, company or organisation, cases are named after the parties (people) who are in disagreement, e.g. *D&C Builders* v *Smith* [1965]. (This was a case where a man called Smith had failed to pay some builders for some work they had done. D&C Builders therefore brought the case against Mr Smith so that they could get the money that Mr Smith owed them.)

When cases are named like this the person or persons coming after the 'v' are the ones accused of doing wrong – whether the case is in a criminal or a civil court.

Decided cases

Decided cases are cases which have gone before a judge and in which a decision has been reached. They can be used as precedent (something which has gone before) to decide a second case.

Imagine there are two cases, A (in 1977) and B (in 2006). Imagine that they are both about cricket balls falling into people's gardens. The judge hearing Case B might well use Case A to help him reach a decision. The same principle is true of any other kind of case, civil or criminal, where there is a precedent (an earlier example of the same kind of case).

The importance of decided cases is that they help to keep the law fair and consistent. It is important that an offender who is tried in, say, Newcastle, gets the same judgment that another person who committed exactly the same crime would get if they were tried in Exeter.

Stated cases

The law is not always right. Sometimes courts can come to the wrong decision, and it may be that an innocent person is put in prison, or has to pay compensation when in fact they did nothing wrong.

Where a mistake is believed to have been made, the person who has been wronged can (through lawyers) lodge an appeal. An appeal is a request to a higher court to overturn (change) the decision of a lower court.

Appeals can be based on two grounds:

1. New evidence, which shows that the original decision was made in ignorance of some of the facts.

2. Legal arguments showing that the law was misinterpreted, misunderstood or wrongly applied in the lower court.

In cases of type (2) a stated case can be used.

A stated case consists of:

(a) A statement of the *facts* of the case which is going to appeal. These facts must be agreed by both sides of the case (i.e. both the plaintiff and the defendant, or the prosecution and the defence, depending on whether the case involves civil or criminal law).

(b) A statement of the *legal reasons* why the case should be reconsidered.

The value of having stated cases is that they enable appeals to go ahead, and wrong decisions to be overturned. This is good for the court system (since it helps it to keep a reputation for fairness) and good for the wrongly accused person (who perhaps should never have been punished in the first place).

activity
**GROUP WORK
(9.2)**

Invite a solicitor to talk to you about decided cases and stated cases, and how they are used.

The Codes of Practice Set Out by the Police and Criminal Evidence Act 1984 and Subsequent Amendments which Apply to the Rights of Offenders Throughout the Judicial Process

Police powers are given in the Codes of Practice for the Police and Criminal Evidence Act 1984 (PACE). These Codes of Practice give full instructions on how the police must go about collecting evidence of crimes. From time to time they are updated, so check that you are using the latest edition.

As the Codes of Practice are over 70,000 words long, you will need to pick out the main points.

There are seven Codes of Practice. A new edition is coming out at the end of 2005. Information in this book is based on the draft versions of these new codes (so you may find slight alterations have been made).

The seven PACE codes of practice (and subjects covered) are:

A Stop and search

B Searching premises

C Detention, treatment and questioning

D Identification of persons

E Audio recording of suspects

F Video recording of suspects

G Statutory power of arrest

Summary of police powers – Police and Criminal Evidence Act 1984

Code A – Code of Practice for the exercise by police officers of statutory powers to stop and search

1. *Main principles*. Police have the power to stop and search if:

   ■ people are suspected of carrying stolen goods or dangerous weapons

   ■ there is a risk of violence

   ■ their premises are also being searched.

   There must be 'reasonable suspicion'.

2. *Explanation of powers*, e.g. Police can remove face disguises.

3. *Conduct of search*. Searches must be courteous and take no longer than necessary.

   ■ Outer clothing. Police can require a person to remove an outer coat, jacket or gloves.

   ■ Intimate searches. Can be done at a nearby police station.

   What the officer tells the suspect:

   ■ that they are being detained for the purposes of a search

   ■ the officer's name and police station

   ■ the legal search power, e.g. under section 139B of the Criminal Justice Act 1988

   ■ what they are looking for

   ■ the grounds for suspicion.

4. *Record of search* – must be written down. Vehicles can be searched.

5. *Monitoring and supervision*. Supervising officers must monitor the use of stop and search powers.

NB. Stop and search must not be done in a discriminatory way – e.g. picking on people of a particular colour, dress or appearance. 'The Race Relations (Amendment) Act 2000 makes it unlawful for police officers to discriminate on the grounds of race, colour, ethnic origin, nationality or national origins when using their powers.'

Code B – Code of Practice for searches of premises by police officers and the seizure of property found by police officers on persons or premises

1. *Introduction*

2. *General*. Searches of premises can be done to find:

   - property and material relating to a crime

   - wanted persons

   - children who abscond from local authority accommodation where they have been sent by a court.

3. *Search warrants and production orders*. Warrants should normally be used. They are issued by a magistrate or a judge. The warrant should state:

   - the premises to be searched

   - the object of the search

   - the grounds for the search.

4. *Searches without warrants*. Police can search to make an arrest and they can apply for a search warrant after making the search.

   Manner of search:

   - Officers must be polite and only use reasonable force.

   - The premises must be secured afterwards if the occupier is not there, and the occupier must be given a written notice saying what has been taken.

   Authorisation for searches must come from an officer of the rank of inspector or above.

   Effect on the local community. If it is thought that a search might have a bad effect on relations between the police and the community, the officer in charge must consult the local police/community liaison officer.

   Search record. There must be a written search record.

5. *Searching with consent*. Caution – the person concerned must be clearly informed that they are not obliged to consent and that anything seized may be produced in evidence

6. *Searching premises – general considerations*

   Timing of search:

   - Searches with a warrant must be made within three months of the warrant's issue.

   - Searches must be made at a reasonable hour 'unless this might frustrate the purpose of the search'.

   Multiple entry – the police have powers to enter the same premises several times, for a big search.

   Reasonable force may be used.

   Compensation can be paid for damage if premises were searched by mistake etc.

7. *Seizure and retention of property*. Any property can be seized and kept if it is evidence of an offence. Premises may be searched only to find the object of the search.

8. *Action after search*.

    Return of property – people whose property has been taken in a police search can apply to a court to get it back. Stolen property may be returned to its owner.

    Search Register – a book containing records of searches must be kept at each sub-divisional police station.

Code C – Code of Practice for the detention, treatment and questioning of persons by police officers

1. *General*.

    Length of time in police detention – no longer than needed.

    Protection of vulnerable or young people – an appropriate adult must be present for juvenile/mentally vulnerable suspects.

2. *Custody records*. The Custody Officer (who is not connected with the case)

    - is in charge of looking after detained people
    - must ensure that detainees are correctly treated
    - must keep a written custody record.

3. *Initial action*.

    Rights of detained people. Detained people must be told their rights – i.e.

    - to have someone told of their arrest
    - to consult privately with a solicitor
    - to have free independent legal advice on request.

    Health. The Custody Officer must find out if detained persons need a health check or medical treatment. Risk assessments must be done to find out whether people detained might harm themselves or others. Police can call doctors to examine suspects.

    Language. Interpreters must be provided if necessary.

4. *Detainees' property*. The Custody Officer must check and keep the property of the detained person.

5. *Right not to be held incommunicado*. Detained people have *some* right to communicate with the outside world.

6. *Right to legal advice*. Detainees have the right to see their solicitor, or to have a solicitor free of charge.

7. *Commonwealth or foreign nationals*. They have a right to communicate with their high commission, embassy or consulate. BUT 'if the detainee is a political refugee whether for reasons of race, nationality, political opinion or religion, or is seeking political asylum, consular officers shall not be informed of the arrest of one of their nationals or given access or information about them except at the detainee's express request.'

8. *Conditions of detention*.

   Number of detainees per cell. 'So far as it is practicable' – one in each cell.

   Conditions of cells. Cells must be adequately heated, cleaned and ventilated. They must also be adequately lit, with lights that can be dimmed.

   Meals. Two light meals and one main meal must be provided in any 24-hour period. Drinks must be provided at meal times and 'upon reasonable request'.

9. *Care and treatment of detained people*. They must be medically checked. If drunk or drugged they must be roused every half hour. The Custody Officer must arrange medical attention if the person:

   ■ appears to be suffering from physical illness

   ■ is injured

   ■ appears to be suffering from a mental disorder

   ■ appears to need clinical attention.

   Records must be kept of health problems, minor injuries etc.

10. *Cautions*. The wording for suspects is: 'You do not have to say anything. But it may harm your defence if you do not mention when questioned something which you later rely on in Court. Anything you do say may be given in evidence.'

11. *Interviews*:

    ■ must be carried out under caution.

    ■ suspects must be told the nature of the offence

    ■ should be done at the police station

    ■ there must be no oppression (threats, ill-treatment etc.)

    ■ must be accurately recorded.

    The interview record must give:

    ■ the place of interview

    ■ the time it begins and ends

    ■ any breaks

    ■ the names of all those present.

12. *Time limits of interviews*. In any 24 hours a detainee must have at least 8 hours for rest, normally at night, and refreshment breaks every 2 hours.

13. *Interpreters* should be provided for people who cannot speak English, or who are deaf.

14. *Special restrictions* – a doctor must be present if people are questioned in hospital.

15. *Reviews and extension of detention*. There must be a review officer.

    Length of time in police custody before being charged – the normal maximum time is 36 hours.

See page 229 below.

16. *Charging detained persons* – suspect should be charged when police have enough information.

17. *Drug tests* – must be done for a range of 'trigger' offences (see Case study 9.1).

Annex

Intimate searches

■ must be done by a registered doctor or nurse.

Strip searches

■ the police officer doing a strip search must be the same sex as the detainee

■ the search must be done out of sight of anyone who does not need to be present

■ X-ray and ultrasound may be used to search for hidden drugs.

Code D – Code of Practice for the identification of persons by police officers

1. *Introduction*. Identification by witnesses:

   ■ tests witnesses' recollection

   ■ safeguards against mistakes.

   It includes:

   ■ appearance of suspect

   ■ voice recognition

   ■ fingerprints

   ■ footwear

   ■ DNA

   ■ photographic evidence

   ■ tattoos, scars etc.

2. *General points*. The Code of Practice can be used by the police, detained people and members of the public.

3. *Identification by witnesses* – a record must be kept of witnesses' first description of alleged offender.

   ID parades are held when the suspect disputes that the witness has seen him or her. Suspects who refuse will be cautioned that their refusal will be taken in evidence.

   Precautions – care must be taken not to direct the witness' attention to any individual and to keep witnesses separate.

   Main ID methods are:

   ■ video identification

   ■ identification parade

   ■ group identification.

   Reasonable force can be used if suspect does not consent to ID procedures.

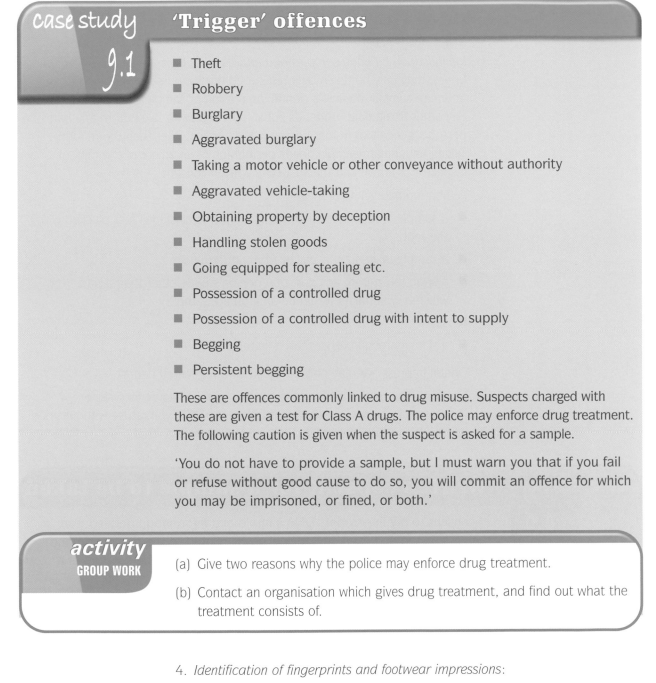

case study 9.1 'Trigger' offences

- Theft
- Robbery
- Burglary
- Aggravated burglary
- Taking a motor vehicle or other conveyance without authority
- Aggravated vehicle-taking
- Obtaining property by deception
- Handling stolen goods
- Going equipped for stealing etc.
- Possession of a controlled drug
- Possession of a controlled drug with intent to supply
- Begging
- Persistent begging

These are offences commonly linked to drug misuse. Suspects charged with these are given a test for Class A drugs. The police may enforce drug treatment. The following caution is given when the suspect is asked for a sample.

'You do not have to provide a sample, but I must warn you that if you fail or refuse without good cause to do so, you will commit an offence for which you may be imprisoned, or fined, or both.'

activity
GROUP WORK

(a) Give two reasons why the police may enforce drug treatment.

(b) Contact an organisation which gives drug treatment, and find out what the treatment consists of.

4. *Identification of fingerprints and footwear impressions*:
   - fingerprints may be taken
   - reasonable force may be used to take fingerprints without suspect's consent
   - suspects must be told why their fingerprints are being taken
   - rules are similar for footwear impressions.

5. *Examinations to establish identity and the taking of photographs*. The police have powers to find out if suspects have any marks, features or injuries that might identify them and to photograph those marks.

6. *Identification by body samples and impressions*. Intimate samples (excluding urine), may only be taken by a registered doctor, nurse or paramedic. An 'intimate sample' means 'a dental impression or sample of blood, semen or any other tissue fluid, urine, or pubic hair, or a swab taken from any part of a person's genitals or from a person's body orifice other than the mouth'. Taking an intimate sample needs permission of an officer of the rank of inspector or above and the suspect's written consent.

A 'non-intimate sample' means:

- a sample of hair, other than pubic hair, which includes hair plucked with the root
- a sample taken from a nail or from under a nail
- a swab taken from any part of a person's body other than a part from which a swab taken would be an intimate sample
- saliva
- a skin impression other than a fingerprint.

Dental impressions may only be taken by a registered dentist.

Caution: 'You do not have to provide this sample/allow this swab or impression to be taken, but I must warn you that if you refuse without good cause, your refusal may harm your case if it comes to trial.'

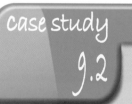

case study 9.2 — Written consent for a sample to be taken

'I consent to my fingerprints/DNA sample and information derived from it being retained and used only for purposes related to the prevention and detection of a crime, the investigation of an offence or the conduct of a prosecution either nationally or internationally.

'I understand that this sample may be checked against other fingerprint/DNA records held by or on behalf of relevant law enforcement authorities, either nationally or internationally.

'I understand that once I have given my consent for the sample to be retained and used I cannot withdraw this consent.'

(*Source*: PACE Code D)

activity
GROUP WORK

(a) To what extent does this written consent protect the human rights of the suspect?

(b) Research fingerprints and DNA samples and their use. How reliable are they, as evidence against an offender?

Figure 9.1

A DNA profile – our individual barcode

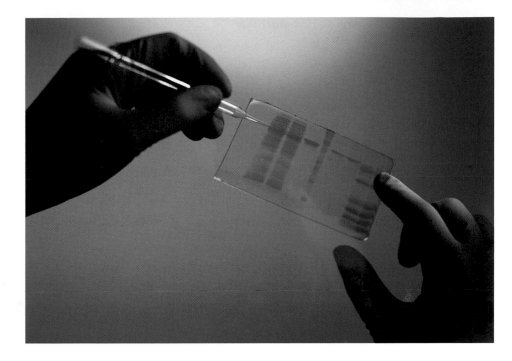

Code E – Code of Practice on audio recording interviews with suspects

1. *General*. 'Recording media' is defined as tapes, optical disks etc.

   Uses of audio recording – for interviews of suspects. The interview can be recorded in writing if the recording machine is not working.

2. *Recording and sealing master recordings*.

   ■ The recording equipment must be loaded with the recording medium (tape etc.) – unwrapped in the suspect's presence – and set to record.

   ■ Two or three recordings should be made, and their security ensured.

3. *Interviews to be audio recorded* – if video recording is not available or appropriate.

4. *The interview*. The interviewer must:

   ■ say the interview is being audibly recorded

   ■ give name and rank and that of other interviewers present

   ■ ask the suspect and any other person present, e.g. a solicitor, to identify themselves

   ■ state the date, time and place of the interview

   ■ state that the suspect will be told in writing what will happen to the copies of the recording

   ■ caution the suspect

   ■ remind the suspect of their entitlement to free legal advice

   ■ ask the suspect about any significant statement or silence.

Information for the suspect. The suspect is handed a notice which explains:

- how the audio recording will be used
- the arrangements for access to it
- that if the suspect is charged they will get a copy of the recording.

5. *After the interview*. The tape must be identified and kept safe.

6. *Media security* – keeping tapes safe and ensuring that they cannot be tampered with or lost.

Code F – Code of Practice on visual recording with sound of interviews with suspects

1. *General*. Definitions

2. *Recording and sealing of master tapes*.

'The visual recording of interviews shall be carried out openly to instil confidence in its reliability as an impartial and accurate record of the interview.

'The camera(s) shall be placed in the interview room so as to ensure coverage of as much of the room as is practicably possible whilst the interviews are taking place.

'The certified recording medium will be of a high quality, new and previously unused. When the certified recording medium is placed in the recorder and switched on to record, the correct date and time, in hours, minutes and seconds, will be superimposed automatically, second by second, during the whole recording.'

3. *Visually recorded interviews* should be used whenever possible, but they are not used in terrorism cases.

4. *The interview* – as in audio interviews above.

5. *After the interview*. The recording media (tapes etc.) are identified, dated and kept safely.

6. *Master copy security* – the master copy is sealed and the seal can only be broken in the presence of the Crown Prosecution Service. When the master copy seal is broken, a record must be made of the procedure followed and the date, time, place and persons present.

Code G – Code of Practice for the statutory power of arrest by police officers

1. *Introduction*

2. *Arrest under section 24 PACE. A lawful arrest* needs two elements:

- A person's involvement, suspected involvement or attempted involvement in carrying out a criminal offence

and

- Reasonable grounds for believing that arrest is necessary.

3. *Information to be given on arrest*. The person must be told they have been arrested and the reasons why.

   When to arrest. A constable may arrest without warrant in relation to any offence.

   Reasons for arrest:

   - to find out the name of a possible suspect
   - to find out the person's address
   - to protect a child or other vulnerable person from the suspect
   - to allow the prompt and effective investigation of an offence.

   Or to prevent the person:

   - causing physical injury to self or others
   - suffering physical injury
   - causing loss or damage to property
   - committing an offence against public decency
   - causing an unlawful obstruction of the highway.

   An arrest may be necessary if the person:

   - has made false statements
   - has presented false evidence
   - may steal or destroy evidence
   - may contact other suspects
   - may intimidate, threaten or contact witnesses.

   Also, to

   - enter and search premises
   - search the person
   - prevent contact with others
   - take fingerprints, footwear impressions, samples or photographs of the suspect
   - carry out statutory drug tests
   - prevent the person's disappearance.

4. *Records of arrest*. The arresting officer must record:

   - details of the offence leading to the arrest
   - why arrest was necessary
   - the giving of the caution
   - anything said by the person at the time of arrest.

   On arrival at the police station, the Custody Officer must open the custody record and record details given by the arresting officer about the arrest.

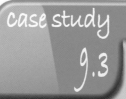

case study 9.3 — General protection for police officers

Statements like this are found in many parts of the PACE Codes of Practice:

'Officers can withhold their own identities from suspects

(a) in the case of enquiries linked to the investigation of terrorism or

(b) if the officer or police staff reasonably believe recording or disclosing their name might put them in danger'

activity
GROUP WORK

(a) Research and outline the differences in police powers between the Terrorism Act 2000 and PACE.

(b) Do you agree that the police need more protection when dealing with terrorist suspects than when dealing with 'ordinary' suspects? Give reasons for your point of view.

Talk to police officers.
Read the relevant parts of the Codes of Practice for the Police and Criminal Evidence Act 1984 – freely available from www.homeoffice.gov.uk

---

Analysis of police powers – main points

The police powers are written down in Codes of Practice (booklets). They are read by the police who use them and by suspects and members of the public.

Police powers control the way the police treat suspects and witnesses. They are intended to be realistic and practical, so the wording often includes phrases such as 'as is practicably possible'.

The main purposes of the powers are:

- to ensure that evidence of crimes is as valid as possible
- to protect the police from accusations of wrongdoing and brutality
- to ensure that suspects are treated fairly and equally by all police forces
- to protect the human rights of suspects
- to ensure that accurate records are kept of police activities.

The powers allow for suspects and witnesses to consent to

- being searched
- having their houses or workplaces searched
- having fingerprints or even 'intimate samples' taken.

If they don't consent, however, 'reasonable force' can be used so that the police can get the evidence they want.

The Police and Criminal Evidence Act makes police leave a 'paper trail' of written (or taped) evidence of all their dealings with suspects. This makes the police accountable: their actions can, if necessary, be investigated by the courts.

Human rights

Police powers also protect suspects from the risk of abuse, ill-treatment, wrongful arrest etc. There are strict rules on how long suspects can be kept in police detention.

There appear to be many limitations to police powers, but in fact the police have very great powers if they believe they have to be used. They *can* arrest anybody if an officer has 'reasonable grounds' for thinking that the person is involved in an offence.

If police officers go beyond their powers, they rarely lose their jobs or get taken to court.

However, breaking the Codes of Practice can have very serious results. If evidence is wrongly obtained, the courts may have to release a dangerous criminal. And if a suspect dies because more than 'reasonable force' is used in an arrest, officers might end up facing a charge of manslaughter.

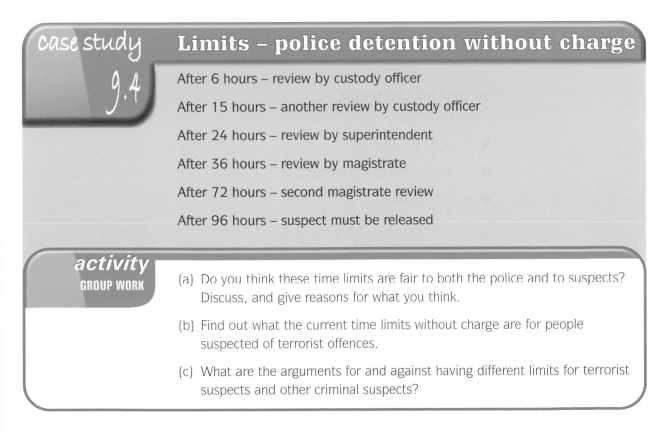

case study 9.4

Limits – police detention without charge

After 6 hours – review by custody officer

After 15 hours – another review by custody officer

After 24 hours – review by superintendent

After 36 hours – review by magistrate

After 72 hours – second magistrate review

After 96 hours – suspect must be released

activity
GROUP WORK

(a) Do you think these time limits are fair to both the police and to suspects? Discuss, and give reasons for what you think.

(b) Find out what the current time limits without charge are for people suspected of terrorist offences.

(c) What are the arguments for and against having different limits for terrorist suspects and other criminal suspects?

Why police powers must be used

The PACE Act was passed in 1984, following the publication of the Scarman Report on the Brixton Riots of 1981. The powers under PACE replaced the relatively uncontrolled police powers which existed before 1984.

The main justifications for using police powers are:

To get reliable evidence

If we take Code D, the Code of Practice for the identification of persons by police officers as an example, we can see what this means. There can be serious problems with evidence based on identification. This is because:

(a) some people have a poor memory for people's faces, appearance and what they are wearing

(b) if someone witnesses a crime they are under stress, and may be too scared, disturbed or angry to notice much about a suspect

(c) people can have poor eyesight, or the lighting may be bad, or they are too far away when they see an incident, or things happen too quickly to be seen properly

(d) suspects may be disguised, or wearing different clothes from the ones they normally wear

(e) criminals themselves are under stress when committing crimes, and often look different as a result

(f) the police can bias or encourage witnesses to identify the person they (the police) think is the suspect.

Code D reduces the risk of (f).

To protect the police

In the past the police were often accused of obtaining evidence wrongly – e.g.

■ by bullying, oppression, coercion and physical violence

■ by rewriting or falsifying their police notebooks

■ by telling lies in court.

Maybe they didn't do these things, but they couldn't prove it because the system wasn't transparent: there was no 'paper trail'. PACE allows police actions to be checked.

Deaths in police custody can also be properly investigated (because better records are kept) and police are less likely to be falsely accused of killing someone in the cells.

Good for society

Thanks to PACE we have a police service which is accountable. This means:

(a) people are more willing to trust and cooperate with the police

(b) human rights are respected – and seen to be respected

(c) the police get more respect from the community, and there is less risk of communities rioting (as they did in 1981) because they are angry at police unfairness.

activity
**GROUP WORK
(9.3)**

Invite a police officer to talk to you about PACE, how it is used, and the advantages and disadvantages.

Rights of suspects in police custody

Under PACE, suspects are protected by a number of important rights while they are in police custody.

1. To have a solicitor (free of charge)
    - to talk privately to the solicitor at any time, by phone or face to face at the police station
    - to talk to the solicitor before being questioned
    - to have the solicitor in the same room while being questioned.

2. To have someone know that they are in police custody – the police must contact a relative, friend etc. to say that the person is in police custody.

3. To see the PACE Codes of Practice so that they know their own rights while in police custody.

4. To see the custody record – the official record of their time in police custody. This right lasts for 12 months after being detained.

5. To communicate
    - make phone calls (with permission only)
    - have a pen and paper
    - to have visitors (with the Custody Officer's permission).

6. Accommodation
    - in a clean, warm room, adequately lit
    - with clean, suitable bedding
    - toilet and washing facilities.

7. Clothes – clean, comfortable clothes.

8. Food and drink – three meals a day, and drinks when required.

9. Exercise – out of doors.

10. Health

   ■ free medical care

   ■ medication (if approved by the police doctor)

   ■ to see a nurse.

11. Length of detention – see Case study 9.4 on page 229 above – the right to be let out immediately if there is no longer any reason for keeping the person.

12. Questioning

   ■ in a clean, warm, lit room without having to stand

   ■ the right to know the name and rank of the police asking questions

   ■ with breaks at normal meal times, and breaks for a drink after every two hours

   ■ 8 hours' sleep in any 24 hours spent in custody.

13. Rights for young or vulnerable people to have an 'appropriate adult' present while being questioned, searched, cautioned, charged etc.

---

activity
GROUP WORK
(9.4)

Obtain a copy of the articles of the Human Rights Act 1998. What human rights are being infringed, from the suspect's point of view? Does it matter?

---

keyword

Bail
the act of releasing an accused person from custody after being charged, on a promise that they will appear in court, or at the police station, on a given date.

Bail

There are two kinds of **bail** – unconditional bail and conditional bail.

Unconditional bail

If the courts or the police think that the accused will turn up on the date decided, and is no risk to the public or themselves, they will give them unconditional bail. This means the person promises to go to the court or the police station at the time arranged and can otherwise lead a normal life.

Conditional bail

If the courts or police think it would be risky giving the accused unconditional bail, they might give conditional bail. This means that the accused has to follow certain conditions or rules.

Refusing bail

Refusing bail means keeping the accused in custody. This can be at a probation hostel, bail hostel or full-blown prison. If the custody is in a prison it is called imprisonment on remand.

The reasons for refusing bail are as follows:

■ The court or police believe the suspect will:

   ▪ abscond

   ▪ reoffend

   ▪ interfere with witnesses or the victim.

case study 9.5 — Bail conditions

(a) Typical bail conditions:

- Curfew (this can be checked by visits to the home by police, probation etc.)

- Keeping away from someone such as a witness who might be at risk of being intimidated by them

- Reporting at a police station at certain times

- Wearing an electronic tag

- Having someone else provide a surety (a sum of money to guarantee that the offender turns up at the court or police station at the stated time)

- Forfeiting a passport

- Having drug or alcohol assessment and follow-up treatment

- Living at a specific address

(b) Differences between police and court bail conditions

'Police powers to impose conditions are not identical to court powers to impose conditions. Specifically, police may not impose a condition to reside at a bail hostel, to attend an interview with a legal adviser, nor require the suspect to make him or herself available for inquiries and reports'

(*Source*: CPS)

activity
GROUP WORK

(a) Arrange the bail conditions under (a) in order of seriousness as you see them. Compare your findings with your partner and, if you differ, try to reach agreement.

(b) Why do you think the police have fewer powers to impose bail conditions than the courts?

- The suspect
  - is accused of a very serious crime like murder or rape
  - has refused drug or alcohol assessment or treatment
  - has a history of breaching bail (i.e. failing to turn up at court or at the police station when supposed to)
  - has made threats of violence
  - has no fixed home.

Figure 9.2
Electronic tagging – effective
or not?

Bail for juveniles (under 17)

The courts can give young people either unconditional or conditional bail. Conditional bail can be for the same reasons as for adults, and also for the young person's 'welfare or own best interests'.

There are more types of conditional bail for juveniles than for adults (see Case study 9.6).

Young offenders can be remanded to local authority accommodation, and to secure accommodation if they are a risk to others – i.e. have committed violent or sexual offences which would have carried a sentence of more than 14 years' imprisonment if they had been done by an adult. Local authorities can apply to have a young person in their care sent to a secure accommodation by applying

---

case study
9.6

Types of conditional bail for people aged 12–17

Youths aged 12 to 17 may be remanded on unconditional bail, conditional bail, conditional bail with electronic monitoring, bail supervision and support, bail supervision and support with electronic monitoring, Bail Intensive Support and Surveillance Programme (ISSP), Bail Intensive Support and Surveillance Programme with voice verification and/or with electronic monitoring.

(*Source*: CPS)

activity
GROUP WORK

Contact your local probation service and find out what is meant by 'supervision', 'support' and 'intensive support and surveillance'.

to a court for a secure accommodation order. This is done if it is felt that the young person will almost certainly abscond, or is at risk of harming themselves or others.

The points to prove to support a successful prosecution
The 'burden of proof'

In English law a person is innocent of crime unless they can be proved guilty 'beyond all reasonable doubt'. In court it is therefore up to the prosecution to prove that an offence (crime) has been committed, and that the accused person did it. The prosecution do this by producing evidence, either through witnesses who come to court and say what they know, or through forensic science facts such as bullets, bloodstains, footprints or CCTV footage which link the accused with the offence. Even if the accused pleads guilty the evidence is needed – nobody can be convicted simply on the basis of their own confession.

Murder – points to prove

'It is an offence for a *person* (*1*) to *unlawfully* (*2*) *kill* (*3*) any *person* (*4*), *under the peace* (*5*), *with malice aforethought* (*6*), *express or implied* (*7*).'

Each of the italicised points has to be proved for a person to be convicted of murder.

1. Person (1) – the killer must be a human being.

2. 'Unlawfully' means in a way or in circumstances which are against the law. It is not unlawful to kill someone in self-defence.

3. Kill. The victim must die, and the death must be the result of the murderer's action.

4. 'Person' here means that only a human being can be murdered.

5. 'Under the peace' means in peacetime. If soldiers are at war, they are not breaking the law if they kill enemy soldiers.

6. 'With malice aforethought' means 'with the intention of doing harm'. Accidental killing is not murder.

7. 'Express or implied' relates back to the 'malice aforethought'. 'Express' means that the intention to kill was shown openly – e.g. by saying, 'I'm going to kill X!' 'Implied' means that the intention to kill was shown in an indirect way – e.g. by digging a grave in your back garden and claiming it was a fishpond.

activity
PAIR WORK
(9.5)

Find a law in a police law book, study what it says, and say what proof is needed by the courts that that law has been broken.

Police Law and Procedure, Police Law, Ninth Edition, 2005, Jack English and Richard Card, ISBN 0-19-928405-9

A–Z of Policing Law, Roger Lorton, London: The Stationery Office, 2001.
www.police-information.co.uk

The Role of the Prosecution, the Defence and the Courts

The Crown Prosecution Service (CPS)

The Crown Prosecution is a body of lawyers which was set up in 1985 to take over from the police the job of prosecuting offenders.

Its roles are:

- giving pre-charge advice to the police
- reviewing all cases and deciding whether to proceed
- overseeing the progress of cases
- conducting the prosecution of cases in the magistrates' courts
- instructing counsel in the Crown Court.

The CPS take all the evidence that the police collect about an offence and the person charged with it, and decide whether it will stand up in court. The advantages of having the CPS rather than leaving prosecution up to the police are that:

- it reduces the police workload
- cases are prosecuted in a fairer and more consistent way
- disclosure is more consistent (see pages 239–40).

There is a branch of the Crown Prosecution Service in each of the 42 areas of the criminal justice system in England and Wales.

Defence

The criminal court system in England and Wales is **adversarial**: the prosecution are on one side and the defence on the other. The accused have defence lawyers (solicitors in the magistrates' courts, barristers in the Crown Court) to help them put forward their case.

If they plead not guilty and the case goes to trial, the defence lawyer tries to show that:

- the accused is innocent, or
- they are guilty of a lesser crime or
- even if they are guilty as charged, there are reasons why they should not be treated too harshly.

Defence lawyers can be provided free (under the legal aid scheme) if people cannot afford their fees. This is because, in the UK, everybody is supposed to be equal under the law.

The courts

Magistrates' courts

Most criminal courts in England and Wales are magistrates' courts. They deal with about 96 per cent of all criminal cases. Two or three lay (paid expenses only) magistrates usually sit on the 'bench' and judge the cases that come before them. Most magistrates have no legal training.

Magistrates get legal advice from a trained lawyer, the Clerk of the Court. Some cases are heard by District Judges, who are legally qualified and paid. Magistrates' courts are open to the public. Cases are argued by prosecution and defence lawyers, and many take only a few minutes to hear. Magistrates' courts deal with 'less serious' crimes, for which the penalties are imprisonment of 6 months or less, or fines of £5000 or less.

Youth Courts are a special kind of magistrates' court which are not open to the public. Instead of magistrates they have specially trained justices and deal with matters relating to people under 18.

The Crown Court

There are 78 branches of the Crown Court in England and Wales. These courts try the major criminal cases for which the penalties could be imprisonment of over 6 months or fines of over £5000. The cases are heard by judges, who are highly qualified lawyers, and argued by barristers, who are specialists in criminal law. The Crown Court is open to the public.

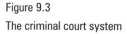
Figure 9.3
The criminal court system

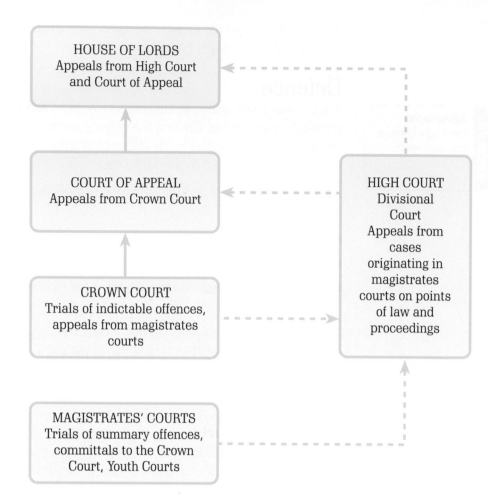

Civil courts

The main civil court is the county court, sometimes called the Small Claims Court. This deals with disagreements over money, family law etc.

Tribunals

These are specialised courts which deal with things like unfair dismissal, discrimination at work, immigration and asylum appeals, tax disagreements, the Data Protection Act. The most well known are Employment Tribunals.

High Court and Court of Appeal (Civil Division)

These hear appeals in civil law.

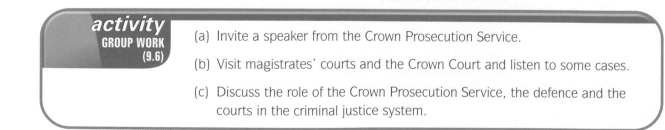

activity
**GROUP WORK
(9.6)**

(a) Invite a speaker from the Crown Prosecution Service.

(b) Visit magistrates' courts and the Crown Court and listen to some cases.

(c) Discuss the role of the Crown Prosecution Service, the defence and the courts in the criminal justice system.

Disclosure

'Disclosure' means telling defence lawyers all the evidence which has been collected about an alleged offence. In particular it concerns evidence which has been discovered by the police but which will not be used by prosecution lawyers.

Such evidence is not used by prosecution lawyers because it does not greatly help the prosecution's case. However, it might help the defendant – which is why defence lawyers need to know about it as soon as possible.

Documentation used in disclosure (forms on which material about the case and evidence is listed):

MG6C – for non-sensitive material

MG6D – for sensitive material

MG6E – the disclosure officer's report

'MG' stands for 'Manual of Guidance' – the official CPS guidelines on disclosure.

Other relevant documents:

(a) Parts 25–28 of the *Criminal Procedure Rules 2005* (the Rules)

(b) The *Criminal Procedure and Investigations Act 1996 (Defence Disclosure Time Limits) Regulations 1997* issued under section 12 of the Act (the Regulations).

(c) Code of Practice issued under Section 23 of the Criminal Procedure and Investigations Act 1996 as amended (the Act).

case study 9.7 The disclosure process

The *disclosure officer* is the person responsible for examining material retained by the police during the investigation; revealing material to the prosecutor during the investigation and any criminal proceedings resulting from it, and certifying that he has done this; and disclosing material to the accused at the request of the prosecutor.

What the disclosure officer does:

1. The officer gets advice as to which evidence is relevant to the prosecution.

2. A list or schedule is made by the disclosure officer of material which will probably not form part of the prosecution's case.

3. Non-sensitive material is listed on a non-sensitive schedule.

4. Sensitive material is listed on a schedule of sensitive material.

5. Extremely sensitive material may be revealed to the prosecutor separately.

6. These schedules must be prepared for all serious offences which are likely to be tried in the Crown Court, and some others if it is fairly certain that the accused will plead not guilty.

7. Each item of material must be listed (and described if necessary) separately on the schedule and numbered consecutively so the prosecutor knows whether to see the material before disclosure.

8. The schedules should be given to the prosecutor at the same time, if possible, as the evidence itself is given to the prosecutor.

9. The disclosure officer should tell the prosecutor if any material has been retained by the police investigators, and if so why.

10. The disclosure officer must also give the prosecutor any information from an accused person which explains the offence, or casts doubt on the reliability of a confession (i.e. suggests the accused may not be guilty).

11. Additional schedules must be given to the prosecutor of further relevant material unless the prosecutor intends to reveal the information to the defence.

12. The disclosure officer must check any material retained by the police and, if it seems to help the accused, must reveal it to the prosecutor.

13. Schedules given to the prosecutor must be signed and certified by the disclosure officer.

    Disclosure of material to accused (i.e. the lawyers of the accused)

14. If the prosecutor wants, or if the court wants, the disclosure officer must send copies of material to the accused.

15. The disclosure officer must disclose material to the accused either by giving him a copy or by allowing him to inspect it (unless there is good reason – size or sensitivity) not to.

16. Tapes etc. must be transcribed and certified as a true record of the material which has been transcribed.

17. If a court concludes that an item of sensitive material must be disclosed, then it can be.

(*Source*: Summarised from the Code of Practice)

activity
GROUP WORK

(a) Invite a speaker from the CPS who knows about disclosure and the documentation used.

(b) Ask for an account of a case involving disclosure, showing how disclosure is carried out and how the documentation is used.

www.cps.gov.uk (search for 'The CPS Disclosure Manual')
www.hmcourts-service.gov.uk (search for the CPS website)
www.opsi.gov.uk (search for: Criminal Procedure Rules 2005)
Legal words defined in plain English: www.plainenglish.co.uk

*progress
check*

1. What is the difference between common law and statute law?

2. What is the difference between a stated case and a decided case?

3. Outline the role of the custody officer.

4. Give five rules relating to police interviews of suspects.

5. How long can a suspect be kept in police custody before being charged?

6. List six ways in which a suspect can be identified.

7. Why are ID parades held?

8. State four possible bail conditions

9. What are the main roles of the prosecution and the defence?

10. What is disclosure?

Crime and its Effects on Society

This unit covers:

- the impact of criminal behaviour
- investigating local crime reduction initiatives
- the methods used to report and record crime
- the options available to effectively manage offenders

Open any newspaper or watch any television news and you will find reports and comment about crime. Major crimes can dominate the media for days on end, and everybody talks about them. This is because crime means a lot to us all and, directly or indirectly, affects all our lives.

In this unit you will learn about crime as the police and other public services see it. You will also learn about victims of crime and how they are helped by the public services. You will look at what crime costs, not just to a victim but to the whole country, and what is being done to try to reduce crime and the damage it causes.

The investigation and recording of crime are covered in this unit, and so are new methods of policing. Finally, you will learn about crime figures, and the basics of how offenders are dealt with by the criminal justice system.

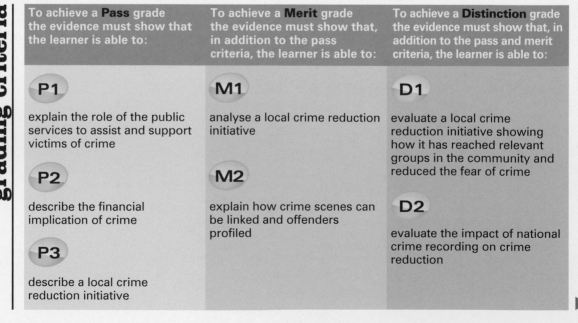

grading criteria

To achieve a **Pass** grade the evidence must show that the learner is able to:	To achieve a **Merit** grade the evidence must show that, in addition to the pass criteria, the learner is able to:	To achieve a **Distinction** grade the evidence must show that, in addition to the pass and merit criteria, the learner is able to:
P1 explain the role of the public services to assist and support victims of crime	**M1** analyse a local crime reduction initiative	**D1** evaluate a local crime reduction initiative showing how it has reached relevant groups in the community and reduced the fear of crime
P2 describe the financial implication of crime	**M2** explain how crime scenes can be linked and offenders profiled	**D2** evaluate the impact of national crime recording on crime reduction
P3 describe a local crime reduction initiative		

grading criteria

To achieve a **Pass** grade the evidence must show that the learner is able to:	To achieve a **Merit** grade the evidence must show that, in addition to the pass criteria, the learner is able to:	To achieve a **Distinction** grade the evidence must show that, in addition to the pass and merit criteria, the learner is able to:
P4 explain the process involved to report and record crime	**M3** analyse how the National Crime Recording Standards impacted nationally upon the police service and the effect on crime statistics	
P5 describe the role of the Crime Scene Investigation unit		
P6 explain how the National Intelligence Model and Intelligence Led Policing has led to new policing practices		
P7 explain the ways to an offender can be effectively dealt with describing the consequences that can follow		

The Impact of Criminal Behaviour

The most direct impact of crime is on the **victims**. They are the people who suffer, and whom the public services need to help. Following some complaints by the public and by politicians, the police and other services in the criminal justice system are now working hard to help the victims of crime.

There is increasing interest by the government and the public services in looking after and helping the many thousands of people who, each year, become victims of crime.

activity
GROUP WORK
(10.1)

List 10 crimes and then discuss the different ways victims suffer as a result of those crimes.

Table 10.1 Public services that help and support the victims of crime

Service	Role
Police	They investigate the crime and the Safety Unit helps the victim at court and in other ways – for example with crime prevention advice (see Case study 10.1).
Lawyers	They keep in touch with the victim, explain what is going on in court, and inform victims of their rights (see Case study 10.1). In criminal cases lawyers are normally free of charge to the victim. But victims *may* have to pay if they seek compensation from an offender through a civil court.
Victim Support	This voluntary organisation liaises with the police and the victim to make sure victims get all the help they need. They also provide a witness service to help the victim – who is usually a witness – in court.
The courts	They have introduced many features (e.g. video links for vulnerable witnesses) and can now, with the police, offer protection for victims – and witnesses – who feel at risk of intimidation).
Prison service	They keep offenders under lock and key, where they cannot try to do further harm to victims.
Probation service	They manage non-custodial (non-prison) sentences – e.g. sentences in the community – which aim to rehabilitate offenders so they do not break the law again.
NHS	They give medical help (or psychiatric help) to victims who have been physically or mentally damaged by the offender.
Universities and researchers	They carry out research on things like 'repeat victimisation' (the tendency for offenders to target the same victims again and again) and suggest ways of reducing crime levels (and therefore the number of victims).
Specialist voluntary organisations	Victims of specific types of crime are helped by specialist groups – for example Rape Crisis, Local Authority Child Protection teams, the National Society for the Protection of Children (NSPCC) and Voice UK (protecting people with learning difficulties who are victims).
Criminal Injuries Compensation Scheme	Compensation for personal injury; losses because of theft of, or damage to, property; losses because of fraud; loss of earnings while off work; medical expenses; travelling expenses; pain and suffering; and loss, damage or injury caused to, or by, a stolen vehicle. In some cases, surviving dependants of a victim who died during, or as a direct result of, a crime may be entitled to compensation.

Victim help and support

Police – Safety Units

The Safety Unit makes contact with the victim within 24 hours of the offence being reported. It provides a range of services such as:

- keeping in touch with the victim throughout the proceedings
- attending court with the victim
- representing the victim, at pre-trial reviews in the magistrates' courts
- and acting as a referral point for clients seeking services for their children.

Lawyers

The CPS and the Bar are working with the Local Criminal Justice Boards (LCJBs) in agreeing a new standards of Victim Care document for prosecutors. These include:

- the prosecutor introducing him or herself to the victim before the case starts

- assuring the case will be prosecuted fairly

- assuring that the prosecutor will challenge any unfair cross-examination by the defence

- explaining that the prosecutor is fully prepared to meet the victim at the end of each day of the trial to answer procedural questions.

- meeting the victim at the end of the trial to deal compassionately with queries the victim may have, for example the right of appeal.

(*Source*: Office for Criminal Justice Reform (2004) *Increasing Victims' and Witnesses' Satisfaction with the Criminal Justice System: Delivering a High Quality Service*; www.cjsonline.org/victims)

activity
GROUP WORK

(a) What do you think are the main fears of witnesses who go to court?

(b) Contact your local court and find out what help and protection they offer to witnesses.

The way the different public services, which help victims of crime, interact is shown in Figure 10.1.

The aims of victim support services which operate in and around the criminal courts are indicated in Figure 10.2.

www.bromsgrove.gov.uk (witness support)
www.crimereduction.gov.uk (repeat victimisation)
www.victimsupport.org.uk

The costs of crime

Crime is expensive for the victims, and for the rest of us.

Costs – before and after crime

A major study into the costs of crime was carried out by the Home Office in 2000. It was called *Home Office Research Study 217: The Economic and Social Costs of Crime*.

It broke down the financial implications of crime into three types. The first was 'in anticipation of crime'. This included the cost of crime prevention and insurance premiums. The second type of financial implication was 'as a consequence of

Figure 10.1

Victim role and public service role

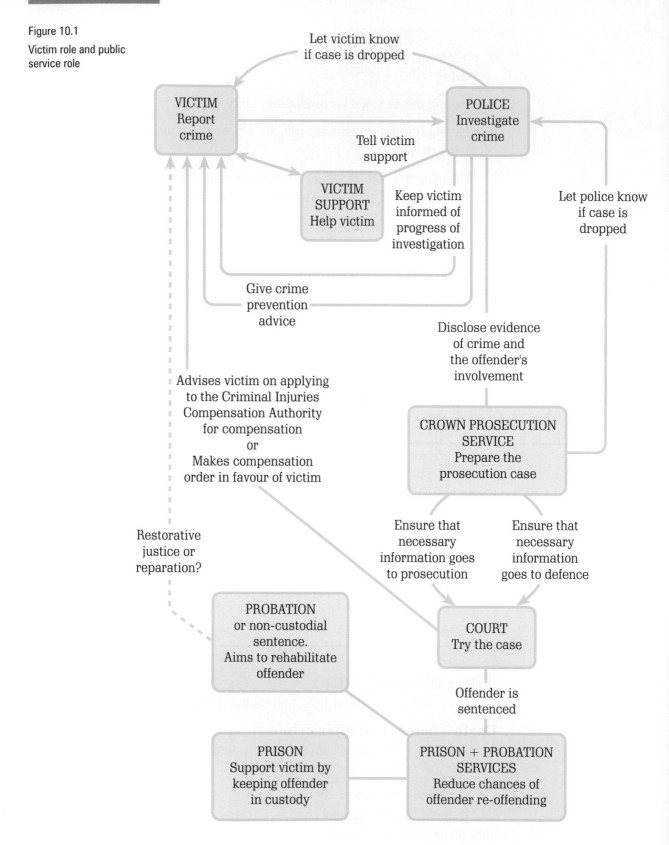

Figure 10.2

Improving victim and witness satisfaction

crime'. This included things like the cost of property stolen and damaged, of working hours lost, and the cost of health and victim support services. The third type of financial implication was 'in response to crime' and this included the cost of all the public service work (such as the police and the prison service) which is done to solve and follow up crime.

An edition of *The Economic and Social Costs of Crime* came out in 2005, and deals with 2003/4. It estimates that crime cost the UK economy £36.2billion for that year. This is only the cost of crime against individuals and households, not industry.

Figure 10.3

Estimated total cost of crime against individuals and households in 2003/04 by cost category

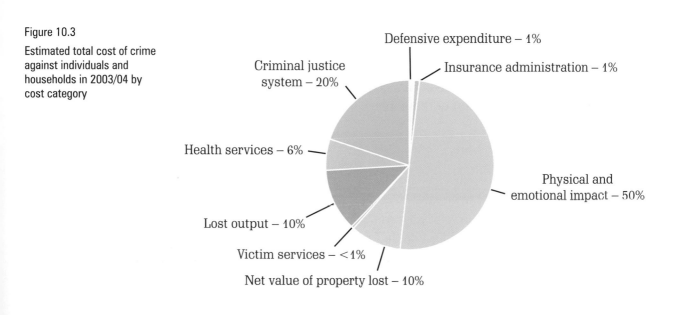

The financial implications of crime

In anticipation of crime

Security expenditure

Insurance resources

Precautionary behaviour*

Collective/community defensive expenditure*

Government crime prevention activity*

Insurance premiums*

Non-financial costs:

Fear of crime*

Lower quality of life of potential victims*

As a consequence of crime

Property stolen and damaged

Lost output

Emotional and physical impact

Health services

Victim support services

Insurance claims*

Quality of life of victims*

In response to crime

Police

Prosecution

Legal aid and non-legally aided defence costs

Magistrates' and Crown Courts

Probation Service

Prison Service

Jury Service

Criminal Injuries Compensation resources

Criminal Injuries Compensation Payouts*

Witness costs*

Miscarriages of justice*

Offender and his/her family*

*The researchers decided they couldn't assess the financial implications (costs) of these items.

(*Source*: *Home Office Research Study 217: The Economic and Social Costs of Crime*, Home Office website)

activity
GROUP WORK

(a) In what ways can 'fear of crime' and 'emotional and physical impact' have an effect on the financial cost of crime?

(b) Why is the cost of 'fear of crime' hard to assess?

Relative costs of different kinds of crime

The pie chart in Figure 10.4 shows which crimes carry the biggest financial implications. Violence against the person and sexual offences are the costliest. These are serious crimes and cost a great deal to solve. They are tried in the Crown Court, which is much more expensive than the magistrates' court. Large numbers of police and lawyers are involved and the offenders spend many years in prison, so the cost to society is high. Theft and burglary are far more common, but they cost much less to deal with, so the overall financial implications are less.

Figure 10.4

Estimated total cost of crime against individuals and households in 2003/04 by crime type

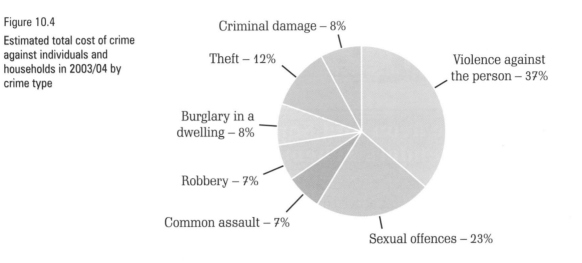

- Criminal damage – 8%
- Theft – 12%
- Violence against the person – 37%
- Burglary in a dwelling – 8%
- Robbery – 7%
- Common assault – 7%
- Sexual offences – 23%

activity
GROUP WORK
(10.2)

Visit www.homeoffice.gov.uk and find the latest edition of *The Economic and Social Costs of Crime against Individuals and Households*.

Then find out the average cost of (a) a homicide, (b) a rape and (c) a car theft.

Investigating Local Crime Reduction Initiatives

Local crime reduction initiatives are widely used by the 43 local police forces in England and Wales. Case study 10.3 provides an example of one.

Analysis of the Avon and Somerset Prolific Offenders Scheme

Avon and Somerset Constabulary point out: 'The scheme is based on the proposition that in a given area, up to 80 per cent of crime is attributable to 20 per cent of the offenders living there.' These are the prolific offenders which give the initiative its name.

We've been burgled three times since that Neighbourhood Watch started up in the next street!

case study 10.3

The Avon and Somerset Prolific Offenders Scheme

The purpose of the Avon and Somerset Prolific Offenders Scheme is to target the most active criminals, seeking to reduce crime in the communities it serves, through rehabilitation, enforcement and surveillance.

The Avon and Somerset Prolific Offenders Scheme was set up in April 2002 under the auspices of the Bristol Crime and Disorder Partnership with the aim of targeting the most prolific offenders in the Bristol area. The first partnership of its kind within the Avon and Somerset Police force area, and possibly anywhere in the country, the Prolific Offender Unit brings the police, prison and probation services together at both a strategic and an operational level. It is this unique combination that has contributed to the strength and the success of the scheme and which has attracted considerable interest both locally and nationally.

Beginning in one police station in Bristol, the scheme swiftly spread to all three force districts in Bristol and has now been launched force-wide with units being set up in Staple Hill, Bath, Weston-super-Mare, Taunton and Yeovil.

Avon and Somerset Prolific Offenders Scheme (ASPOS) targets those offenders who are causing the most damage to the community and for whom other sentencing options have failed. They concentrate on house burglars and car thieves, almost all of whom are driven to steal by the need to support a long-standing drug addiction.

activity
GROUP WORK

(a) What are 'prolific offenders'?

(b) Why has the scheme attracted national interest?

How ASPOS works
Selection

The police select offenders on the basis of 'age, frequency and nature of previous offences and custodial history'. They choose young adults who have many convictions and have done time in prison. If they can stop these prolific offenders from offending, then the crime rate in the area will go down.

Supervision

Offenders who are chosen for the scheme are forced to go on it. The main feature of the scheme is the level of supervision the offenders get. Normally offenders may have only one appointment a week with a probation officer or other worker. On the ASPOS scheme offenders get much more supervision: 'Specifically in the first six months the requirements would include:

- 4 appointments per week for the first 12 weeks
- 2 appointments per week for the second 12 weeks
- a review of level of reporting after 24 weeks
- drug-testing twice per week in the first 4 weeks following custody.'

Partnership

The scheme involves a lot of cooperation between police and probation officers: 'The exchange of information between probation and police ensures that each agency is intervening with the offender with the optimum amount of information.'

Tailored to offenders' needs

The ASPOS programme uses a range of methods to help prolific offenders kick the burglary habit. 'Each offender has an individual programme of intervention which includes surveillance, drug treatment, cognitive skills training, employment training and education, and challenges to offending.'

- *Surveillance* means watching their behaviour, to make sure they don't reoffend and restricting the places they are allowed to go to.
- The *drug treatment* aims to break the offenders' addiction to class A drugs.
- *Cognitive skills training* helps them to understand why they offend and teaches them to behave differently.
- *Employment training* prepares the offender for a useful job.
- *Education* develops their thinking skills which, up till now, have been used in planning burglaries.
- *Challenges to offending* are any arguments or actions which will show them the futility of wasting their lives in crime.

activity
GROUP WORK
(10.3)

What do you think are the two main rewards of running a scheme such as ASPOS?

Evaluating crime reduction initiatives

It is necessary to evaluate crime reduction initiatives to see whether they work, and whether they give value for the taxpayer's money.

A very important question is: 'How can its success be measured?' Possible answers are:

- Through statistics (these may not be reliable, however, if the scheme is a small-scale local one).

- Through public awareness surveys. This shows that people know about the initiative, but not whether it works.

- Through individual case studies. These don't really measure the success – they only show that the initiative worked for one person.

Two more questions which people ask when they are evaluating a scheme are:

1. Do the benefits of the scheme outweigh the costs? (The costs are not just money, but also the time and effort of all the people involved.)

2. How does the scheme compare with others of its type?

Figure 10.5

Questions to ask when you evaluate a local crime reduction initiative

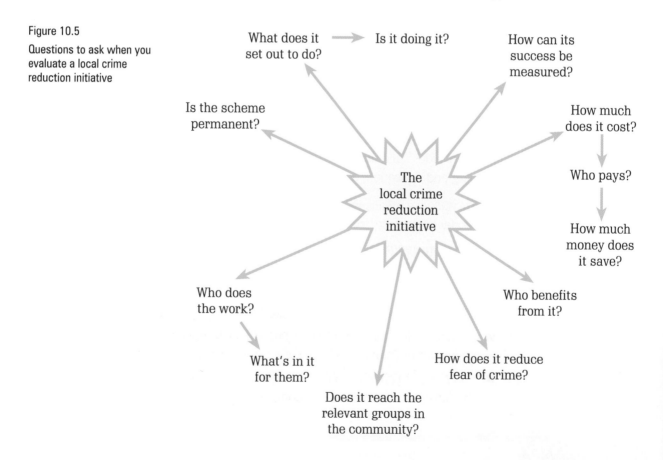

activity
GROUP WORK
(10.4)

Ask someone (police, probation officer, social worker, volunteer etc.) who works for a local crime reduction initiative to give you their views on how successful it is, and how it might progress or be improved.

Methods Used to Report and Record Crime

Ways of reporting crime

Reporting crime telling the police about it.
keyword

There are a number of ways in which a crime can be reported. These depend on the urgency of the situation and the type of crime.

(a) Calling 999. This is the urgent number to call if a crime is happening or about to happen, and an immediate police attendance is needed. (112 can also be used – it is the European emergency number.)

(b) Contacting the police in person. The victim or witness of a non-urgent crime goes to the police station and reports it at the desk.

(c) Phoning the police on a non-urgent line. The victim or witness calls the local police station on a normal phone number. This is the way most crime should be reported, as long as the caller is not at immediate risk.

(d) Phoning the local community safety unit. This is the place to report non-urgent crime (i.e. when the immediate danger is past) of the following types:

- domestic violence
- homophobic crime
- racial crime
- rape
- sexual assault.

Community safety units specialise in dealing with these types of crime. But in situations of danger the victim should always ring 999.

(e) Reporting internet crime:

- Child pornography, obscenity and race-hate. This can be reported to the police directly, or to the Internet Watch Foundation – a partnership between the police and major internet firms. The report can be made online (see Figure 10.6).

- Hacking and virus writing. Contact the Crime Management Unit or the local police station.

www.met.police.uk

Figure 10.6

Reporting internet crime (child pornography, obscenity and race-hate)

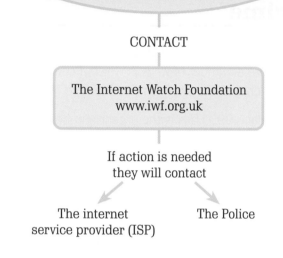

Internet crime
- Child pornography anywhere in the world
- Obscene material on British sites only
- Criminally racist material on British sites only

CONTACT

The Internet Watch Foundation
www.iwf.org.uk

If action is needed
they will contact

The internet
service provider (ISP)   The Police

(f) Reporting fraud. This would normally be done through the local police station. The Metropolitan Police have a special fraud squad for investigating high-value fraud (more than £750,000).

(g) Phone scams. These can be reported to the Independent Committee for the Supervision of Standards for Telephone Information Services (ICSTIS) which has a helpline. The police will then record and investigate the offence if ICSTIS reports it to them.

(h) Suspected terrorist activity. This can be reported on a special hotline: 0800 789 321. If there is a bomb warning or other immediate threat, 999 should be called.

NB: The information given in this section relates to the Metropolitan Police. Details will be different in other parts of the country.

keyword

Recording crime
when the police put a crime on their database (list) of crimes.

Recording crime

Police methods of **recording crime** changed in April 2002 when a new system of counting crimes was introduced by all 43 local police forces in England and Wales. This new system is called the National Crime Recording Standard (NCRS).

1. All incidents reported to the police, whether they are crimes or not, are recorded. An incident record, however, is not a record of a crime, and will not come into the recorded crime figures.

2. An incident is recorded as a crime if 'on the balance of probability'

   (a) The circumstances as reported amount to a crime defined by law

   (b) There is no credible evidence to the contrary.

case study 10.4 — Examples of NCRS counting rules

The test to be applied in respect of recording a crime is that of the balance of probabilities i.e. is the incident more likely than not the result of a criminal act? In most cases, the belief by the victim (or person reasonably assumed to be acting on behalf of the victim) that a crime has occurred is sufficient to justify its recording, although this will not be the case in all circumstances.

...

The concept of 'No Victim No Crime' as contained within paragraph 3.9 of the NCRS is a guiding principle and should generally be adhered to. However, in exceptional cases where there is overwhelming evidence that a serious crime has been committed, a force may decide to record even though the victim has declined to confirm or cannot be found.

(*Source*: Home Office, *Home Office Counting Rules for Recorded Crime*)

activity — INDIVIDUAL WORK

(a) How would a police officer assess 'the balance of probabilities' that a crime had happened?

(b) Give examples of crimes which might not be reported to the police for each of the following reasons:

- nobody knows about the crime except the offender
- there is no clear victim
- the crime is considered unimportant
- people don't believe the police can (or will) do anything
- the victim feels ashamed
- the victim is frightened.

(c) Is there such a thing as 'victimless crime'? If so, how many examples can you think of?

3. The crime is recorded even if the victim doesn't want anything to be done about it.

4. A crime is usually not recorded as a crime unless there is a victim (see Case study 10.4 above).

5. A crime is recorded as soon as the recording officer is satisfied that a crime has been committed.

6. The date given to the crime is the date it was recorded, not the date it happened

7. Once a crime is on the record it must stay on the record unless later information proves that it didn't happen or it wasn't a crime.

8. There are other rules, such as 'one crime, one victim' and 'the finished incident rule' which aim to stop the same crime being recorded twice.

activity
GROUP WORK (10.5)

Ask a police officer to talk to you about the reporting and recording of crime.

Figure 10.7
The process of recording crime

(*Source*: *Home Office Counting Rules for Recorded Crime*, 2005; www.homeoffice.gov.uk)

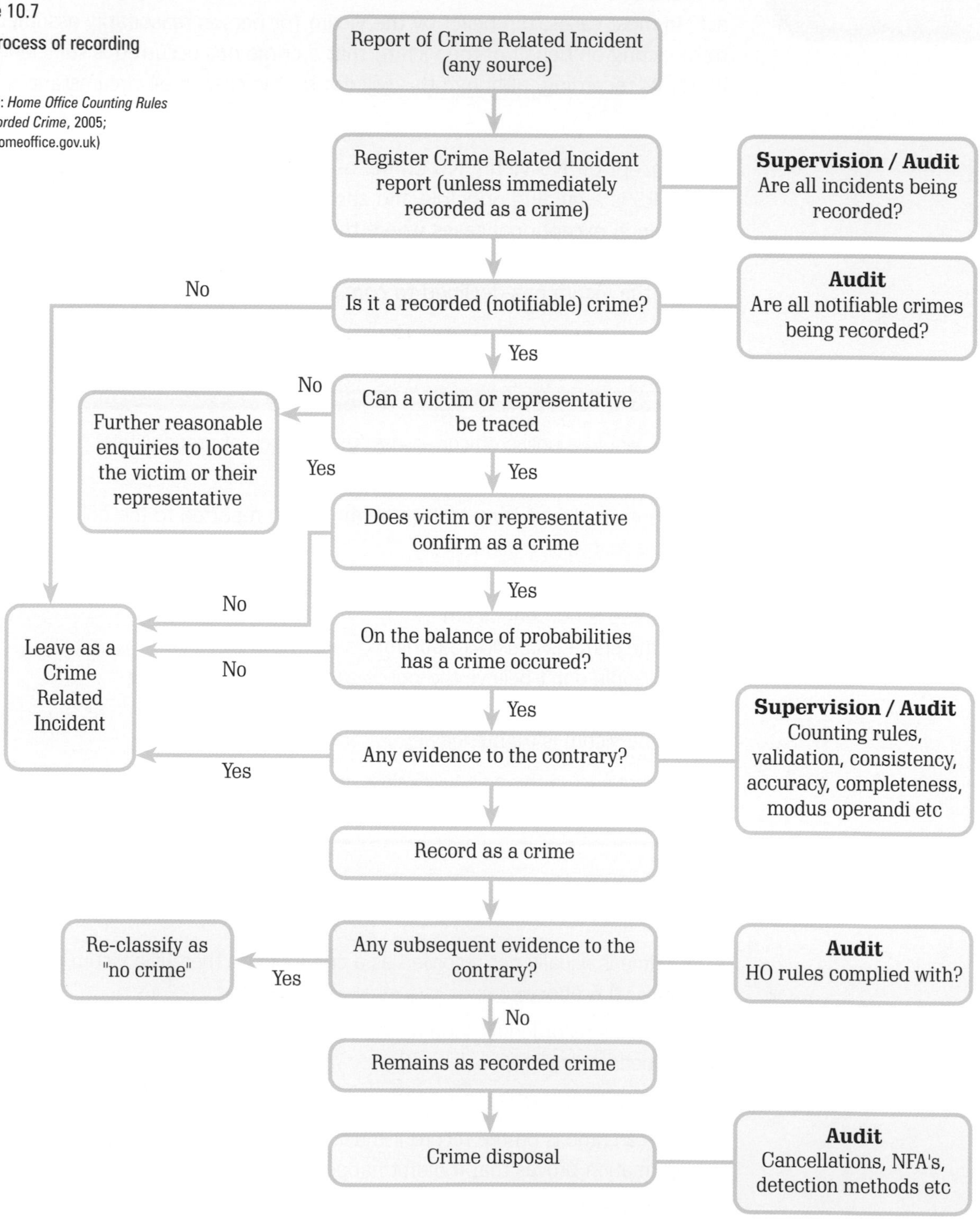

www.homeoffice.gov.uk (Search for 'counting rules' and 'National Crime Recording Standard')
www.audit-commission.gov.uk

The National Crime Recording Standard

The National Crime Recording Standard (NCRS) was introduced in 2002. It was devised by the Home Office and supported by the Association of Chief Police Officers (ACPO).

The NCRS is a set of rules for recording crimes. The Home Office audits (studies) the figures and produces from them reliable statistics showing the true figures of recorded crime in all parts of England and Wales.

The chief aims were:

- To promote greater consistency between police forces in the recording of crime.
- To take a more victim-oriented approach to crime recording.

Impact on the police service

The adoption of the NCRS had three main impacts (effects) on the police service, two which were positive and one which, for a time (until people got used to the new counting system), was negative.

1. *More reliable crime figures*. The greater consistency of crime recording brought about by the NCRS made crime figures more believable. It enabled the government to audit (inspect) the performance of different forces more effectively, and to find out which forces were more effective in recording and solving crimes. It also helped researchers to understand patterns of crime across the country more accurately, and to plan future policing needs.

2. *More helpful to victims*. A second impact on the police service was to encourage a trend which had been going on for some time before 2002 – a trend in paying more attention to the victims of crimes. There has been an increased awareness of what people suffer when they are victims of crime (due mainly to research in the USA, and opinion polls in the UK). This has led to ideas such as 'zero-tolerance', and also to the development of schemes which help victims and witnesses of crime.

For more on help for victims and witnesses, see pages 243–45.

3. *Paperwork*. Another impact was to increase the amount of paperwork, and the amount of special training given to officers (now known as 'recording officers') whose job was to record crime. Changing from one system to another was understandably difficult for people who were used to recording crimes in other ways.

Impact on crime statistics

The introduction of the NCRS standardised the ways in which individual police forces collected their crime figures. The effect on individual forces was variable because each force previously had its own methods, and some were closer to the NCRS method than others. However, the overall national impact was to increase the total number of recorded crimes by 10 per cent.

This is an average figure. The effect was different for different types of crime, because the recording systems used previously varied from one type of crime to another. The figures for individual types of recorded crime are:

Violence against the person	+20%
Burglary	+3%
Robbery	+3%
Theft	+9%
Vehicle theft	−1 to −9%
Criminal damage	+9%

(*Source*: Home Office Research Development and Statistics (2003)
*National Crime Recording Standard (NCRS):
An Analysis of the Impact on Recorded Crime*)

The impact was most marked for the months immediately following the introduction of the new counting system in April 2002.

Visit www.homeoffice.gov.uk and read up about the NCRS.

Impact 2002–2005

The effect of the NCRS in the next three years was to cause the police to record a higher proportion of the crime reported to them than they did before the changes in the counting rules brought about by NCRS. As the Home Office puts it in *Crime in England and Wales 2004–2005* (the annual crime figures):

'The rate of victims' reporting of crimes to the police has remained broadly stable since 1997, whereas the rate of recording of crimes by the police has been increasing, especially in the last three years, largely as a result of the national introduction of the National Crime Recording Standard (NCRS).'

The reason why it is known that the police are recording more of the crimes that are reported to them is because there are two types of crime statistics – those collected by the police and those collected by the British Crime Survey.

The British Crime Survey

The British Crime Survey (BCS) is based on the questioning of over 45,000 people about the crimes they have suffered in the past 12 months. It gives information about all types of crime against individuals (but not about crimes against, say, industry). These figures can then be used to give a picture of crime rates in the country which is more accurate than the police figures. The reason why it is more accurate is because very many crimes are never reported to the police, but people will report them in a survey. More detailed explanation is given in Case study 10.5.

---

case study 10.5

The British Crime Survey

BMRB Social Research carried out 45,120 face-to-face interviews with adults aged 16 or over living in private households in England and Wales. Interviews took place between April 2004 and March 2005. The sample was designed to be representative of private households, and of adults aged 16 and over living in private households. The overall response rate for calendar year 2004 was 75 per cent.

BCS respondents are asked about their experiences of crime-related incidents in the 12 months prior to their interview. In addition, the respondents are asked about their attitudes towards different crime-related issues such as the police, Criminal Justice System, perceptions of crime and anti-social behaviour.

The BCS figures are based on the interviews between April 2004 and March 2005 (BCS year ending March 2005) and incidents experienced by survey respondents in the 12 months prior to their interview, with the estimates centring on March 2004. Averaging over the moving recall period of the BCS generates estimates that are most closely comparable with police recorded crime figures for the 12 months up to the end of September 2004.

The police recorded crime figures relate to the crimes recorded by the police in England and Wales in the financial year 2004/05.

(*Source*: Home Office, *Crime in England and Wales 2004–2005*; www.homeoffice.gov.uk)

---

activity
GROUP WORK

(a) What problem is caused by the fact that the police normally record crime figures for each financial year, while the BCS records crime figures from September to September?

(b) Why does a crime survey give a more accurate picture of crime figures than police records?

The British Crime Survey was done in the years before the change in police crime counting rules brought about by the NCRS in 2002, and has been done in the years since then. By comparing the figures for different types of crime in the British Crime Survey and the police figures for recorded crime, we can find out how many of the crimes that actually happen the police are recording. And that is why we know that under the new system the police are recording more of the crimes that are reported to them than they were under the old system.

The impact of national crime recording on crime reduction

Crime reduction

Crime reduction can mean two things:

(a) any lessening of crime, for whatever reason

(b) strategies, schemes and plans (by the police, partnerships and local authorities) to prevent, limit or reduce crime – either in a given area or the country in general.

Crime recording

As we have seen, this is simply the inputting of crimes reported into the police system. Changes in crime recording cannot, in themselves, reduce crime in any way. Changes in the recording system may make it seem as though crime numbers have gone up or down, but this is simply because they are being counted differently.

Crime trends

One major importance of national crime recording is that it shows **crime trends**.

Crime trend data, collected using reliable methods such as the National Crime Recording Standard and the BCS survey, are used to set policing targets.

Setting targets

A target is a figure, based on recent trends, designed to improve the performance of a public service. The aim is to reach the target after a given period of time. Many police targets are to do with crime reduction (see Case study 10.6).

Some of these targets are set for the whole of England and Wales by the Home Office; others are set locally. They are meant to be realistic (i.e. possible) but challenging (i.e. a definite improvement from the previous year). A realistic target for reducing crime must be linked to present crime levels. Present crime levels can only be known if the counting system is good. Both the government and the police hope that by having valid figures for recorded crime based on the NCRS, it will be possible to set realistic targets which will motivate the police to bring about a real reduction in crime levels.

keyword

Crime trend
an increase or decrease in crime over a period of time.

Figure 10.8

Crime trends measured by
the British Crime Survey,
1995–2004/5

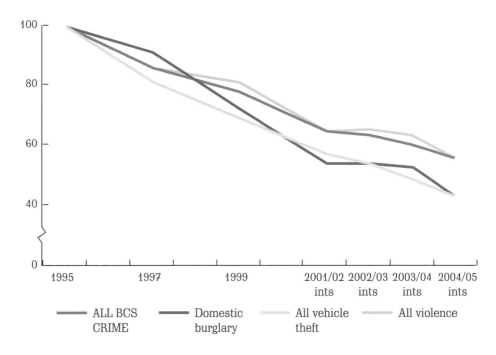

| — ALL BCS CRIME | — Domestic burglary | — All vehicle theft | — All violence |

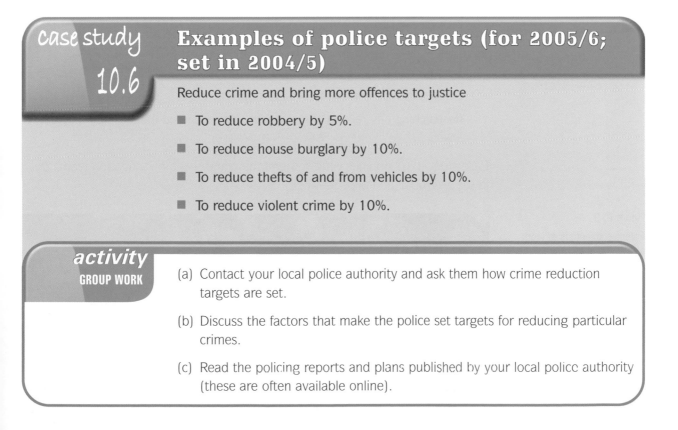

case study 10.6

Examples of police targets (for 2005/6; set in 2004/5)

Reduce crime and bring more offences to justice

- To reduce robbery by 5%.
- To reduce house burglary by 10%.
- To reduce thefts of and from vehicles by 10%.
- To reduce violent crime by 10%.

activity
GROUP WORK

(a) Contact your local police authority and ask them how crime reduction targets are set.

(b) Discuss the factors that make the police set targets for reducing particular crimes.

(c) Read the policing reports and plans published by your local police authority (these are often available online).

Look at www.homeoffice.gov.uk for
- police crime figures from 2002 to the present time
- BCS crime figures from 2002 to the present time
- information on how local and national police use statistics to plan future methods of crime reduction

The Crime Scene Investigation unit

The police must gather as much evidence about a crime as possible if they want to solve it. One way they do this is by investigating the **crime scene**, often using the expert help of **forensic scientists**.

Basic crime scene examination follows the steps given below:

1. Attending the scene, making contact with the victim
2. Assessing the scene (forensically)
3. Considering health and safety risks
4. Carrying out a forensic examination of the scene
5. Completing relevant documentation
6. Providing advice and guidance
7. Maintaining continuity and integrity of samples
8. Disseminating the results of the examination
9. Liaising with officers who have attended the crime scene(s)
10 Researching any related crime scenes and recovered items which may be linked.

Case study 10.7 outlines what some of the crime scene investigation teams do in the Metropolitan Police Service.

> **keyword**
>
> **Crime scene**
> the place where a crime happened, or any place where evidence of a crime is found.

> **keyword**
>
> **Forensic scientists**
> experts trained in collecting and examining evidence of crimes.

Figure 10.9

Forensic scientists at work at a scene of a crime

> **remember**
>
> 'Crime scene investigation' is sometimes called 'crime scene examination'.

case study 10.7

Crime scene investigation teams

The Forensic Services Command Unit is responsible for the forensic examination of all crime scenes. A Borough Forensic Manager has a team of Crime Scene Examiners who cover the examination of volume crime scenes and support Crime Scene Managers at more serious crime scenes, including murder.

Forensic Investigation Specialist Crime conducts forensic investigations of homicide, armed robbery and any other crime that falls within the remit of Specialist Crime. The Unit also has a Forensic Intelligence Unit to gather intelligence on crime scenes linked by forensic evidence.

The Fingerprint Bureau searches and compares finger and palm marks from crime scenes against offender databases, arrestee fingerprints against databases of unidentified marks, and fingerprints of suspects specified by investigating officers. The unit also retrieves finger and palm marks by physical and chemical means and coordinates fingerprint evidence for presentation in court. Furthermore, the unit stores and retrieves archived material from forensic investigations and is also responsible for searching and comparing the fingerprints of all arrestees in London, in order to establish their true identity.

The Evidence Recovery Unit involves the chemical treatment prior to fingerprint examination, DNA and firearms examination and use of specialised photographic lighting techniques.

(*Source*: www.met.police.uk)

activity
GROUP WORK

(a) Why is it necessary to have specialist forensic teams?

(b) How is forensic material stored?

(c) How is forensic information stored?

(d) What kinds of samples are searched for at crime scenes? List as many as you can and discuss what they might reveal.

In the Metropolitan Police officers who work at the scene of a crime (where a crime has happened) are called Crime Scene Examiners.

Crime Scene Managers are in charge of crime scenes. They:

- preserve the scene of crime
- organise the investigation of the scene
- ensure that evidence is collected and dealt with correctly.

They can call in help from outside specialists – especially the Forensic Science Service, which is independent of the police and also works for other organisations such as HM Revenue and Customs.

Invite a visiting speaker from the forensic science service.
Visit these websites:
www.forensic.gov.uk
www.acpo.police.uk (A top site!)

How crime scenes can be linked and offenders profiled

Crime scenes are important because they contain evidence about the crime and whoever did it. In the case of a murder this evidence may include a dead body, bloodstains, a murder weapon and other obvious 'clues'. But there will also be some less obvious clues which can only be found by skilled and painstaking search – for example hairs, dust or spots of dried body fluids. All these details, big and small, make up the scene of crime.

Linking crime scenes is done by inputting key details of every crime onto a computer database. Special software then picks out similarities between crimes, and groups them according to these similarities. Repeat criminals usually commit their crimes in a particular way – a way which they have found is effective. This tends to be true for any kind of crime – murder, burglary, rape, mugging or even shoplifting. The criminal's special way of carrying out a crime is called a modus operandi (MO). This is Latin for 'method of operation'.

Crime scenes can be linked by:

- location
- times at which the crimes take place
- type of victim
- how the crime is committed
- methods of disposing of stolen goods (for burglary or theft)
- other characteristics.

Linked crime scenes may tell the police that the crimes are probably committed by the same person. By using evidence from several crimes they can learn more about the offender's character, needs and interests. With this collected information the police can use 'offender profiling' (see below) to build up a picture of the offender.

Another form of crime scene linkage helps the police to predict the type of crime likely to happen in a particular area. An example is given in Case study 10.8.

case study 10.8

Crime pattern analysis

Crime pattern analysis is a generic term for a number of related analytical disciplines such as crime, or incident series identification, crime trend analysis, hot spot analysis and general profile analysis. Above all, crime pattern analysis looks for linkages between crimes and other forms of offending to reveal similarities and differences. It can help to reveal the relationships between crimes and offer opportunities to link committed offences quickly to possible offenders.

(*Source*: National Criminal Intelligence Service)

activity
GROUP WORK

(a) Why does crime pattern analysis work well with prolific offenders?

(b) Investigate crime trends in local or national crime figures, and suggest reasons for these trends.

Offender profiling

Offender profiling is a technique for linking different types of offender with different types of crime.

Psychological studies of offenders (using prison interviews, pre-sentence reports and other information) show that different types of crime are carried out by different types of people with different needs.

Arsonists, for example, are a type of offender which can be profiled, as Case study 10.9 shows.

The aims of offender profiling are:

- to build up a psychological picture of an offender so that he or she can be identified, found and charged

- to understand better the motivation which makes some people commit certain types of crime (and use this knowledge to stop them offending in the first place).

The National Intelligence Model

The National Intelligence Model (NIM) is a code of practice governing the way the police use 'intelligence' – information about crimes and offenders. It came into operation in January 2005. The aim is for all the police forces in England and Wales to have the same ways of classifying and storing this information so that it can easily be shared and used by other forces.

Included in the National Intelligence Model is the Serious Organised Crime Agency, formed in 2006 from the National Crime Squad and the National Criminal Intelligence Service. NIM incorporates other codes of practice, especially those drawn up by the Association of Chief Police Officers (ACPO), to deal with serious crime – e.g. the *ACPO Manual of Standards on Surveillance*, the *ACPO Manual of Professional Standards in Policing*, the *ACPO Kidnap Manual of Guidance* and *The Murder Investigation Manual*.

The National Intelligence Model and policing practices

1. Purpose of NIM – to standardise and coordinate the fight against crime at all levels.

2. Aim – to analyse and use information to maximum benefit.

---

case study 10.9

Offender profiling

In the USA, research has been undertaken to define the characteristics of children who put themselves at risk of setting further fires so that appropriate intervention programmes can be developed. Differences between groups of fire-setters and non fire-setters have been found, these included:

■ more curiosity about fire and involvement in fire-related activities in the past and present

■ more frequent exposure to peers and family members who were involved with fire

■ more frequent complaints or concerns from adults about the child's behaviour with fire.

(*Source*: D.J. Kolko and A.E. Kazdin (1989). Assessment of dimensions of firesetting among patient and nonpatient children: The Firesetting Risk Interview, *Journal of Abnormal Child Psychology*, 17, 157–76.)

In England and Wales, in every year between 1995 and 1999, around a half of those found guilty or cautioned for arson were males aged under 18.

(*Source*: www.crimereduction.gov.uk)

---

activity

GROUP WORK

(a) Suggest as many reasons as you can why young males are more likely to be arsonists than any other section of the population.

(b) Can you think of any kinds of crime which are more likely to be committed by (a) older people and (b) women?

3. NIM classification of crime

   Level 1: local crime and anti-social behaviour

   Level 2: regional criminal activity usually requiring additional resources

   Level 3: the most serious and organised crime.

4. Responsibility

   - Within each force an assistant chief constable (or higher) must ensure that the force conforms to the standards needed.

   - Each force must hold high-level meetings on Strategic and Tactical Tasking and Coordination (effective planning, and sharing information with other forces or agencies).

5. Knowledge, systems, sources and people – forces must make the most of their knowledge, systems, sources and people.

   - Knowledge: the knowledge of the area, the crimes that have taken place, and the knowledge of how to do policing.

   - Systems: computer networks.

   - Sources: informers and other sources of information about crime and crime patterns.

   - People: all the staff who are involved with policing.

6. Technology and software

   - Standardised IT facilities for all forces good enough to carry out NIM effectively.

   - Consistency of storage, processing and communicating intelligence.

7. Security – good data protection measures (since NIM makes information about people much more widely available, yet privacy must be protected).

8. Profiling – profiles are drawn up of 'targets' (criminal individuals or groups) and 'problems' (special types of crime).

9. Level of response – proportional, in other words NIM neither over-reacts nor under-reacts to a problem.

10. Human rights – human rights are respected.

Intelligence-led policing

Intelligence-led policing is policing which acts on the basis of intelligence (information) about possible crimes, rather than waiting for the crime to happen. It can be a very effective way of either catching criminals in the act, or preventing the crime from even happening.

case study 10.10

Intelligence-led policing

'Over the last few years, police activity has shifted its centre of balance away from the reactive investigation after events, towards targeting active criminals on the balance of intelligence. We have [invested] much in developing new intelligence practices and skills in analysis. Intelligence usually means making inferences from large amounts of data. This process is only possible if we can mix and match information across the board. To this end, it is essential that common standards and discipline attach to the intelligence process. Aside from professionalising police efforts to target local criminals, we should be able to aggregate the national picture in a much more informative way. The evaluation of this programme is one of the main planks to the ACPO Crime strategy.'

(*Source*: Sir David Phillips, QPM, Chief Constable of Kent County Constabulary, March 2000 in NCIS, *The National Intelligence Model*; www.ncis.co.uk)

activity
INDIVIDUAL WORK

(a) Using the internet or newspapers, find stories where intelligence-led policing has led to the solving of crimes or the arrest of criminals.

(b) Intelligence-led policing can lead to the use of 'stings'. What are stings, and what are their advantages and disadvantages?

New policing practices

These should be researched through the help of visiting speakers from your local police force. Some of the points are:

- that the computerisation of records is more important than ever

- that officers require a good deal of training in the National Intelligence Model and the techniques of intelligence-led policing

- that policing is more proactive (catching criminals before or during, rather than after, they have committed the crime). Proactive policing includes 'stings', where criminals are tempted into a trap, and infiltration of criminal networks

- the police spend more time listening to informants and collecting information

- there is much more liaison between different forces than there used to be.

 Visit www.policereform.gov.uk and research 'National Policing Plan'.

The Options Available to Effectively Manage Offenders

> **keyword**
>
> **Sentence**
> a punishment –
> involving some loss
> of freedom – given
> to a guilty person
> by a criminal court.

If offenders are found guilty in court they are sentenced. **Sentences** are either non-custodial (outside prison) or custodial (inside prison).

There are three basic levels of non-custodial (not prison) sentence, and a range of custodial sentences.

Different levels of sentence

Low

For offences such as persistent petty offending, some public order offences, some thefts from shops, or interference with a motor vehicle, the following can be used:

- 40 to 80 hours of unpaid work
- a curfew up to 12 hours per day for a few weeks
- exclusion from an area etc., without electronic tagging for a few months
- a prohibited activity requirement
- an attendance centre requirement.

Medium

> **remember**
>
> A suspended
> sentence is a
> sentence which is
> not served, but
> appears in the
> offender's criminal
> record.

For offences such as handling stolen goods worth less than £1000, burglary in commercial premises, some cases of taking a motor vehicle without consent, or some cases of obtaining property by deception:

- 80 to 150 hours of unpaid work
- an activity requirement 20 to 30 days
- a curfew up to 12 hours for 2 to 3 months
- an exclusion requirement lasting 6 months
- a prohibited activity requirement.

High

For offences such as a standard domestic burglary committed by a first-time offender:

- an unpaid work order of between 150 and 300 hours
- an activity requirement up to the maximum 60 days
- exclusion order lasting 12 months
- a curfew up to 12 hours a day for 4 to 6 months.

Other options for more serious offences:

- electronic monitoring (used to enforce compliance with other requirements)
- a possible lightening of the sentence where the offender has spent time in prison on remand before trial

■ breaches of any conditions will result in re-sentencing, or in increasing the severity of the original sentence

■ deferred sentences: these are sentences where the offender follows certain conditions such as training or drug treatment, rather than receive a direct 'punishment', e.g. imprisonment, even though the offence was serious enough to be custodial. These are used when it is expected that the offender will be of good behaviour after sentencing.

Custody

This means imprisonment. Under the 2003 Criminal Justice Act prisoners may be let out of prison before the full sentence is complete, but they must then be under supervision outside prison for the rest of the period of their original sentence.

Intermittent custody

This new form of custody means the offender stays in prison at the weekend, but may be allowed to study, work or care for someone during the week.

activity
INDIVIDUAL WORK
(10.6)

(a) What are 'an activity requirement and 'a prohibited activity requirement'?

(b) Go through each sentence and decide how effective you think it is (i) as a punishment, (ii) as a deterrent to others and (iii) as an aid to rehabilitation.

case study

10.11

Fines

Fines are penalties available to courts for a wide variety of offences. In the Magistrates' Courts offences that attract fines are subject to maximums from level 1 to level 5.

Level 1: £200
Level 2: £500
Level 3: £1,000
Level 4: £2,500
Level 5: £5,000

There is no limit to the amount the Crown Court can fine, but the amount will take into account the seriousness of the offence and the offender's ability to pay.

(*Source*: www.cjsonline.gov.uk)

activity
GROUP WORK

(a) Discuss the advantages and disadvantages of fines as a form of punishment.

(b) At the time of writing, some 75,000 people are being held in Britain's prisons. Are we imprisoning too many people, too few or about the right number? What do you think?

www.sentencing-guidelines.gov.uk

progress check

1. State how three public services help the victims of crime.
2. Give two financial costs and two non-financial costs of crime.
3. Which type of crime is the most costly for the taxpayer?
4. What happens to offenders when they receive 'cognitive skills training'?
5. What types of crime do community safety units specialise in?
6. What is the National Crime Recording Standard, and why is it useful?
7. Why are the crime figures in the British Crime Survey different from police crime figures?
8. What are the 10 steps of crime scene examination?
9. What is the National Intelligence Model?
10. State four types of non-custodial sentence

UNIT 12

Driving and its Relationship to the Public Services

This unit covers:

- the requirements of pre- and post-test driving
- common traffic offences and driver attitudes
- the role of emergency services in responding to road traffic collisions
- the importance of road safety campaigns, initiatives and strategies in accident prevention

Learning to drive is a 'must' for most people, and passing the test is likely to get more difficult as the years go by. You should therefore learn as much about driving as you can, at the earliest possible age, and pass your driving test if you haven't already done so.

The need is even greater if you want to join the uniformed public services, although the armed forces will sometimes teach you to drive after you have joined.

This unit will not teach you to drive, but it will give you a lot of useful background information about driving. You will find out about the legal requirements for learning to drive and about safety on the roads. And you will learn what the emergency services do when there is an accident. Finally, you will study accident prevention and the various schemes and campaigns used to make driving safer on British roads.

grading criteria

To achieve a **Pass** grade the evidence must show that the learner is able to:	To achieve a **Merit** grade the evidence must show that, in addition to the pass criteria, the learner is able to:	To achieve a **Distinction** grade the evidence must show that, in addition to the pass and merit criteria, the learner is able to:
P1 identify the stages of learning to drive and documentation associated with car ownership	**M1** explain the legal requirements of car ownership and learning to drive	**D1** evaluate the importance of the emergency services working together when dealing with collisions

grading criteria

To achieve a **Pass** grade the evidence must show that the learner is able to:	To achieve a **Merit** grade the evidence must show that, in addition to the pass criteria, the learner is able to:	To achieve a **Distinction** grade the evidence must show that, in addition to the pass and merit criteria, the learner is able to:
P2 explain how driver attitudes and behaviour contribute to traffic offences	**M2** explain how the emergency services work together when dealing with collisions	**D2** evaluate the success or failure of a local and national campaign in accident prevention
P3 identify common traffic offences which cause road traffic collisions	**M3** explain how successful road safety campaigns have been in accident prevention	
P4 describe the responsibilities of both individuals and employees regarding driving safely and within the law		
P5 outline the responsibilities of the emergency services when dealing with road traffic collisions		
P6 describe national and local road safety campaigns, initiatives and strategies in accident prevention		

The Requirements of Pre- and Post-test Driving

Stages of learning to drive

1. Getting a licence

Driving licences are issued by the Driver and Vehicle Licensing Agency (DVLA). The type of licence you need for learning to drive is called a provisional licence. Without it you cannot drive on a public road. You apply by completing a form called D1 which comes either from a post office, or through the DVLA form ordering service.

You need to prove your identity and provide a photograph. Means of identification are:

- full valid current passport
- UK birth certificate
- certificate of registry of birth (provided your name is present on the certificate)
- adoption certificate
- ID card issued by a member state of the EC/EEA
- travel documents issued by the Home Office
- certificate of naturalisation.

The photograph must be:

- colour passport style and size (size of image 45mm × 35mm)
- a recent and true likeness, showing the full face, with no hat, helmet or sunglasses, although you can wear everyday glasses
- taken against a plain, evenly lit and light background
- signed on the reverse by the person who has completed Section 7 of your D1 form (previously D750) if you enclose any document other than a full valid current UK passport.

(*Source*: www.dvla.gov.uk/drivers)

If the identification document is anything except a full passport the photograph must be validated by having somebody who knows you sign on the back to say that it is a true likeness. A list of people who can validate the photograph (and complete Section 7 of the D1 form) is given below:

- a local business person or shopkeeper
- a librarian
- a professionally qualified person, for example, a lawyer, teacher or engineer
- a police officer
- a bank or building society officer
- a civil servant
- a minister of religion
- a magistrate
- a local councillor or an MP (AM, MEP and MSP).

Warning: This person must have known you personally for at least two years and must not be a relative.

Note: Some professionals may charge you for this.

The DVLA will make random checks on people who sign photocard driving licence applications.

(*Source*: www.dvla.gov.uk/drivers)

Proving identity at a post office

If your proof of identity is a passport, and you don't want to send it through the post to Swansea, you can get it validated (checked) at a post office for an additional fee of £4.00 (2005 figure). The validation will then be sent with the rest of your application to the DVLA.

The completed application and fee (£38 in 2005) for a provisional licence is sent to the DVLA, Swansea, SA99 1AD.

---

activity
GROUP WORK (12.1)

(a) Why do drivers need licences and identification? Think of as many reasons as you can.

(b) Why can only 'a professionally qualified person' complete Section 7 of the D1 form?

(c) Would a bus driver or a window cleaner be allowed to complete Section 7?

---

2. Learning to drive

You cannot start learning to drive on a public road until you have received your provisional licence.

Most people learn to drive by taking driving lessons, and doing some private driving practice.

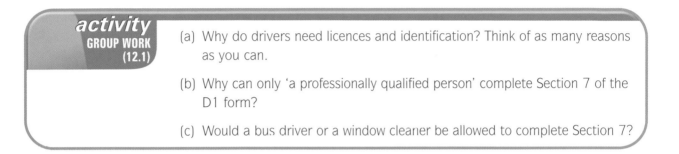

case study 12.1

Driving lessons and practice

Those who pass their driving test have had, on average, about 45 hours of professional training combined with 22 hours of private practice. Learners who prepare this way, with a combination of plenty of professional training and plenty of practice, do better in the test.

(*Source*: Driving Standards Agency www.dsa.gov.uk/)

activity
GROUP WORK

Why are both professional training and plenty of practice so useful for someone preparing for the test?

The syllabus of driving lessons includes:

- controlling the car

- dealing with different road, traffic and weather conditions

- manoeuvres such as emergency stops, three-point turns, reversing etc.

Private practice must be done with someone who is at least 21 years old and has had a full UK driving licence for the same type of vehicle for at least three years. Learner drivers must display L-plates.

While learning to drive you should study the *Highway Code*. Knowledge of this is needed for driving in general, and for the theory test (see below). The *Highway Code* can be bought, or downloaded from the internet.

www.highwaycode.gov.uk

3. The tests

There are two types of test – the theory test and the practical test. You have to take both.

The theory test was introduced in 1996 and upgraded in 2002. It consists (2005) of 35 multiple-choice questions, and 14 film clips showing potential **hazards**. It is done on a touch-screen computer. This test has to be done after your 17th birthday and before you take the practical test.

> **keyword**
>
> **Hazard**
> anything that can cause harm.

When you take the practical test you need all your car documents with you. The test lasts 40 minutes. You will drive in various road situations and carry out some manoeuvres such as reversing or an emergency stop. If you drive without any major faults, and with no more than 15 minor faults, you will pass. The pass rate is 43 per cent.

After passing the test you must obtain a full licence by completing the declaration on your test pass certificate and sending it to the DVLA. Then you can drive alone on the public road. However, there is a probationary period of two years. If you get six or more penalty points during these two years your licence will be revoked (taken away) and you will have to take the theory and practical tests again.

The process of learning to drive – i.e. getting better – continues long after drivers have passed their test.

There are organisations which offer advanced driver training and tests – one of the main ones is the Institute of Advanced Motoring.

The Advanced test lasts for 90 minutes and covers about 40 miles of roads.

Documentation

The documents needed are:

- a driving licence
- a valid vehicle licence disc
- an MOT (Ministry of Transport) certificate if the car is more than 3 years old
- car insurance.

There are three types of car insurance:

- third party (covers injuries to other people, including passengers; damage to other people's property; liability for accidents caused by passengers; liability from a caravan or trailer attached to the car)
- third party, fire and theft (like third party but also covers the driver for fire and theft of vehicle)
- comprehensive (like the above *and* accidental damage to own car; personal accident benefit – covers injuries to yourself; death or long-term injury cover; medical expenses; loss of personal belongings in the car).

Want to find out more?
Go to www.dvla.gov.uk

Legal requirements of owning a car

In addition to the documentation shown above there are other requirements relating to car ownership.

The DVLA must be told if you change your name, address or vehicle.

Laws about the car

1. *Tyres*. It is against the law to have:
   - car tyres with tread worn to below 1.6mm
   - a mix of radial and cross-ply tyres
   - over- or under-inflated tyres
   - tyres with cuts, lumps, bulges or tears
   - the wrong sort of tyre fitted to a vehicle or trailer.

2. *Seatbelts*. The law about seat belts is summarised in Table 12.1.

3. *General roadworthiness*. It is the responsibility of the car owner to ensure that the car is in a fit condition to go on the road. The car should be regularly and thoroughly serviced by someone who knows how to do it. After the car is 3 years old it must have an MOT test every year to check that it is in a roadworthy condition. In cars, the features tested in the MOT are given in Case study 12.2.

Table 12.1 Seatbelt law

	Front seat	Rear seat	Who is responsible
Driver	Seatbelt must be worn if fitted		Driver
Child under 3 years of age	Appropriate child restraint must be worn.	Appropriate child restraint must be used if available.	Driver
Child aged 3 to 11 and under 1.5 metres (approx 5ft) in height	Appropriate child restraint must be used if available. If not, an adult seatbelt must be worn.	Appropriate child restraint must be used if available. If not, an adult seatbelt must be worn if available.	Driver
Child aged 12 or 13 or younger child 1.5 metres (approx 5ft) or more in height.	Adult seatbelt must be worn if available.	Adult seatbelt must be worn if available.	Driver
Adult passengers (aged 14 and upwards)	Seatbelt must be worn if available.	Seatbelt must be worn if available.	Passenger

case study 12.2 — MOT checks

Vehicle identification number – a vehicle identification number must be permanently displayed and legible on a vehicle first used on or after 1 August 1980

Registration plate – condition, security, legibility and format of letters/numbers

Lights – condition, operation, security and correct colour. The headlamps will also be checked to see if the aim is correct

Steering and suspension – correct condition and operation

Wipers and washers – operate to give the driver a clear view of the road

Windscreen – condition and driver's view of the road

Horn – correct operation and type

Seatbelts – all seatbelts installed are checked for type, condition, operation and security. All compulsory seatbelts must be in place

Seats – front seats secure. Front and rear backseats can be secured in the upright position

Fuel system – no leaks, fuel cap fastens correctly and seals securely. The fuel cap will need to be opened. Make sure the key is available

Exhaust emissions – vehicle meets the requirement for exhaust emission. These vary on the age and fuel type of the vehicle

Exhaust system – complete, secure, without serious leaks and silences effectively

Vehicle structure – free from excessive corrosion or damage in specific areas. No sharp edges

Doors – open and close. Latch securely in closed position. Front doors should open from inside and outside the vehicle. Rear doors may need to be opened to gain access to testable items

Mirrors – presence, condition and security

Wheels and tyres – condition, security, tyre size and type, and tread depth. Spare tyres are not tested

Brakes – condition, operation and performance (efficiency test). Suitable vehicles will be tested on a roller brake tester. Vehicles such as those with permanent 4-wheel drive will be tested either on a suitable road using a properly calibrated and maintained decelerometer or, if one is installed at the test station, a plate brake tester

(*Source*: www.direct.gov.uk/Motoring)

---

activity

INDIVIDUAL WORK

Research:

(a) the history of the MOT test

(b) the effect it has had on road safety.

Legal requirements for learning to drive

The legal requirements for learning to drive are outlined in Case study 12.3.

case study

12.3

Legal requirements when learning to drive

To drive a car you must:

- hold the appropriate driving licence
- be 17 or over
- meet the legal eyesight standards
- have at least third party insurance

As a learner driver you must:

- be supervised by a qualified driver (aged 21+ and who has had a full licence for at least three years)
- display L plates

The car must:

- be registered with the Driver and Vehicle Licensing Agency (DVLA)

- have a valid vehicle tax disc

- hold a current MOT certificate (if this is required)

(*Source*: Adapted from www.direct.gov.uk)

activity
INDIVIDUAL WORK

(a) Why is it necessary to be insured?

(b) What information is given on a vehicle tax disc?

All these requirements relate to safety. The reason why safety is so important is that around 3500 people are killed each year on Britain's roads (3221 in 2004). Many more are injured, and accidents are extremely expensive. Having strict laws about learning to drive, and about the cars we drive in, saves lives and money.

Table 12.2 Average value of prevention per casualty and per accident in Great Britain, 2004 (£)

Accident/Casualty type	Cost per casualty	Cost per accident
Fatal	1,384,440	1,573,220
Serious	155,560	184,270
Slight	11,990	18,500
Average all severities	43,650	62,200
Damage only		1,650

(*Source*: *Road Casualties Great Britain 2004*, published September 2005)

www.dsa.gov.uk

Common Traffic Offences and Driver Attitudes

Traffic offences

Traffic offences are incidents on the road where a driver breaks the laws of driving. They are defined under the Road Traffic Act 1988. Many of them are listed below. The wording has been simplified. Section numbers (as they appear in the original Act) are given after each one.

- Causing death by dangerous driving, s.1
- Dangerous driving, s.2
- Driving without due care and attention, s.3
- Driving without reasonable consideration for other persons using the road or public place, s.3
- Refusing to stop when required to do so by a uniformed constable, s.163(3)
- Causing death by drunken or drugged driving, s.3A Road Traffice Act 1991
- Being unfit to drive through drink or drugs, while attempting to drive, s.4(1)
- Being unfit to drive through drink or drugs while in charge of a vehicle, s.4(2)
- Driving over the limit, s.5(1)(a)
- Being in charge of a vehicle while over the limit, s.5(1)(b)
- Failing to provide a specimen of breath, s.6(4)
- Failing to provide specimens (breath, urine or blood) when required to do so, s.7
- Driving without MOT, s.47(1)
- Driving without a licence, s.87(1)
- Driving without insurance, s.143(1)(a)
- Driving while disqualified, s.103
- Breaking speed limits, s.81; s.86

www.opsi.gov.uk/acts

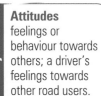

Attitudes
feelings or behaviour towards others; a driver's feelings towards other road users.

Behaviour
actions in general; the way the person drives.

The **attitudes** and **behaviour** which lead to these offences can be worked out by looking at the offences themselves.

'Dangerous driving' is driving too fast, not keeping to the correct side of the road, showing off to passengers, not paying attention, being aggressive to other drivers, and so on.

Attitudes leading to dangerous driving include:

- anger towards other drivers
- disregard for human life
- a sadistic desire to frighten people
- a suicidal desire to put oneself at risk
- being in an extreme hurry to get somewhere
- anger or frustration at something unconnected with driving
- mental or emotional illness or imbalance
- tiredness or stress which the driver has been unable to recognise.

Traffic law is based on behaviour, since this can be witnessed. Strictly speaking, attitudes are hidden inside people's minds.

Nevertheless, attitude is something drivers should be aware of, as the advice in Case study 12.4 shows.

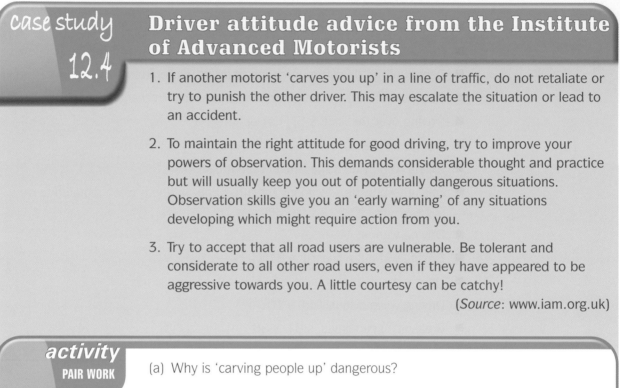

case study 12.4 — Driver attitude advice from the Institute of Advanced Motorists

1. If another motorist 'carves you up' in a line of traffic, do not retaliate or try to punish the other driver. This may escalate the situation or lead to an accident.

2. To maintain the right attitude for good driving, try to improve your powers of observation. This demands considerable thought and practice but will usually keep you out of potentially dangerous situations. Observation skills give you an 'early warning' of any situations developing which might require action from you.

3. Try to accept that all road users are vulnerable. Be tolerant and considerate to all other road users, even if they have appeared to be aggressive towards you. A little courtesy can be catchy!

(*Source*: www.iam.org.uk)

activity
PAIR WORK

(a) Why is 'carving people up' dangerous?

(b) Research techniques for improving your powers of observation.

(c) What is courtesy on the road, who does it benefit, and why?

Figure 12.1
Why driver attitudes matter

Traffic offences which can cause collisions

The main traffic offences are defined in the Road Traffic Act 1988.

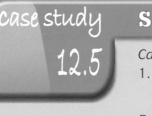

Collision
a crash between a vehicle and another vehicle; a vehicle and a pedestrian; a vehicle and an animal; a vehicle and any other object.

A **collision** is usually an accident but because cars can be used to murder people, when there is a serious collision the police have to consider the possibility that it was deliberate.

The first three sections of the Road Traffic Act 1988 give three serious traffic offences (see Case study 12.5).

The first one has, by definition, caused a collision, and is clearly the most serious of the three offences.

In the case of offences 2 and 3, drivers are likely to be charged with them after a collision has taken place (because the nature of the collision, as described by witnesses, or shown in the damage, makes it clear that the driving was reckless or careless).

case study 12.5

Sections 1–3 of the Road Traffic Act 1988

Causing death by reckless driving
1. A person who causes the death of another person by driving a motor vehicle on a road recklessly is guilty of an offence.

Reckless driving
2. A person who drives a motor vehicle on a road recklessly is guilty of an offence.

Careless, and inconsiderate, driving
3. If a person drives a motor vehicle on a road without due care and attention, or without reasonable consideration for other persons using the road, he is guilty of an offence.

(*Source*: www.opsi.gov.uk)

activity
GROUP WORK

What is the difference between:

(a) reckless driving

(b) driving without due care and attention

(c) driving without reasonable consideration for other persons?

Talk to traffic police, or get them to talk to you.

Visit a magistrates' court and listen to traffic cases.

Read accident reports in local newspapers.

Talk to driving instructors.

Watch television programmes which deal with traffic offences.

Talk to people who do a lot of driving.

Check out: Roger Lorton, *A–Z of Policing Law* (Latest edition), The Stationery Office (or any other up-to-date book on police law).

Responsibilities of drivers

Responsibilities are things that drivers have a duty to do. Most responsibilities are laid down in law, and if drivers ignore these responsibilities they are liable to be accused of dangerous driving.

All drivers have a responsibility to follow the Highway Code when they are on a public road. Drivers who are employees (i.e. paid to drive) have some extra responsibilities, mainly laid down by law, to ensure that they don't put themselves and others at risk.

Individual responsibilities

The responsibilities of drivers under the Highway Code are to drive legally and safely, minimising the risks and inconvenience. The responsibility of the individual driver is basically to be as safe as possible.

These responsibilities are:

- to have a valid driving licence (for you and the car)
- to be medically fit to drive
- to have all necessary documentation
- to be insured
- to have a car which is in good enough order to pass an MOT
- to have seatbelts, and to make sure that you use your own (you should try to make your passengers use them, but you are not legally responsible if they don't)
- to understand and obey road signs and road markings
- to understand and follow the rules of the road
- to overtake safely
- to obey lane discipline
- to obey speed limits
- to signal correctly
- to respect the safety of all other road users
- to be aware of potential hazards
- to stop if the police tell you to stop
- to report all accidents to the police if someone is hurt, however slightly

- to give and receive insurance details if you are in a collision
- never to drive under the influence of drink or drugs
- not to drive if you are in an unsuitable emotional state, or too tired
- not to allow yourself to be distracted by passengers
- not to use a mobile phone in the car
- to park correctly
- to carry first aid
- to drive according to the weather conditions.

Responsibilities of employees

People employed to drive heavy vehicles – such as lorry drivers, coach drivers and ambulance drivers – have an extra set of rules to follow. These are about how long they can drive each day.

They are called the Road Transport (Working Time) Regulations 2005. They affect mobile workers (mainly drivers, crew and other travelling staff) who are travelling in vehicles subject to the Community Drivers' Hours regulation (3820/85/EEC) or, in some cases, the AETR (The European Agreement Concerning the Work of Crews of Vehicles Engaged in International Transport).

Such employees must not work more than:

- an average 48-hour week
- 60 hours in any single week
- 10 hours in any 24-hour period, if working at night.

Working time means the time spent on all road transport activities including:

- driving
- loading /unloading
- driver training, if it is part of the normal workload
- helping passengers to get on and off a vehicle
- cleaning and maintaining the vehicle.

These rules affect drivers of, or workers in, vehicles which weigh more than 3.5 tonnes and are equipped with a tachograph (an instrument fitted to the vehicle which records the time spent working and/or driving).

Employees working on these kinds of vehicle have a responsibility to follow the Road Transport (Working Time) Regulations 2005. Their working practices are inspected by the Vehicle and Operator Services Agency (VOSA) – formerly called the Vehicle Inspectorate, in Great Britain.

Coach drivers on an international unscheduled (non-regular) journey can work longer than 60 hours in a week. At night, the working time should not exceed 10 hours in any 24-hour period.

Figure 12.2
Road Transport (Working Time) Regulations 2005

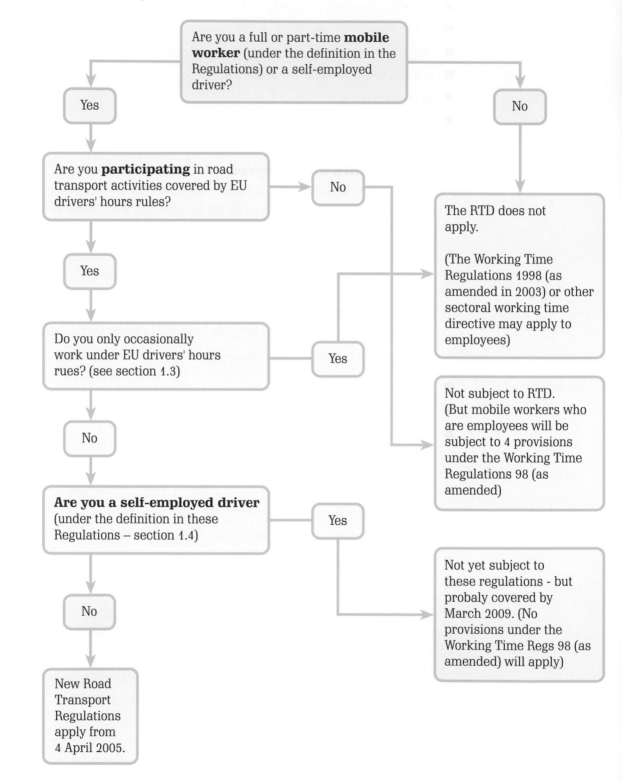

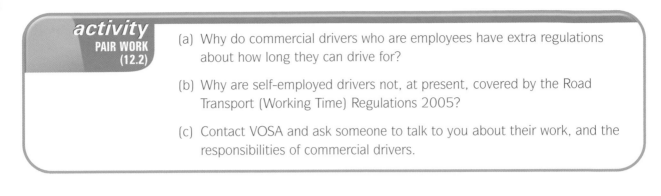

activity
PAIR WORK
(12.2)

(a) Why do commercial drivers who are employees have extra regulations about how long they can drive for?

(b) Why are self-employed drivers not, at present, covered by the Road Transport (Working Time) Regulations 2005?

(c) Contact VOSA and ask someone to talk to you about their work, and the responsibilities of commercial drivers.

Talk to an experienced coach or lorry driver.
Visit these websites:
www.vosa.gov.uk
www.dft.gov.uk

The Role of Emergency Services in Responding to Road Traffic Collisions

What happens at a road traffic collision depends on the seriousness of the incident. The more serious the incident the bigger the response, and the more people are likely to be involved.

When the incident is first reported as a 999 call it is treated as an emergency. The first role of the police, or the control centre which receives the call, is to get information.

case study 12.6

Road traffic collisions

Initial information needed on a road traffic collision:

- Name, home address and telephone number of informant

- First account of informant

- Precise details of location of scene

- Vehicle identification

- Details of other witnesses/persons present at scene.

In cases where the caller attempts to remain anonymous, every effort should be made to discover their identity. If however they terminate a telephone call, steps should be taken to establish its origins. The call records and tapes of other emergency services should identify caller numbers for investigative purposes. Control room staff and individual force policies should guide immediate police response.

(*Source*: © Centrex 2004 *Road Death Investigation Manual* Version 2, 2004)

activity
INDIVIDUAL WORK

(a) For what reasons might a caller try to remain anonymous?

(b) What kinds of guidance can control staff give?

(c) Why does each police force have 'individual force policies' for responding to traffic collisions?

In a serious collision where people are injured all the emergency services are likely to be alerted. The initial response to a serious collision is much the same for all three blue light services (see Table 12.3).

Table 12.3 SAD CHALET: Consideration should be given to the following when approaching an incident

Survey	Survey the scene from a distance having regard to your personal safety
Assess	Assess the incident
Disseminate	Disseminate the information below to your force control room and others as necessary
Casualties	Approximate number of casualties – fatal, injured and not injured
Hazards	Present and potential e.g. fuel spillage, debris, weather and road conditions, terrain, gas, chemicals, fire or danger of explosions
Access	Best routes for emergency vehicles and suitable provisional rendezvous point (RVP)
Location	Exact location (road junction or map reference to pinpoint the scene)
Emergency services	Emergency services present and required
Type and timescales	Type of incident with details of types and numbers of vehicles involved

activity
INDIVIDUAL WORK (12.3)

Why are casualties not the first priority when the emergency services arrive at the scene of a collision?

The police must protect the scene – since a collision, especially when people are injured, could be a crime or evidence of a crime, and there may need to be an investigation.

Scenes can be protected by:

- tape
- individual officers
- vehicles
- road closures and diversions
- temporary fencing.

Whatever emergency services are working at the accident scene, the police have overall control. This is called managing the scene.

---

case study 12.7 — Managing the scene

The SIO (Senior Investigating Officer) has overall responsibility for making decisions regarding the scene.

Consideration should be given to the following:

- evidence
- surface marks on the road – these may be hidden by other vehicles and should be identified, preserved and marked where possible
- debris – do not move debris unless it is absolutely necessary and in any case mark its position
- a record of the weather, road and driving conditions made upon arrival – these can change rapidly and these observations will benefit the subsequent investigation
- landing of a helicopter
- body fluids on surfaces which can, in some cases, be used to identify persons involved in the collision or even position them at the point of impact (all officers should guard against coming into contact with body fluids)
- all items recovered from the scene (items not needed for evidential purposes should be recovered by a suitable contractor)
- a final search to ensure no victims or evidence is missed.

(*Source*: ACPO)

---

activity
INDIVIDUAL WORK

(a) Give examples of the kinds of evidence the police would seek at the scene of a collision.

(b) What is 'debris' – and why might it matter?

(c) Why is information about weather, road and driving conditions needed?

(d) What is the role of the private contractor?

Investigation

The police collect evidence on the causes of the collision especially if it is serious or fatal. The fire and rescue service plays a major role if there is a fire or chemical spillage.

Ambulance service

The ambulance service, with paramedics:

- gives primary care to the injured

- carries out triage (sorting out the most seriously hurt)

- takes the injured to hospital.

Paramedics make use of the 'golden hour' – treating people as soon as possible, sometimes even before they have been cut out of the wreckage. This is because seriously injured people have a much better chance of recovery if they are treated in the first hour after the collision.

Fire and rescue service

Firefighters have a special role in putting out fires and cutting injured (and dead) people out of wrecked vehicles. They also deal with chemical spillages. They give emergency care to the injured. After the investigation they may be involved in a clean-up if dangerous or toxic materials are present.

Contact the traffic police, fire and rescue service and ambulance service. Visit www.acpo.police.uk (*Road Death Investigation Manual* Version 2, 2004)

How the emergency services work together when dealing with collisions

In serious RTAs (road traffic accidents) there is a combined response from the emergency services, with fire, ambulance and police all having a role to play.

This is triggered by a 999 call that normally goes through a shared control centre, automatically alerting all three blue light services. The services try to reach the scene as soon as possible (under 5 minutes in the town; up to 20 in the country).

Combined response for tanker crash
Fire and rescue service response:

1. Bring two 'pumps' (containing firefighting equipment), from different directions, and an 'emergency tender' (containing equipment for first aid and for cutting people out of crashed vehicles).

2. Assess what the tanker is carrying, using the orange HAZCHEM placards, and any indication of what extinguishing agent (foam, powder etc.) should be used.

3. Call for more backup – and technical help – if needed.

4. Approach the crash downhill and downwind.

5. Prevent fire spread – e.g. by using water jets to cool the tanker or anything else which is dangerously hot.

6. Carry out snatch rescues – perhaps of the driver, or people at serious risk in nearby houses.

7. Damp down or divert gases and vapours with a wall of spray, if the gas reacts to water.

8. Keep some of their vehicles in 'fend-off' positions to protect rescue workers from other traffic, if the accident has happened on a motorway.

9. Investigate the accident (together with the police and, perhaps, health and safety (HSE) inspectors).

10. Take part in debriefing.

Police response:

1. Saving lives in conjunction with the other emergency services.

2. Coordinating the emergency services where necessary (though if fire is involved in the accident, the fire and rescue service may do this as they are more aware of the hazards).

3. Protecting and preserving the scene – including controlling traffic and any crowds that might gather.

4. Investigating the accident – together with others (e.g. the fire and rescue service fire investigation team) if appropriate.

5. Collecting and communicating information on casualties.

6. Identifying any dead victims on behalf of the coroner.

7. Prevention of crime (if necessary).

8. Liaison with families (if necessary).

7. Restoring normality at the earliest opportunity.

Ambulance service response:

1. Assessing the scene, calling for backup if needed, contacting receiving hospitals.

2. Giving primary care to any injured people; stabilising the condition of crash victims, e.g. by giving painkillers or by hydrating them.

3. Continuing to give care while the fire and rescue service is cutting out trapped accident victims.

4. Prioritising casualties ('triage') if there are many of them, and not enough ambulances to take them immediately to hospital.

5. Organising parking and loading points for other ambulances.

6. Taking casualties to hospital.

---

activity
GROUP WORK
(12.4)

(a) What does HAZCHEM mean, and why is it necessary?

(b) What is a 'fend-off position'?

(c) What is debriefing?

(d) What is the role of the coroner?

(e) What is the purpose of triage?

In a serious collision the police have overall command of the incident scene, but, where fire or chemical spillage is the main hazard, control passes to the fire and rescue service, at least until the area is safe. The three main emergency services each keep their own control over their own areas of expertise, and the other services make sure that all services can do their specialist work to the best of their ability.

keyword

Debriefed
asked to say exactly what happened.

The emergency services carry out frequent training exercises based on simulated collisions and other incidents where they all have to work together. After these exercises the people taking part are **debriefed**. Problems are noted and training given. When real collisions happen, the training received for simulated collisions enables the emergency services to act promptly and correctly.

Invite a speaker from the police, fire and rescue or ambulance services.
Ask your library to get hold of all the Fire Service Manuals published by the IFE – www.ife.org.uk

Why the emergency services work together when dealing with collisions

The main reason why police, fire and rescue services and the ambulance service work together in collisions (and this goes for train collisions as well as collisions on the roads) is that each service has different but complementary areas of expertise. What this means is that each service specialises in part of the job of dealing with a collision. The present system of having three emergency services dealing with collisions ensures that each aspect of rescue work is done to the highest possible standard.

A fatal road accident – as we have seen – usually costs more than a million pounds to deal with (see page 332). The actions of the emergency services are complex because of the value placed on human life and the possibility that criminal activity is involved.

Figure 12.3 shows how the roles of emergency services at the scene of a collision are organised.

The fire and rescue service rescues people and cuts them out – giving priority, of course, to the living. They may be involved in an investigation and in the clear-up of the scene afterwards. However, the final clear-up is usually done by private firms.

The ambulance service deals mainly with survivors of the collision. They work with the fire and rescue crews in giving life-saving aid to victims, sometimes while they are still trapped. When victims have been freed they are taken to hospital, but they may still be receiving emergency treatment – for bleeding, shock, dehydration etc. – from paramedics on the way in. Ambulance crews try to give as much primary care as possible to accident victims on site (without delaying

Figure 12.3

The role of emergency services at a major road collision

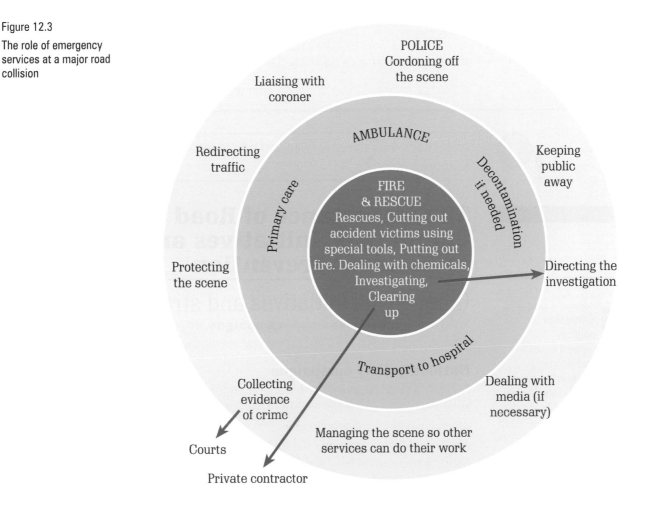

their transport to hospital) because immediate care is the most effective. The ambulance service can provide decontamination facilities if needed.

The police manage the scene and the surroundings so that the other services can get on with their urgent work. They also protect the scene, take a record of what is happening, and collect evidence. This includes finding witnesses, taking statements and taking photos, videos and measurements of the scene. Forensic teams may examine vehicles, body fluids and other evidence. The police liaise with their control centre to find out all they can about the vehicles and their owners or drivers. If the media arrive, the police may talk to them. The public are normally kept away, for fear of delaying the work, endangering themselves and others and contaminating the scene.

In a major collision there will be debriefing of rescue workers involved, to find out what can be learnt from it. The review of real incidents, like the review of training and practice, is important for improving the response to future accidents.

activity
GROUP WORK
(12.5)

(a) Why do the emergency services have to train to work together at scenes of collisions?

(b) Why do the police normally have overall management of the scene?

(c) What happens in a debriefing after a collision?

---

i Ask experts from the police, fire and rescue service and the ambulance service to speak to you.

The Importance of Road Safety Campaigns, Initiatives and Strategies in Accident Prevention

Campaigns, initiatives and strategies

Road safety **initiatives** include **campaigns**, education, police going to schools, road signs, road works and traffic calming.

National safety campaigns

National safety campaigns are planned and run by central government – in this case, the Department for Transport. They highlight particular road safety dangers which have been causing accidents. Normally they give a simple, memorable message. Many campaigns run for a limited period of time, since people stop noticing them when they are no longer new.

Campaign
publicity (advertisements and slogans), designed to make people more aware of a specific danger.

Initiatives
new actions planned to achieve an aim

case study

12.8

Time-line: campaigns, initiatives and strategies

1997: New Zebra, Pelican and Puffin crossing regulations introduced. Road Traffic (New Drivers) Act 1995 comes into force, withdrawal of licence and compulsory retesting for new drivers who accumulate 6 or more penalty points within 2 years of passing their driving test.

1998: Transport white paper published: 'A New Deal for Transport: Better for Everyone'. Drink-drive rehabilitation experiment expanded to cover around one-third of courts in Great Britain and extended for 2 years to the end of 1999. Publication of 'Combating Drink-drive: Next Steps' consultation paper.

1999: Kill your Speed campaign launched (six weeks: £3.5m). GLA Road Network announced (220 miles of trunk roads and 105 miles of borough roads). Revised edition of *The Highway Code* published. 'Cycle Smart' campaign for child cyclists launched. First BBC simulcast commercial for £2.6m Millennium Drink-Drive campaign.

2000: The government announced a new road safety strategy and casualty reduction targets for the year 2010 in *Tomorrow's Roads – Safer for Everyone*. A review of speed policy was conducted and reported in *New Directions in Speed Management*. £1.4bn targeted programme of improvements announced in *A New Deal for Trunk Roads in England* following the Roads Review. Think! Road Safety Campaign launched.

2001: The government announced a £10 million pilot of road safety schemes for children in deprived areas. *Road Safety Good Practice Guidance* published. First national campaign launched for fitting child car seats correctly. Road Safety website launched for children.

2002: The government seeks views on banning mobile phones whilst driving. £6 million was made available to improve road safety in most deprived cities. A new motorcycle safety campaign is launched, as is a campaign urging parents to check their child's car seat every trip. The Dangerous Driving report was published in February.

2003: The phased introduction of the hazard perception test into the theory test was completed. As of 1 December the new offence of using a hand-held mobile phone while driving is introduced.

2004: The first three-year review of the Government's road safety strategy published. The World Health Organisation dedicated World Health Day to the issue of road safety. The United Nations issued a resolution on global road safety. Launch of the new National Cycle Training standard.

2005: Publication of the Government's Strategy for Motorcycling.

(*Source*: *Road Casualties: Great Britain 2004*, published September 2005; www.dft.gov.uk/)

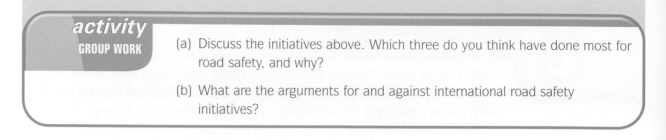

activity

GROUP WORK

(a) Discuss the initiatives above. Which three do you think have done most for road safety, and why?

(b) What are the arguments for and against international road safety initiatives?

The poster in Figure 12.4 is an example of a national campaign. It is one of several posters on the theme of 'Tiredness Kills'.

There are large numbers of safety campaigns, and they keep changing. Many of them, such as the 'Hedgehogs' campaign, are for children. Unlike the campaigns for adults, children's campaigns last a long time, and are much less horrific. They are intended to educate, not to frighten.

The government uses all the mass media to try to get its road safety message across. Television and local radio, cinemas, newspapers, posters and even the internet carry road safety messages.

Check out www.thinkroadsafety.gov.uk (a very useful website, full of campaigns)

Figure 12.4
Tiredness kills

Local safety initiatives

Local government spends a good deal of money on making roads safer. Some of this money is spent on redesigning the roads themselves.

The redesigning is done at places where there is a history of accidents. The cost has to be balanced against the expected reduction in casualties.

Case study 12.9 shows one such scheme in Buckinghamshire. The alterations were done at a place where there had been seven slight accidents between 1999 and 2003.

case study 12.9

Collision factors

Poor visibility at the junctions of Bicester Road/ West Street and Bicester Road/ Mount Pleasant. This is due to the proximity of parked vehicles, making egress from the side roads difficult.

Implementation and Consequent Improvements

The 'Give Way' lines have been moved forward by around 2.0m. This allows better vision for the traffic pulling out of the junction.

Cost – £43,000.

Scheme implemented – between the 10th June 2003 and 4th July 2003.

Photos showing the change in the line of the pavement and new bollards. These changes enabled vehicles to come safely out of side roads.

(*Source*: www.buckscc.gov.uk)

Figure 12.5
Photo of road before changes

Figure 12.6
Photo of same road with changes to the line of pavement and bollards

activity
GROUP WORK

Contact your local council and ask them for information about similar road safety schemes in your area. Do you think they are good value for money?

Strategies

Strategies often take the form of new laws. The Road Safety Bill 2005, a law which has not yet been passed (at the time of writing) and is therefore subject to change, makes strategic (long-term) proposals.

Check out:

- television campaigns, if there are any
- publicity in newspapers.

Visit:

- your local police, who will have plenty of leaflets
- your local council for information on local schemes

Internet sites concerned with road safety:

www.surrey.police.uk (some local initiative)

www.protectchild.co.uk (child safety)

www.dft.gov.uk (Road Safety Bill 2005 – new laws on road safety – not yet passed)

How successful are road safety campaigns in accident prevention?

There are three ways of assessing the success of road safety campaigns: **statistics**, **surveys** and **focus groups**.

Statistics

Can accident statistics tell us how successful road safety campaigns are?

Road accident figures in the UK have gone down very much over the years (see Figure 12.7). But the reasons why are rather complex.

If you look at Case study 12.8 on page 295 above, showing government road safety initiatives since 1997, you will see that there have been many initiatives of various types. Not all of them are road safety campaigns. It is therefore not clear from the statistics whether casualty numbers have gone down because of the campaigns, or because of the other initiatives.

And there are other reasons why road casualties have been falling. Car design is getting safer all the time, with the introduction of airbags and anti-crush technology; roads are being resurfaced, signs are better, traffic-calming systems have been introduced in many places, and dangerous junctions are being remodelled. True, there are more cars on the roads, but they are moving more slowly due to traffic congestion, so accidents that do happen are less likely to injure or kill people.

Figure 12.7

Killed or seriously injured casualties: 1990–2004

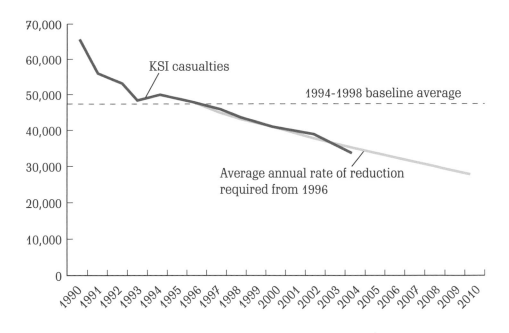

The UK's roads seem surprisingly safe – especially if we look at figures for serious road accidents in other European countries. Almost all of them have a worse rate of serious accidents, especially road deaths, than the UK (see Figure 12.8). The UK has been far more active in promoting road safety than most other European countries, and the effort appears to have paid off. But the figures cannot prove that the road safety campaigns have achieved this.

Figure 12.8

Road deaths per 100,000 population

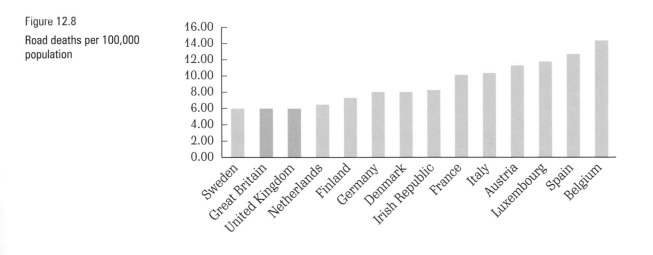

activity
GROUP WORK
(12.6)

Think of as many possible reasons as you can why UK roads are safer than those in continental Europe.

Because it is hard to link campaigns with accident statistics, most research on the success of road safety campaigns has been done using either surveys or 'focus groups'.

Surveys

These are carried out every month by agencies working for the Department for Transport. The basic rules are given in Case study 12.10.

---

case study

12.10

Surveying road safety campaigns

'The monthly Road Safety Campaign tracking research by TNS for the Department for Transport is now in its eighth year.

Each month a set of questions is placed on the RSGB General Omnibus Survey and a representative sample of 2,000 adults aged 16+ from a minimum of 139 sampling points in England, Scotland and Wales is interviewed face-to-face in home.

This report covers the survey conducted in the fieldwork period 6–10 July 2005. ... The July survey focused particularly on the Drinking and Driving campaign about which detailed questions were asked.'

The survey examines public awareness of safety campaigns which took place before or during the survey period. In the survey mentioned in the case study the campaigns were:

- *Drinking and Driving*. The summer THINK! Drink driving campaign was launched on 9 June highlighting that it takes less than you may think to become a drink driver. The Crash TV ad was on air from 9–12 June and the Your Round radio from 10–12 June. Cinema advertising appeared in the week beginning 24 June. All of these were in advance of the July fieldwork.

- *Speed*. National TV and radio advertising played in the week beginning 27 June ending 3 days before fieldwork started. Cinema advertising was played in the week starting 1 July, so overlapped with the fieldwork dates.

- *Child Seat Restraints*. There has been no more activity since posters appeared in motorway service area baby change rooms from 28 March through to 27 April.

- *Seatbelts*. Seatbelts TV advertising aired in the week beginning 30 May.

- *Fatigue*. Fatigue radio advertising aired in the weeks beginning 16 May (young male drivers) and 23 May (leisure drivers).

- *Teenage Road Safety*. Radio advertising featured in the weeks beginning 9 and 23 May.

■ *Child Road Safety*. Hedgehogs TV advertising played from the week beginning 23 May, through to the week beginning 6 June. The Hedgehogs cinema advertising is running throughout July.

■ *Looking Out for Motorcycles*. Continued BSkyB activity takes place from 4 April 2005 to 27 April 2006. There is also press advertising from 4 April through to week beginning 26 September. Both of these overlapped with fieldwork for the July survey.

(*Source*: Department for Transport)

activity
GROUP WORK

Child road safety is the one area in which UK road safety is worse than some continental countries. Examine Hedgehogs and other road safety campaigns aimed at children. Do they seem less effective than campaigns for older people?

The findings of these surveys are processed into tables, graphs or charts. An example is given in Figure 12.9.

Figure 12.9

Spontaneous awareness of publicity about teenagers crossing the road safely

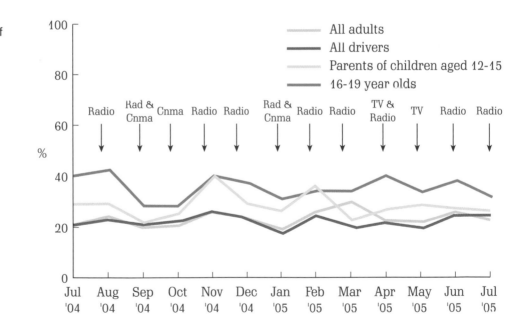

The graph shows variations in public awareness of campaigns about teenagers crossing the road safely. The peaks are for times when the different groups of people surveyed were more aware of recent campaigns; the troughs are for times when the people surveyed were less aware of the campaigns. The conclusions to be drawn are that where there are peaks, the publicity (campaign) was effective, and where there are troughs, it was not. The effective campaigns can be studied in more detail to find out why they were remembered, and lessons learned can be used in planning future campaigns.

Focus groups

A focus group is a group of, say, 10 or 12 people chosen from suitable backgrounds to discuss the effectiveness of particular road safety campaigns. Their role is to give the views of ordinary members of the public. Sometimes they are chosen from the target group – i.e. if the campaign was about teenagers crossing the road safely, the focus group would consist of teenagers. The questions asked are more in-depth than the questions asked in surveys (which have to be 'yes–no' questions whose answers can then be put into tables or graphs).

Evaluating campaigns

Road safety campaigns are usually evaluated on the basis of how aware people are of them.

To do your own evaluation, choose campaigns that have been going on for at least a week or two, so that people have had time to see or hear them.

Then try to use the methods that are used by the professionals.

When you have collected your information using surveys or focus group(s) you should write it up so that the information is recorded, and so that you can say, on the basis of the evidence collected, whether the road safety campaigns you have chosen are effective or not.

In most cases a road safety campaign is effective up to a point. To make a really good judgment you might get some information on how much the campaign has cost, and balance this against lives saved. On the other hand, you might feel that if a campaign saves only one life on the roads, it has paid for itself – especially as the average cost of a fatal road accident is over £1 million.

> **remember**
>
> Unless you have accident statistics, you cannot evaluate the success or failure of a local and national campaign in accident prevention. Even if you do have the statistics, how can you prove that a drop in the figures is due to a campaign?

> **activity**
> **GROUP WORK**
> **(12.7)**
>
> (a) Choose two road safety campaigns – one local and one national.
>
> (b) Carry out an evaluation either by survey or focus group of its effectiveness.
>
> (c) Check local and national websites (or your local council) to see if there are any relevant accident figures.

Figure 12.10

Steps involved in an evaluation

(*Source*: Adapted from Department for Transport)

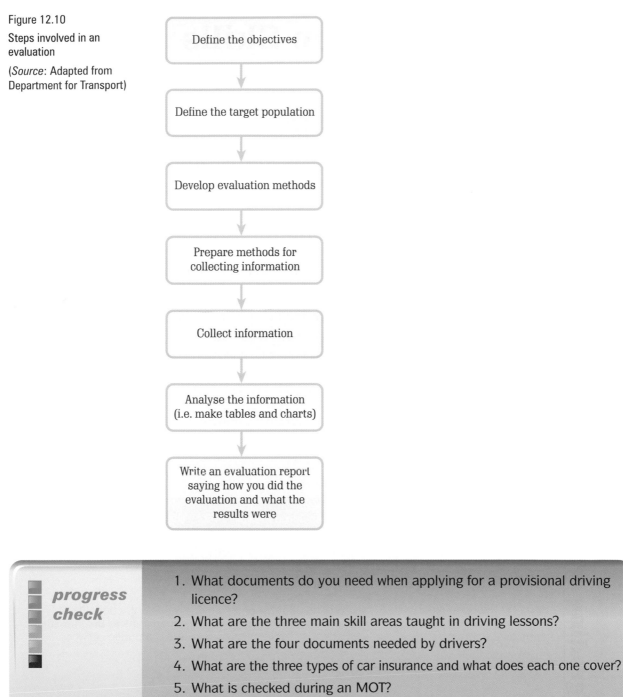

Define the objectives

Define the target population

Develop evaluation methods

Prepare methods for collecting information

Collect information

Analyse the information (i.e. make tables and charts)

Write an evaluation report saying how you did the evaluation and what the results were

progress check

1. What documents do you need when applying for a provisional driving licence?
2. What are the three main skill areas taught in driving lessons?
3. What are the four documents needed by drivers?
4. What are the three types of car insurance and what does each one cover?
5. What is checked during an MOT?
6. Name five common driving offences.
7. How long can a coach driver working for a company work in a week?
8. What does SAD CHALET stand for?
9. What are the main roles of the police, fire and rescue, and ambulance services at a collision?
10. What is the difference between a campaign, an initiative and a strategy in road safety?

Expedition Skills

This unit covers:

- the benefits of expeditions for the public services
- the correct equipment needed to take part in expeditions in the three areas of personal, group and safety
- planning and carrying out a multi-day expedition involving an overnight stay
- evaluating individual and team performance during the expedition

You will go on an expedition lasting at least two days with at least one night spent under canvas. Travel will probably be on foot, though it might include kayaking, sailing, mountain biking or travelling on horseback.

The expedition may be organised by your tutors, a public service group such as an army youth team, or some other organisation. Before going you will learn about the relevance of expeditions to public service work, the equipment and planning needed, and the practical skills and teamwork needed to make an expedition reasonably comfortable and enjoyable.

You will then go on the expedition itself, using the skills you have been learning about, and afterwards you will assess what you did.

grading criteria

To achieve a **Pass** grade the evidence must show that the learner is able to:	To achieve a **Merit** grade the evidence must show that, in addition to the pass criteria, the learner is able to:	To achieve a **Distinction** grade the evidence must show that, in addition to the pass and merit criteria, the learner is able to:
P1 describe the benefits of expeditions to the public services	**M1** analyse the benefits of expeditions to the public services	**D1** evaluate the benefits of expeditions to the individuals and the public services
P2 describe the equipment needed for a multi-day expedition including personal and group safety	**M2** explain the purpose and function of equipment needed for a multi-day expedition	**D2** justify choice of equipment for a multi-day expedition
P3 contribute to the planning and preparation required for a multi-day expedition	**M3** explain the process of planning and the preparation required when planning an expedition	**D3** evaluate the expedition process from start to finish, making recommendations and justifying decisions made

grading criteria

To achieve a **Pass** grade the evidence must show that the learner is able to:	To achieve a **Merit** grade the evidence must show that, in addition to the pass criteria, the learner is able to:	To achieve a **Distinction** grade the evidence must show that, in addition to the pass and merit criteria, the learner is able to:
P4 use camp craft and navigational skills during the expedition	**M4** describe individual performance and that of group members, identify strengths, weaknesses and areas for improvement	
P5 define the responsibilities of the individual when in the countryside		
P6 participate in a multi-day expedition, identifying own roles and responsibilities		

Benefits of Expeditions for the Public Services

Those who organise expeditions say they have many benefits. The public services believe they are good for their own members and good for other people. See Figure 13.1.

In Figure 13.1, the benefits of expeditions come under four main headings: 'hard skills', 'soft skills', physical benefits and public service-related skills.

Hard skills means the practical abilities needed for camping and expeditions carried out in open country. They include:

■ choosing a campsite and pitching tents

■ cooking and using stoves

■ navigation skills

■ understanding weather and terrain

■ using camping and other equipment

■ packing and carrying rucksacks and other equipment

■ knowledge and awareness of safety.

The purpose of hard skills is to enable expeditions to be carried out in comfort and safety, and to achieve their objectives.

Figure 13.1
The benefits of expeditions

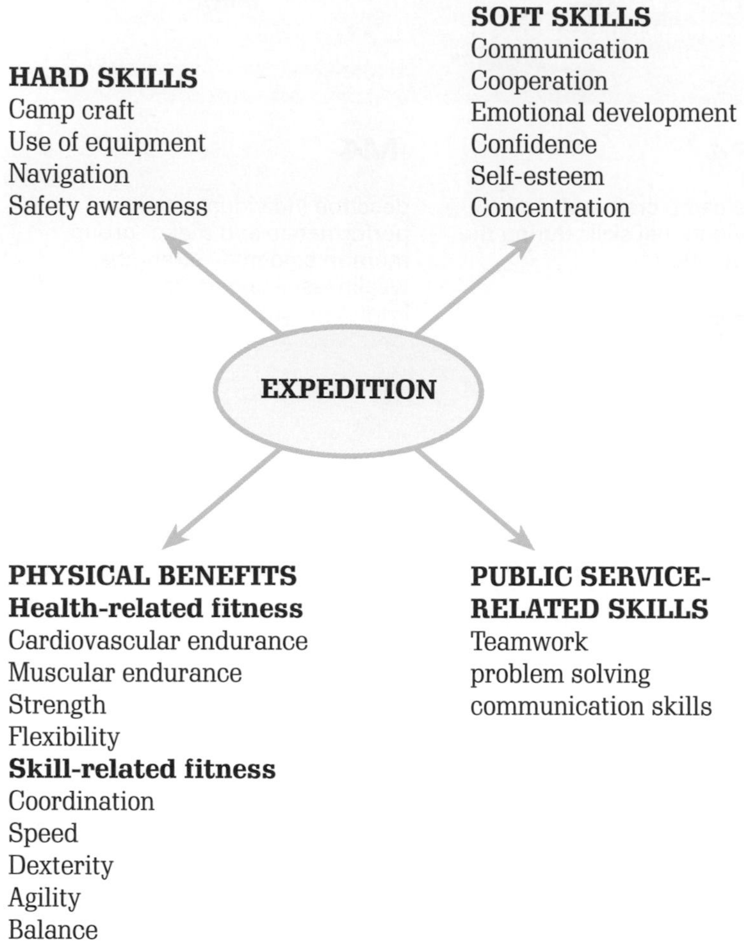

SOFT SKILLS
Communication
Cooperation
Emotional development
Confidence
Self-esteem
Concentration

HARD SKILLS
Camp craft
Use of equipment
Navigation
Safety awareness

EXPEDITION

PHYSICAL BENEFITS
Health-related fitness
Cardiovascular endurance
Muscular endurance
Strength
Flexibility
Skill-related fitness
Coordination
Speed
Dexterity
Agility
Balance

PUBLIC SERVICE-RELATED SKILLS
Teamwork
problem solving
communication skills

Soft skills involve personality development and the ability to get on with other people. They include:

- communication
- cooperation
- emotional development
- rapport with others
- confidence
- self-esteem
- ability to concentrate.

The purpose of soft skills is to make people more effective in work, in study and in their everyday lives.

We thought Jenny ought to get out of the house a bit more, so we sent her to Kyrgyzstan -

Physical benefits are the benefits in fitness and strength which can come from taking part in expeditions. These can be split into health-related fitness benefits and skill-related fitness benefits.

Health-related fitness is linked to our body systems working well. It includes:

- cardiovascular endurance (the heart, lungs and blood vessels are in good shape)
- muscular endurance (muscle tone is good and the muscles can work hard for long periods of time)
- strength (powerful muscles)
- flexibility (joints bend well).

Skill-related fitness is linked to the speed, control and efficiency with which we move. It includes:

- coordination
- speed
- dexterity
- agility
- balance.

link

There's more about these in Unit 3: Uniformed Public Service Fitness, page 78.

Public service-related skills are mainly soft skills used in expeditions which are also needed in public service work. The main ones are:

- teamwork
- problem solving
- communication skills.

Why expedition skills can benefit the public services

Every one of the skills listed above is useful in one or more public services and is needed by people who are employed in them.

The hard skills are needed in the armed forces, especially in some of the basic training. As Case study 13.1 shows, the army uses expedition skills widely in training.

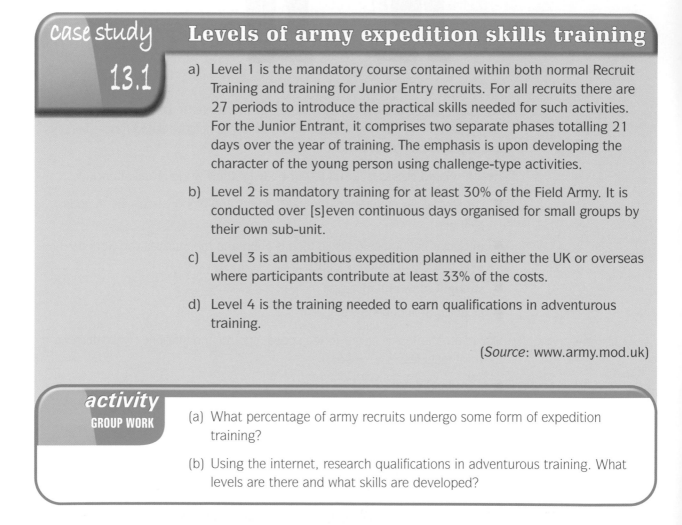

case study 13.1   Levels of army expedition skills training

a) Level 1 is the mandatory course contained within both normal Recruit Training and training for Junior Entry recruits. For all recruits there are 27 periods to introduce the practical skills needed for such activities. For the Junior Entrant, it comprises two separate phases totalling 21 days over the year of training. The emphasis is upon developing the character of the young person using challenge-type activities.

b) Level 2 is mandatory training for at least 30% of the Field Army. It is conducted over [s]even continuous days organised for small groups by their own sub-unit.

c) Level 3 is an ambitious expedition planned in either the UK or overseas where participants contribute at least 33% of the costs.

d) Level 4 is the training needed to earn qualifications in adventurous training.

(*Source*: www.army.mod.uk)

activity
GROUP WORK

(a) What percentage of army recruits undergo some form of expedition training?

(b) Using the internet, research qualifications in adventurous training. What levels are there and what skills are developed?

Expedition skills are linked to adventurous training in the army, especially at levels 1 and 2. Level 3 is different, since, though the expeditions are run by the army, they are not compulsory, and the army pays only 67 per cent of the total cost. Level 3 expeditions are to places like the Himalayas – they are serious expeditions and are meant to put participants to the test, physically, mentally and emotionally. See Case study 13.2.

case study 13.2 — Army expeditions – level 3

Expeditions, whether in the UK or overseas, are expected to be adventurous: they should be of a physically and mentally demanding nature, putting the expedition members under some pressure that cannot be experienced in normal military training. Leadership and personal skills will be developed, and interdependence enhanced. Some time may be spent on local leave, but this is to be no more than two days rest for every 10 days training.

Approved expeditions are primarily for Service personnel – regulars or reserves – and a civilian will only be authorised exceptionally if considered essential to the expedition. All participants are required to contribute at least a third of the cost themselves, therefore participation is on a voluntary basis, but with duty status. Expedition parties should be of manageable size, and contain the statutory ratios of qualified/unqualified personnel relevant to the activities to be undertaken. Members of an expedition are usually drawn from a Single Service for convenience of planning, but may be Joint Service.

(*Source*: www.army.mod.uk)

activity
GROUP WORK

(a) What kind of pressures might be experienced in a level 3 expedition that are not found in normal training?

(b) What are the benefits for the army in carrying out this sort of expedition?

The soft skills are of major importance in all kinds of public service work – both uniformed and non-uniformed. They are used every day, in every job. This is because all public service work involves teamwork and teamwork is a learnable skill that can be developed and practised on expeditions. Good teamwork is linked to morale – the fighting spirit of the armed forces – and the professional pride of the other public services. Soft skills take a long time to develop – some would say a lifetime – but they are developed faster and more effectively on expeditions than in many other situations.

The physical benefits matter, especially for people wishing to join public services where a high degree of strength and fitness are needed, such as the armed forces, the fire and rescue service, the ambulance service and some units in the police.

Expeditions by themselves will not develop all these physical qualities to the highest level but they are certainly useful, especially for improving cardiovascular and muscular endurance.

Benefits of Expeditions for the Public Services

<table>
<tr><td>

Psychomotor
to do with muscular coordination and dexterity.

</td></tr>
</table>

<table>
<tr><td>

Cognitive
to do with learning and understanding.

</td></tr>
</table>

<table>
<tr><td>

Affective
to do with emotion and sympathy.

</td></tr>
</table>

Why expedition skills can benefit the individual

Individual benefits brought about by expeditions are very similar to the benefits for the public services. What is good for the public service is good for the individual. So individual benefits come under the same headings: hard skills and soft skills. Hard can themselves be divided into two types – **psychomotor** and **cognitive** skills. Soft skills can be divided into psychomotor, cognitive and **affective** skills.

Hard skills

The hard skills are linked to the activities carried out on the expedition. For example, if the expedition includes canoeing, then participants will improve their canoeing skills. If they keep pitching and dismantling tents, they will get better at that too.

- *Psychomotor skills* (coordination). Skills like canoeing and pitching tents develop psychomotor skills (the ability to coordinate and control the movements of our muscles). They are therefore related to components of skill-related fitness such as dexterity (the ability to use our hands skilfully). Similar skills are widely used in the public services, especially where people are working with machines or equipment of any kind. Gunners in the armed forces, police drivers, prison officers practising control and restraint and firefighters all need good psychomotor skills.

- *Cognitive skills* (developing understanding and knowledge). Expeditions develop cognitive skills. Because they put us in new situations and force us to learn how to do things we have not done before, they make us better at the act of learning. Learning how to navigate, or where to pitch a tent to be out of the wind, uses cognitive skills – memorising, practising, asking questions etc. – which we then apply to other learning situations. Similar cognitive skills are used, for example, when learning techniques of primary care as a paramedic, or when learning about any new piece of equipment or process. Cognitive skills are learning skills, which can be used whatever we are learning about. Watching carefully, listening to instructions, making notes if necessary, practising a task and then reviewing how well we did it: these learning processes are just as important in real public service work as they are on expeditions.

Soft skills

These include communication, cooperation, developing the emotional intelligences, problem solving, confidence, self-esteem, self-reliance, resilience, managing emotions of fear, anxiety, anger, frustration, elation, working under pressure, concentration and so on. These are thinking and communication skills. They are described as 'soft' not because they are signs of weakness (they are not), but because they are to do with the mind, emotions and spirit rather than physical objects such as equipment.

- *Psychomotor skills*. Soft skills have a small but important psychomotor element. Expressing emotions such as sympathy, seriousness and determination is done through the body, and skills of self-presentation involve being able to control our bodies, faces and voices so that they express what we want them to express.

- *Cognitive skills*. Soft skills are cognitive in that they involve learning a lot about other people, and about ourselves. Self-knowledge (which includes knowledge about how we relate to other people) is vital in public service work.

- *Affective skills* are soft skills concerning emotion. If we know what frightens, angers, bores, annoys or pleases us, then we can control ourselves and, sometimes, other people. An expedition is a kind of laboratory of human emotions, where people learn and experiment with new roles in a fresh environment. People who have little opportunity to show leadership qualities in real life may find they can do so in the context of an expedition.

All these interpersonal skills are used in, say, the police, where much of the work involves dealing with other people, whether colleagues, offenders, victims of crime or the general public. The people skills needed for such work are considerable, and police officers need a wide range of such skills to deal with different situations, individuals and groups.

Other individual benefits

Expeditions are an escape from the routine of ordinary life, and as such are beneficial to the individual even if they are not directly relevant to their work or their career plans. Being with new people, or the same people outside the classroom or workplace, is refreshing and stimulating. Doing new activities tests resilience (the ability to adapt to new situations) and gives confidence. Being outside, in a natural environment, gives a sense of freedom and allows us to appreciate the beauty of the countryside, and of hills and mountains. There are times when it is a great benefit to get away from ordinary work!

activity
INDIVIDUAL WORK
(13.1)

Examine:

(a) the skills you use in an average day. Are they hard or soft skills, and are they psychomotor, cognitive or affective?

(b) the daily work of a public service which interests you. List in detail the skills which are needed, and say whether they are hard or soft skills.

How great are the benefits of expeditions to the individuals and the public services?

In evaluating the benefits of expeditions to individuals and the public services, there is a risk of exaggeration. For most people expeditions are an enjoyable way of building character and skills. But they can have their limitations. This is because:

1. Individuals are different and expeditions benefit some individuals more than others. The people who benefit most are those who have little experience but are willing to learn and develop. The people who benefit least from a given expedition are either those who don't really want to go on it and don't wish to learn anything, or those who have been on several expeditions already and are therefore less changed by any one expedition.

2. Expeditions are not all the same. For example, an expedition whose members have never been camping before, run by an army youth team, will be a different kind of expedition from one undertaken for the Gold Level of the Duke of Edinburgh's Award by experienced campers and walkers. And this again will be different from the kinds of expedition run by commercial organisations or charities, where people go overseas for weeks or more taking part in expeditions to the Andes, the Himalayas, Kilimanjaro or Malaysia. In addition, a well-organised expedition with motivated participants may achieve much more for the individuals involved than a badly organised or uninteresting expedition.

3. An expedition for students run by the public services will only directly benefit the public services if:

    (a) the students on the expedition later join a public service, or

    (b) if the students enjoy the expedition and tell other people about it – which is good public relations and may encourage other people to apply at a later date.

4. Public services are different. All of them require soft skills, but not all of them require the hard skills developed by going on expeditions. Those that do need people with those hard skills (such as the Royal Marines) will give them training after they have joined up.

Cost

The cost of organising and going on expeditions varies widely depending on who is organising it, and where the expedition is going. Evaluating expeditions involves balancing benefits against costs. For example:

■ Is the experience and educational value of an expedition worth the time, effort and money spent on it?

■ Could the time and money have been better spent in other ways, like helping people in the community, or in environmental work such as planting trees or building footpaths?

Benefits and responsibilities

Expeditions probably bring more benefits if the people going on them take an active part in the planning, preparation and participation.

Expeditions organised by those doing them (such as the Duke of Edinburgh's Award) are valued by employers of all types because they indicate strength of character, organising ability, and independence of mind.

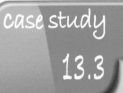

case study 13.3

The Duke of Edinburgh's Award: activities – benefits

Plan and execute a journey – requiring attention to detail and organisational ability

Demonstrate enterprise and imagination – by the Team organising their own venture

Work as a member of a team – all ventures must be a team effort

Respond to a challenge – either planned or unforeseen

Develop self-reliance – by carrying out an unaccompanied journey

Develop leadership skills – members of the Team should have opportunities to take a leading role during different aspects of the venture

Recognise the needs and strengths of others – by involving Team members in mutually supporting each other to ensure the success of the venture

Make decisions and accept the consequences – by the Team making real decisions affecting their well-being

Reflect on personal performance – through reviewing progress during training and at the end of the Qualifying Venture

Enjoy and appreciate the environment – by developing an awareness of the areas visited and issues affecting the environment

(*Source*: www.theaward.org)

---

activity

INDIVIDUAL WORK

Discuss and rate these benefits in order of importance:

(a) to you, if you were involved in this kind of expedition

(b) to a public service that you might hope to join at a later date.

(c) (Group) Compare your findings with others.

The Correct Equipment Needed to Take Part in Expeditions in the Three Areas of Personal, Group and Safety

There are three types of expedition equipment: personal, group and safety.

Personal equipment

This is clothing and equipment that only you will use during the expedition.

Clothing

This depends on the season and where the expedition is taking place.

Your expedition will probably take place in early autumn, spring or early summer, and be somewhere in open hilly country in the British Isles.

Expeditions in continental Europe and beyond are perfectly possible, but the distance is further, the arrangements are more complicated, the dangers are slightly greater, and the cost is likely to be higher.

In the UK conditions are cool and damp, and the clothing you wear on expeditions must take this into account. If you have to carry everything on your back, keep the weight down. If you have a back-up team with a minibus, you may not need to carry everything.

Here is a suggested list for backpacking:

Essential:

1. Anorak or waterproof jacket
2. Loose trousers or jogging bottoms

3. Thermal T-shirts/underwear (+ thermal leggings in winter)

4. Fleeces or woollen pullovers

5. 2 pairs of thick socks

6. Woolly hat or balaclava

7. Gloves

8. Walking boots (get advice)

9. Waterproof bottoms (when it's raining)

Optional:

1. Gaiters (essential in snow)

2. Shorts (in warm weather)

Spare clothes. If you have to carry everything on your back, the spare clothes you take must be light and warm, and you *must keep them dry* (e.g. by wrapping them carefully in a dustbin liner before packing them in your rucksack):

- spare T-shirts and underclothes

- spare fleeces

- spare pair of trousers

- 2 spare pairs of socks.

Other personal equipment

Sleeping bag. A sleeping bag of suitable warmth is vital. Make sure it has a waterproof bag round it when it is not in use. A carry-mat made of light rubber foam is useful to put under the sleeping bag. This can be carried rolled up on the outside of your rucksack.

Hygiene. A small spongebag containing soap, toothbrush, toothpaste etc. and a toilet roll in a plastic bag will do for basic hygiene.

Others. You should have your own watch, torch, water-bottle, tin-opener, matches, plate, knife, spoon and cup, and scouring pad for washing up.

Rucksack. You may have to provide your own, or the expedition organisers may provide one. If you are carrying all or most of your camping equipment and clothes on your back, you will need a big rucksack (65 litres capacity).

Day-sack. If you are camping at a site for several nights, it is useful to have a small rucksack (day-sack) for carrying sandwiches, water bottle, first aid, a map and a few spare clothes during the day.

Group equipment

This may be provided by the organisers of the expedition. They will almost certainly give you training in how to use it and look after it.

Main items are:

- a tent
- a cooker.

Figure 13.2

Camping stove

Tents

If you have to provide your own tent, and you have to carry it any distance, make sure it is light. Find out from the organisers what sort of tent would be best, if you haven't already got a suitable one. Most modern tents are waterproof if they are treated properly, but if you are going to camp in an exposed place you need a tent which can stand up to wind.

Cooker

Most expeditions use portable cookers of the 'Trangia' type. These stoves are cheap, convenient, effective and easy to use – but you should practise with them first to make sure you don't burn your fingers.

These stoves burn methylated spirits, which can be carried in a bottle but are *highly* flammable. The flame is nearly invisible in daylight.

Safety equipment

1. *Maps and compass*. These may be supplied by your expedition organisers. Your main duty is to know how to use them and look after them.

link See Unit 8, page 185–96.

2. *Torch*. A reliable lightweight torch is needed when you are on an expedition.

3. *First aid*. Your expedition organisers should have excellent first aid kits. You should carry sticky plasters (or a roll of sticky plaster plus scissors), and one or two longer lightweight bandages. They should be kept dry in a plastic bag.

4. *Survival or bivvy (bivouac) bags*. These are used if you are likely to sleep out without a tent. They are waterproof plastic bags big enough to contain a human being. They can be carried in a day-sack (small rucksack). You may not need them – ask your tutor.

5. *Whistle* – a light loud whistle should be carried in your pocket or day-sack. It should only be used if you are injured and need to call help. You should then blow six long blasts per minute and keep doing this every other minute.

6. *Flares*. These are for signalling where you are if you are lost at night.

7. *Emergency rations*. Chocolate, spare sandwiches and other calorific food can be used as emergency rations. Instead of eating them during the day, keep them in case you get lost or have to spend an unplanned night out.

8. *Spare clothing*. Always have a spare pullover, woolly hat and gloves in your day-sack (unless you are sure it will be hot all day, and you are at no risk of spending a night out).

9. *Suncream*. If you have light skin, carry suncream and use it in sunny weather. The sun is more powerful on mountains, and in early summer.

10. *Insect repellent*. If insects like you, and you don't like them, take some repellent with you.

11. *Route card*. You should have a route card with you on an expedition, and you should make sure the organisers have a copy of it too.

link

See pages 198–200 for details.

activity
GROUP WORK
(13.2)

Collect brochures etc. giving information on expedition equipment, and make sure everyone in your group has all the information they need.

Understanding your equipment – purpose and function

keyword

Purpose
the intended use of an item.

Function
how it works.

When planning expeditions you should not only obtain your equipment, you must make sure you understand it and can use it.

The **purpose** and **function** of major items are outlined in Table 13.1.

activity
GROUP WORK
(13.3)

Visit a major shop or manufacturer of hiking and camping equipment.

Ask and make notes about the technical principles and design features of clothes, boots, tents etc.

i

Ask experienced walkers and campers, and visit manufacturers' sites on the internet. Also useful is www.ramblers.org.uk

Buying equipment

Some expedition equipment is expensive, and you should not buy it if you are only going to use it once, or if you can borrow it from the organisers of your expedition.

If you enjoy going on expeditions and wish to make a habit of it, buy carefully and take reliable advice. Make sure you know:

■ what the item is needed for

■ how to use the item

■ any technical features about how the item works

■ what the item weighs

■ how much space the item takes up in your rucksack

■ any safety, protection or comfort aspects associated with the item.

Table 13.1 The purpose and functions of equipment on an expedition

Item	Purpose	Function
Clothing	Clothing has two main purposes, from the point of view of an expedition (a) to keep you dry (b) to keep your body at the right temperature	(a) There are two types of waterproof outer clothing. The first type, which is cheaper, is made of thin waterproofed fabric and is very lightweight. It is used in lightweight cagoules. It keeps the water out when new, but after a while the waterproofing wears off, especially near the seams. Unfortunately it suffers from condensation, so the wearer can still get wet. The second type, which is heavier and more expensive, is made of breathable waterproof fabric. It usually stays waterproof and there is minimal condensation. (b) Clothing keeps you warm by insulating you from the cold, so that the heat generated by your body stays in. Insulation works best if you have several layers of thermal clothing, which trap warm air close to your body. In cold weather there should be a windproof layer on the outside to seal warm air in and protect against 'wind-chill'. In hot weather less clothing is needed, but a single layer will protect you from strong sun and insect bites.
Footwear	The functions of footwear are (a) to protect your feet from being bruised, scratched and cut by the hard ground. (b) to stop you from slipping (c) to keep your feet warm (d) to keep your feet dry	(a) Walking boots have thick strong soles which protect the feet from shocks. The inside should be shaped and lined to reduce the risk of blisters, hard skin and cracking of the heels. (b) The soles are of moulded, textured rubber composition, often of a 'vibram' type. They enable you to grip the ground on steep slopes. Rock and snow climbers use specialist footwear. (c) Boots are well insulated both in the soles and the uppers to protect against cold. (In hot weather some walkers use sandals if they are keeping to the path.) (d) Wet feet get cold and blistered. Walking boots are usually waterproof.
Rucksacks	These are sometimes called backpacks. They are used for carrying things.	Modern rucksacks are designed to be carried high up the back: this puts less strain on the spine and uses less energy when walking. Lightweight fabric and aluminium frames keep them light and protect the back. They have small pockets to keep special items in, and a big cavity for holding bulky items.
Tent	A tent is a portable shelter made of fabric and reinforced with 'poles'. It protects campers against cold, wind and rain.	Tents for expeditions are usually light and low. They should be put up with the door away from the wind. They have two layers of fabric, an inner tent and a flysheet, to give good protection against rain. There is a sewn-in groundsheet to make them draughtproof. Pegs and guy-ropes hold the tent firm in strong winds.
Cooker	Most campers use meths cookers of the 'Trangia' type, though some use butane pressure stoves. They are needed for making hot meals and drinks.	It is possible to camp without a cooker if you don't mind cold food. Cookers work well if they are protected from strong wind. You can cook simple meals on them. To avoid injury or fire you must learn how to use them before your expedition. If you carry a cooker you must also carry the fuel for it. You should never use a cooker inside a tent.
Sleeping bag	A sleeping bag is a sack made of duvet-like material in which you can sleep. The insulating material is usually a kind of Terylene fibre, though it is still possible to get expensive ones made of goose-down etc.	Sleeping bags are essential for camping, even on summer nights. They work by insulating the body with warm air which is trapped in the fibres. You should put a carry-mat under the sleeping bag to protect you against the cold of the ground (especially if the ground under the groundsheet is also wet), and to reduce bumps. A pillow is rather bulky to carry on an expedition, and a bag of dry clothes may do just as well. Use your judgment.

If you are seriously interested in expeditions, buy the best quality you can afford.

- *Keep it light.* If you have to walk a long way with a rucksack on your back, it should be kept as light as possible (without leaving out essentials). The total weight of a packed rucksack should be one that you can carry in reasonable comfort. Get advice from your tutor or instructor: the weight must be right for you.

- *Know what to leave out.* Do not take anything with you which cannot be justified. In addition, don't take valuables (or things of sentimental value) on expeditions. Open countryside is a great place for losing things.

activity
PAIR WORK
(13.4)

Give a short presentation:

(a) on the technical and design features of two key items you will take on an expedition (e.g. rucksack, tent, boots)

(b) explaining how they are used and why they are needed.

www.scotlands-best.com

Planning and Carrying Out a Multi-Day Expedition involving an Overnight Stay

Planning and preparation

The overall planning for your expedition may be done by your college, or the instructors/organisation who are taking you on your expedition. But you will need to do your own planning as well.

Sort out some basics

This should be done as early as possible:

1. Find out where you are going, when you are going, and how long you will be staying there.
2. Sort out the money! You may need money:

    (a) to pay the people running your expedition

    (b) for your own food and clothing, and equipment

    (c) for your own spending while on the expedition.

    If you are short of money, see your tutor or the organiser to discuss the problem.

3. Plan with your colleagues/classmates if you are going to be sharing a tent or working as a group. Get to know them and make sure you get on with them. You may want to pool your food resources and plan meals together. This is certainly a good idea if you are sharing a tent.

4. *Food*. Planning what you want can be done weeks before. The buying should be done in the last week. If you are part of a team who will be cooking and eating together, plan your food together. Before you buy food, you need to know:

   ■ how long the expedition is

   ■ what time of year it will be

   ■ whether you will be staying near any shops

   ■ whether you are carrying your own food

   ■ what kind of cooking facilities you will be using

   ■ the food likes and dislikes of your team

   ■ who is paying for the food

   ■ whether you will need to provide your own packed lunches.

   The food you buy must be:

   ■ easy to carry, if you have to carry it. If you are not going to carry your food, you have far more choice.

   ■ high in energy – especially carbohydrates. If you are preparing and cooking meals, cereals, bread, potatoes, rice and beans will give you plenty of energy.

   ■ easy to cook. Bread, dried potatoes and baked beans are good from this point of view. Food that doesn't need cooking, but gives plenty of energy, such as sardines, can be useful. Other people prefer a good fry-up. If you haven't got time to cook vegetables, you can eat bananas, apples and oranges instead.

   ■ agreed with your team if you are sharing the catering.

5. *Clothes*. Planning (and any buying) should be done weeks ahead. Packing should be done in the last couple of days. If you are carrying clothes in a rucksack, you can't take very many. But you must be able to keep warm. Here is a list for four days which you could carry on your back (but it might not be enough in midwinter or on high mountains):

   ■ two changes of underwear
   ■ two shirts
   ■ two pairs of trousers (jogging bottom type)
   ■ three fleeces or pullovers
   ■ two pairs of thick socks
   ■ one pair of leggings
   ■ woolly hat
   ■ waterproof leggings
   ■ one pair of gloves.

   This assumes you are already wearing a full change of clothes, plus a waterproof anorak or jacket.

6. *Boots*. Buy, or arrange borrowing, weeks in advance. Test them to make sure they fit! You need one good pair of boots. They should be waterproof, and you must test them beforehand to make sure they don't give you blisters. Walking boots should be a size bigger than your normal shoes – e.g. 9 instead of 8 – and you should wear two pairs of thick socks with them.

7. Other belongings to take:

   ■ a torch
   ■ watch
   ■ sponge bag
   ■ a tin opener
   ■ knife, fork and spoon
   ■ plastic cup and plate
   ■ pen, pencil and notebook
   ■ pocket money
   ■ water bottle
   ■ completed consent forms etc. (if you haven't given them in already!).

   If your expedition is not arranged by the college you should also take:

   ■ first aid, especially dressings for blisters, bandages, antiseptic ointment
   ■ a small pocket knife
   ■ map, compass, whistle

- money
- watch
- travel tickets
- 2 bin liners
- small roll of string.

---

activity
GROUP WORK
(13.5)

Either:

(a) List the things you need to borrow from the expedition organisers, such as tent, anorak, boots, sleeping bag, rucksack and stove

or

(b) Plan well in advance how you will get these yourself.

---

remember

Don't forget the paperwork (check with your tutor if in doubt).

It is important that you:

(a) Keep a diary or log recording all your planning and preparation. You will need it later on in the unit.

(b) Let your tutor, organisers or instructors know how your plans are getting on.

(c) Make sure that you are medically fit to go on an expedition.

Explaining your planning and preparation

For Unit 13 you will need to prove that you can **plan** and **prepare** for an expedition.

Planning means thinking about *and then writing down*:

keyword

Plan
write down the things you are going to do, giving deadlines and stating who is responsible.

keyword

Prepare
do things that need to be done before the expedition (e.g. packing your clothes).

- the aim of the expedition
- the type of expedition
- where you are going
- when you are going
- how long the expedition will last
- how you will get to the starting point
- who you are going with
- who you will share tent, food etc. with
- the clothes and equipment you need to take
- the things you will need to buy or borrow
- the cost
- the paperwork (e.g. permission or disclaimer forms for your parents or yourself to fill in); contact phone numbers and addresses for the expedition organisers

- the food you will take
- menus for the meals and packed lunches
- who is going to do what
- safety and first aid arrangements
- the route of the expedition (on a route card)
- any other preparation (e.g. testing the cooker; putting up the tent to make sure nothing is missing).

If you are planning with other people this may take some time. You will find it useful to write an action plan. A simple action plan is shown in Table 13.2.

Table 13.2 **A simple action plan**

Action	Responsibility	By (date)	Done?
Buy food	Melanie	12 March	All except fruit; will buy that the day before
Borrow tent	Shazia	11 March	Yes, but I need to buy 10 more pegs
Get maps and compass	Debbie	14 March	Got maps, but compass isn't working. Will check with tutor.

If you are unsure about whether your action plan is complete, show it to a tutor and ask their advice.

Preparation

This means all the things you need to do before setting off on your expedition. With the help of your action plan the preparation should be fairly easy. If you need to borrow things from the expedition organisers, make sure you get your name down on the list. If you have to pay for your expedition, make sure that this is done. Check that you have completed all the paperwork.

Make a full list of all the things you need to take with you. Get someone to check it. Then tick off each item as you pack it in your rucksack. Don't leave all the packing until the very last minute! Keep an eye on the total weight – carrying too much weight can take all the fun out of an expedition.

Contingency plan

If you are ill, or there is some other serious problem that might stop you going on the expedition, tell your tutor as soon as possible, and find out what should be done about it.

> *remember*
>
> You will need to show navigational skills. Make sure you can use a map and a compass.

> **activity**
> **INDIVIDUAL WORK**
> **(13.6)**
>
> Keep a diary or log of your planning and preparation. If you are working as part of a group, make it clear in the record which parts of the planning and preparation you have been personally responsible for. Your tutor will need this information for grading purposes.

Camp craft and navigational skills

When on the expedition you will be expected to show **camp craft** and
navigational skills.

Camp craft includes:

- choosing a campsite
- pitching (putting up) the tent
- cooking at the campsite
- cleaning up after meals
- dealing with water
- keeping the tent and its surroundings clean
- toilets
- not lighting fires (unless you have permission, and a safe place)
- sleeping in comfort
- coping with bad weather, if it happens
- looking after the environment
- not inconveniencing others
- striking camp (leaving the campsite) efficiently
- leaving the site as you found it (or better).

Advice

Choosing a campsite. Pick a place where the ground is dry and smooth, out of
the wind. Position the tent so that the entrance is downwind. Sometimes it is
good to have the back of the tent near a wall or hedge. Leave space between
your tent and the next.

Pitching (putting up) the tent. Read the instructions and try to get some practice
before you go on the expedition. Ask for help if you get stuck. Take care not to
tread on the tent or damage it, once it is up.

Cooking at the campsite. Put your stove out of the wind, but not inside the tent.
Practise using the stove before the expedition (or by daylight). Make sure you
have enough fuel. Take care not to get burnt.

Cleaning up after meals. Do the washing up at the nearest tap or stream. Avoid
polluting stream water any more than you have to. Don't use more plates and
utensils when cooking than you have to.

Dealing with water. Avoid spilling water (or drinks) in the tent.

Keeping the tent and its surroundings clean. If there is a rubbish bin, use it as
you go along. Don't leave dangerous rubbish like empty tins or broken glass
lying about. Keep your boots outside the tent (upside-down).

Toilets. Use the toilets at the campsite (if there are any). If not, go well away from the tents and cover the outcome with moss or turf.

Not lighting fires (unless you have permission, and a safe place). If you want to light a fire, ask your tutors or instructors first. In dry summer weather you should never light a fire outside.

Sleeping in comfort. Don't try to get too many people inside the tent. Don't take up more than your fair share of space. If it's cold, keep some clothes on.

Coping with bad weather, if it happens. Keep all your dry clothes wrapped in plastic bags. Wrap your sleeping bags in bin liners or waterproof covers if you go out walking on a wet day (just in case the tent floods while you're out). Put on plenty of spare clothes and waterproofs, and practise smiling.

Dealing with rubbish. Take it to the bin, or take it away with you.

Looking after the environment. Don't leave rubbish lying about.

Good neighbours. Keep the noise down if people want to sleep. Don't quarrel with people sharing your tent. If there is a dispute, see your tutor about it (or settle it quietly).

Striking camp (leaving the campsite) efficiently. Decide who's going to do what – if there are several people sharing the same tent.

Leaving the site as you found it (or better). Check before you leave that you've left no rubbish.

Figure 13.5
Home from home

activity
INDIVIDUAL WORK
(13.7)

Make a written and/or photographic log of your expedition.

link

For navigation, see Unit 8, pages 185–97.

| keyword | **Responsibilities**
duties. |

Your responsibilities in the countryside

When on an expedition in the countryside you have **responsibilities** to do with safety, getting on with other people, and the environment.

Safety responsibilities

There are certain safety responsibilities which expedition members have towards themselves and one another. These are:

- no drugs
- no alcoholic drinks unless specifically allowed by the expedition organisers
- no hunting knives or other dangerous objects
- don't go off alone without telling people where you are going
- follow the organisers' instructions.

Social responsibilities

Treat people who live in the country with respect.

Environmental responsibilities

Follow the Countryside Code.

link

For the Countryside Code, see page 202.

activity
GROUP WORK
(13.8)

(a) Discuss the damage that camping does to the environment.

(b) Note the ways that individual campers can minimise that damage.

www.thebmc.co.uk
www.defra.gov.uk

| keyword | **Roles**
jobs, and the work
done. |

Going on the expedition – your roles and responsibilities

Your **role** while on the expedition will include navigation, pitching tents, cooking, cleaning, getting on with your companions and doing your best to make the expedition a success.

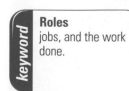

keyword

Responsibilities
duties.

Your main **responsibilities** are to do the expedition, pass the unit, and to take care of your own – and others' – safety.

Checklist of main roles and responsibilities

If you do all the things listed below you should enjoy your expedition and do well.

Before the expedition:

- Inform the organisers if you have any worries or problems as long as possible before the expedition. This includes health problems, disability, phobias, lack of money, possible clash of dates with something else you need or want to do, family difficulties, worries about food, problems with other classmates or problems with staff members.

- Pay for the expedition – if you need to pay – at the earliest possible date.

- Tell your parents or other people all about it well in advance, and keep them in the picture.

- If you are asked to form groups (e.g. to share tents) choose people you are friendly with, but take care not to exclude or be unfriendly to people you don't like.

- Work as a team at all times.

- Have a positive attitude to tutors and instructors – remember your aim is to get a good grade!

- Make lists of what you need and check them off while you do your packing.

- Write an action plan to help your preparation (and as evidence for your grading).

- Arrange well in advance to borrow equipment if you need to do so. If you need to borrow clothes or footwear, be sure of your sizes.

- Be certain how you are travelling to the expedition base (e.g. coach, minibus, train group travel etc.). Follow your tutors' instructions about this (for they will be based on safety and insurance requirements).

- Arrive at the right place and time for setting off.

- Don't pack anything you shouldn't take.

During the expedition:

- Be pleasant and cooperative with other students and with tutors.

- Follow instructions.

- Participate enthusiastically in all activities.

- Do your share of chores, e.g. washing up.

- Be tidy and considerate in the tent or in the outdoor centre/bunk-house/hostel.

- Be punctual – don't keep other people waiting.

- Make sure you understand and follow all safety instructions.

- Never wander off without telling people in charge where you're going.
- If you are walking, never separate from your party.
- Check your equipment before setting out each day.
- Be prepared for cold, wet or horrible weather.
- If you are camping, pitch your tent with the door downwind.
- Don't try to carry too much.
- Remember that a chain is only as strong as its weakest link. Don't force anyone to do more than they are capable of.
- Carry out any exercises, paperwork, record-keeping or self-assessment connected with passing the unit.
- Keep out of pubs unless you have permission to go in.
- Follow agreed sleeping arrangements.
- Avoid quarrelling with other people.
- Tell a tutor if you feel unwell, or have any worries or problems.
- Keep a diary.

After the expedition:

- Tidy the campsite and pack all your stuff away properly.
- Make sure you give back everything you borrowed, to the person you borrowed it from.
- Don't leave your belongings on the coach or train home.
- Carry out all self-assessments set by your tutors so you get the best possible grade for the unit.
- Thank your instructors and tutors for the effort they have put in to make the expedition a success.

---

activity
INDIVIDUAL WORK
(13.9)

Check that you have a written record of your preparations and participation in the expedition. If it isn't finished, bring it up to date.

Evaluating Individual and Team Performance during the Expedition

Self-assessment and group assessment

During and after your expedition you are expected to describe how well you think you and your group members did, and identify your strengths, weaknesses and areas for improvement.

It is for this part of the unit that you should keep a log or diary of your expedition. If your record is detailed enough, it will help you considerably with your grade.

- *Self-assessment*. This is an account of what you yourself did on the expedition, and how well you think you did it. Your tutors or instructors will be able to use this as evidence to help them give you your unit grade.

- *Group assessment*. You also need to give an assessment (appraisal) of what other members of your group did.

Self and group appraisal are widely used during the training of new recruits in the public services, especially the police. Judging yourself and others is not easy, but it is worth making the effort to learn how to do it.

The main rules are:

- mention strengths as well as weaknesses

- be honest without being brutal

- make constructive comments suggesting what you (or someone else) should do in future

- give evidence to support what you say about yourself or your group members.

An example of how this might be done is given in Table 13.3.

activity
INDIVIDUAL WORK
(13.10)

Give an appraisal (written or spoken) of:

(a) what you have done in the expedition

(b) what others in your group (e.g. the people sharing your tent) have done

(c) what you and they could have done better.

A full evaluation of an expedition

To evaluate the expedition in full you need to say:

- how you planned and prepared

- what you did during the expedition

- how well you and your group did

- what you and your group could do to improve your expedition skills in the future

- what skills and abilities you feel you – and your group – learned from the expedition.

Table 13.3 Writing an appraisal

Performance recorded	Simon Wu	Ahmed Bashir	Stephen Knight
CAMPCRAFT			
Pitching tent	The tent was a Lichfield dome tent and I knew how to pitch it because we have a similar one at home. I explained to Ahmed and Stephen how to do it. It was quite windy so I made Ahmed hold the tent down while Stephen and I put in the poles and then while I held it, Ahmed and Stephen put in the pegs.	Ahmed had never put up a tent before so he needed some guidance from me and Stephen. He wanted to be helpful but he didn't always listen to what I said. When we had got the poles in he was very active putting in the pegs, and did it very well. He also organised the layout inside the tent so that we all had enough room.	Stephen did not know much about this sort of tent because he normally uses an old-fashioned ridge tent belonging to his dad. He gave very good advice about where to pitch the tent (against a wall to protect from wind) and about having the door facing downwind. He showed us how to lock pegs and align guy-ropes.
	Areas for improvement.	Areas for improvement	Areas for improvement
	I might have been a bit bossy when telling Ahmed and Stephen how to pitch the tent. I might have given too many instructions and not enough help!	In my opinion Ahmed should try not to panic and get confused when given instructions. When he gets the idea he is careful and well organised.	Stephen knows a lot about expeditions because of walking in Scotland with his dad. But like me he is a bit bossy!

You evaluation might take the form of a written report, a portfolio, a spoken presentation, a slide show, a collection of photographs or any other format agreed with your tutor.

If you do a written report it could follow this format:

Page 1 – Title page

Page 2 – Brief introduction about the expedition and how you recorded what you did

Page 3 – Planning and preparation

Page 4 – The expedition itself

Page 5 – How well you and your group did

Page 6 – Recommendations for improvement

Page 7 – Conclusions on what you learned; the overall value of the experience.

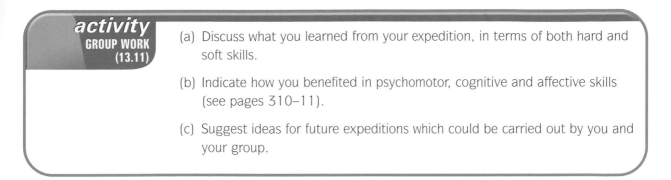

(a) Discuss what you learned from your expedition, in terms of both hard and soft skills.

(b) Indicate how you benefited in psychomotor, cognitive and affective skills (see pages 310–11).

(c) Suggest ideas for future expeditions which could be carried out by you and your group.

progress check

1. Name three hard skills and three soft skills.
2. Why do the armed forces use expeditions in their training?
3. How might going on expeditions benefit an applicant for a public service job?
4. What do 'psychomotor', 'cognitive' and 'affective' mean?
5. What first aid should you take with you on an expedition?
6. What are the four purposes of a boot?
7. What clothes should you carry on a four-day expedition?
8. For what two reasons should you take bin liners on an expedition?
9. Give three rules for pitching a tent.
10. Give five safety responsibilities for expedition members.

Glossary

Accountability – working in such a way that other people can see what you have done, how you have done it, and what it costs. It usually means keeping good records and making them available for inspection.

Adversarial – like a fight between two opponents.

Affective – to do with emotion and sympathy.

Attitudes – feelings or behaviour towards others; a driver's feelings towards other road users.

Audience – any listener or listeners (occasionally it can mean readers).

Awareness – understanding and sensitivity.

Bail – the act of releasing an accused person from custody after being charged, on a promise that they will appear in court, or at the police station, on a given date.

Basic training/initial training – training for new recruits giving general skills which are needed for almost every job in that service

Bearing – a direction measured in degrees counted clockwise round the face of the compass, from 000 to 359. Degrees are given in three figures.

Behaviour – actions in general; the way the person drives.

Benefit – advantage; good outcome.

Calorie – a unit of energy found in food. This energy can be used by the body, or stored in the form of fat.

Campaign – publicity (advertisements and slogans), designed to make people more aware of a specific danger.

Camp craft – the skills used in camping.

Charisma – personality, attractiveness, or leadership qualities.

Chart – a map of an area of sea, showing everything of interest to a sailor.

Citizen – a member of a particular political community or state.

Cognitive – to do with learning and understanding.

Collision – a crash between a vehicle and another vehicle; a vehicle and a pedestrian; a vehicle and an animal; a vehicle and any other object.

Common law – old laws on basic crimes like murder, robbery, rape etc. based on old traditions.

Community – a body of people organised into a political, municipal or social unity.

Components of fitness – types of fitness. Five are 'heath-related' and five are 'skill-related'.

Conditions of service – things like hours, pay, holidays, pension and health arrangements that go with the job.

Contingency plan – a way of getting to safety.

Contours – lines on maps which show the gradients of hills.

Crime scene – the place where a crime happened, or any place where evidence of a crime is found.

Crime trend – an increase or decrease in crime over a period of time.

Cultural – to do with the way people act and think.

Cultural problem – bad feeling or hostility arising out of differences in culture between two groups of people

Culture – the shared beliefs and lifestyle of a community.

Debriefed – asked to say exactly what happened.

Degrees – units for measuring angles.

Diet – intake of food.

Digital mapping – a system of map-making using computers to survey, store, transmit and present information.

Diversity – differences between individuals or groups within a community.

Economic – to do with money, business and trade.

Entry requirements – a list of information about the kind of applicant a public service is looking for. Sometimes entry requirements are called a 'person specification', or 'job criteria'.

Evaluate – to decide, by research and careful thought, how good something is.

Fibre – stringy material found in food. It is not a nutrient, but it helps digestion.

First aid – simple, quick treatment given to people who are injured or suddenly taken ill.

Fitness – the ability to exercise for a long time without getting tired.

Focus groups – small groups of people who are questioned in depth about what they think.

Forensic scientists – experts trained in collecting and examining evidence of crimes.

Glossary

Formal – for use in special situations or business (can refer to writing, speech, behaviour or dress).

Function – how an item works.

Gradient – the steepness of a hill.

Hazard – anything that can cause harm (e.g. chemicals, electricity, working from ladders, etc.).

Human rights – laws or beliefs which protect people against bad government, bad laws, and cruel, oppressive behaviour by people in power.

Inequality – big differences between rich and poor people and their standard of living.

Initiatives – new actions planned to achieve an aim.

Instructor – a teacher of practical or job-related skills and knowledge.

Interpersonal communication skills – reading, writing, listening, speaking and non-verbal communication.

Issues – risks, dangers or problems.

Jargon – language specific to a particular job.

Job description – information about a job, sent out to applicants.

Latitude – lines going round the world parallel to the equator. Latitude lines never meet.

Law, a – a rule which can be enforced by the courts.

Law, the – a system of rules which can be enforced by the courts.

Legislative documents – laws made by Parliament. The big general laws are called Acts; the small specific ones are called Regulations.

Longitude – lines going round the world at right angles to the equator and passing through both poles.

Making way – moving.

Manager – a person who organises, motivates and directs other employees.

Manual handling – 'a wide range of manual handling activities, including lifting, lowering, pushing, pulling or carrying. The load may be either inanimate – such as a box or a trolley, or animate – a person or an animal' (HSE).

Map – a plan of an area showing the main features of interest and the distances between them.

Mission statement – a phrase or sentence which (a) says what a public service aims to do and (b) tries to give a good public image of the service.

Morale – confidence; team spirit and the will to succeed.

Multicultural – describing a diverse society where difference is respected and people from all ethnic and cultural backgrounds live together freely and equally.

Municipal unity – locally based, possibly with local government.

Negligence – failing to do something which should be done.

Norms – lifestyle, customs, habits etc.

Nutrient – any chemical in food which is used by our bodies.

Nutrition – (1) healthy eating; (2) food science.

Organs – particular parts of the body which do a special job. The heart, brain, lungs and glands are all organs, each with a different function.

Outdoor activities – almost any recreation which is done out of doors. It includes outdoor pursuits, but can also include less energetic activities such as angling or gentle walks.

Outdoor pursuits – adventurous activities normally done in open country or wild environments e.g. rock climbing, sailing and caving

Personnel – staff or employees.

Plan – write down the things you are going to do, giving deadlines and stating who is responsible.

Plot – to work out, and mark, positions and courses in pencil accurately on a chart.

Political unity – the community has leaders or some kind of power structure.

Port – the left-hand side of a boat.

Potential – (1) possible or likely; (2) usefulness.

Prepare – do things that need to be done before the expedition (e.g. packing your clothes).

Project – a group, organisation or plan.

Psychomotor – to do with muscular coordination and dexterity.

Purpose – overall aims.

Qualities – ways of behaving or feeling towards other people, e.g. honesty, sympathy, courage etc. Qualities can be either good or bad.

Recording crime – when the police put a crime on their database (list) of crimes.

Recreation – any activity which is done for pleasure.

Regulations – specialised health and safety laws. Unlike the Health and Safety at Work Act they state exact rules for particular jobs.

Repetitions ('reps') – the number of times you do a particular exercise during a training session.

Reporting crime – telling the police about it.

Resources – money, staff, equipment and knowledge.

Responsibilities – duties; and how the public services make sure they give a good service.

Review – explain what you did, and why – after you have done it.

Risk – a chance that somebody might be harmed.

Road atlas – a book of maps for drivers.

Roles – jobs and the work done.

Scale – the size of a feature on a map, in relation to its real size, expressed as a ratio, e.g. 1:25,000.

Segregation – separateness; living and working apart from other ethnic groups.

Self-esteem – feeling good about yourself.

Sentence – a punishment – involving some loss of freedom – given to a guilty person by a criminal court.

Social problem – any aspect of people's behaviour which threatens the well-being of a community.

Social unity – the fact that people mix or communicate with each other.

Society – the public, people in general or 'the community'.

Specialise – to concentrate on one particular kind of work.

Sport – physical activity that is done to improve fitness and may be competitive.

Squad – a small, specialised team which can act quickly.

Stamina – the ability to work for a long time without getting tired; endurance or 'staying power'.

Starboard – the right-hand side of a boat.

Statistics – data, e.g. accident figures.

Statute law – written laws made by Parliament, e.g. the Road Traffic Act 1988.

Statutory – laid down by law.

Strategies – long-term approaches to problems, for example of road safety. The use of speed cameras is an example of a strategy.

Surveys – asking a lot of people what they think by ticking boxes.

Synoptic chart – a weather map.

Taxes – money collected by the government to pay for public services

Team – a small group of people working together towards an agreed purpose.

Teamwork – (1) work done by a team; (2) methods of working together in groups.

Under way – beginning to advance or starting to move.

Uniform – dress of a distinctive design or fashion worn by members of a particular group and serving as a means of identification.

Values – what we think; our beliefs.

Vessels in sight – boats which can be seen from your own boat.

Victim – a person who is robbed, hurt or killed in a crime.

Welfare – health, safety and comfort.

Index

Page reference in italics indicates figures or tables

Index

Index

Index